Winter Wheat©

the memoirs of

RONALD JOSEPH GERHARD

Entering the world as strangers, we found that those whose love had created us were waiting in great anticipation for our arrival.

Delmar, New York
14 April 2017

ISBN-13: 978-1544079042

TABLE OF CONTENTS

DEDICATION   STRANGERS NO MORE

Because we are all immeasurably connected, there is really only one story to tell; and we each have our chapter to contribute to our ever-growing chronicle. This, my chapter, is dedicated to my children, my grandchildren, and their descendants with the hope that they will build a future in which they continue to be connected to each other.

I believe that there was a time when people were more closely connected than they are today, they lived together in clans and tribes and saw few outsiders. However, demographic peer groups are replacing clans, global corporations are replacing tribes, and busy lives and mobility are disrupting family units.

While we may not be able to totally avoid all that tends to separate us, we can choose to build bridges to reduce that which would keep us apart. For we are, I believe, stronger together than we are apart, and it is my hope that you will never be strangers to each other or to your ancestors or descendants.

Everything that is done in this world is done by hope.
Martin Luther

APPRECIATION   GRATITUDE

I offer many thanks to my friend Mary (Mimi) Moriarty, both for editing my preliminary work, and for inspiring me to write, both by her stellar example and by her affirming words.

~

Thanks also to Gail and John Haines, and others in our couples group who have supported me by encouraging me to share my stories and by their assurance that my progeny would be interested in hearing about my life in my own words.

~

I'm forever grateful for my wife Regina, who helped me create and enrich both my story and this written portrayal.

~

Kudos also to the internet contributors who furnished the historical highlights of the events that provided the canvas on which we painted our lives.

Appreciation is a wonderful thing:
It makes what is excellent in others belong to us as well.
Voltaire

INTRODUCTION   FIRST BLESSINGS

Men rise and fall like the WINTER WHEAT, but before they fall each generation provides the seeds for the future harvest. However, unlike the wheat, we also pass on the ageless treasure of our ancestors' achievements, memories, and hopes, which are the roots upon which future lives will be grafted.

My Great-great-great-grandfather was Wilhelm, my Great-great-grandfather was Johann, my Great-grand father was Henrich, my Grandfather was Albert, and my father was Arthur, I knew them all . . . but only by name. I never met any of them, except for my father, and him only for a few moments one afternoon in May. In reading these sketches of my life, I hope that you may come to know me by more than just my name. My life was built upon the achievements of our ancestors, but the impact of your life preceded your birth, by providing an invisible force that motivates me to help prepare for your arrival. While I have inherited some of the resources that I rely upon from my ancestors, the rest I have borrowed from you. We all live in this alliance between the dead, the living, and the unborn; each future generation motivating the living to build upon the work of those who have passed. Neither time nor space can occlude the influence that we have upon one another to learn from yesterday, to live for today, and to plan for tomorrow. I am escorted through life by this beloved entourage.

My life was little more than a collection of mostly unremarkable moments lived in my own brief allotment of the unfolding of eternity. So, some of my vignettes may seem trivial, but even notable events may sound emotional shallow when being recounted. Learning of another's encounter with a tiger may provide a clear picture of the event, but readers will not experience the terror of such an encounter; for the emotional experiences of others, may be understood but rarely felt.

I believe that our identities consist largely of our memories of the past, but since we can only meet one another in the endless flow of the present, we can never truly know one another. Only the chronicles of our pasts can provide insights to others, about whom we really are or who we really were. The perspective of time will add clarity to our shared story when you weave tales from my life, into the fabric of your own life. Those memories will become an integral part of you, so I shall live with you, no longer in the past, but a part of your present. I hope that my memory will bring you happiness, because one of the greatest gifts we can give to one another is a happy memory.

Like all histories, this one only contains that which the author chose to record. Most of the things that happened to me are written upon the pages of my heart; however, some remain just cryptic notes whose meanings are long forgotten as time has rewritten them. Some are too painful to read, and some are too private to write. I have had successes and failures; pains and joys; but this memoir is not written to elicit pity for the hardships that I have endured or admiration for what I may have accomplished. It attempts merely to have you understand who I was, and to realize that I longed to know you and share whatever I could with you.

Despite these limitations, I have tried to tell the true story of my life, even though I realize that what I have created is a mere shadow of the full story. The readers' imagination, intelligence, and wisdom will discover him who has cast this shadow.

It was me.

"We enter the world as strangers who all at once become
heirs to a harvest of memory, spirit and dream that has long
preceded us and will now enfold, nourish and sustain us.
The gift of the world is our first blessing."

John O'Donohue

CHAPTER 1   *THE THIRTIES*

At the beginning of the 1930s, more than 15 million Americans, one-quarter of all U.S. workers, were unemployed. President Hoover did little to alleviate the crisis: Patience and self-reliance, he argued, were all Americans needed to get them through this "passing incident in our national lives." In 1932, Americans elected Franklin Roosevelt, who pledged to use the power of the federal government to make Americans' lives better. Over the next nine years, President Roosevelt's New Deal created a new role for government. Though the New Deal alone did not end the Depression, it did provide an unprecedented safety net for millions of Americans.

Between 1930 and 1933, more than 9,000 banks closed in the U.S., taking with them more than $2.5 billion in deposits. Unemployed people did whatever they could, like standing in charity breadlines and selling apples on street corners, to feed their families.

President Roosevelt passed 15 major laws that reshaped many aspects of the American economy and restored Americans' confidence that, as Roosevelt had declared, "The only thing we have to fear is fear itself."

During the Depression, many people listened to the radio. The most popular broadcasts distracted listeners from their everyday struggles: comedies such as Amos 'n' Andy, soap operas and sporting events. Swing music encouraged people to cast aside their troubles and dance. Bandleaders like Benny Goodman and Fletcher Henderson drew crowds to ballrooms and dance halls. In addition, even though money was tight, people kept going to the movies. Musicals, "screwball comedies," and hard-boiled gangster pictures offered audiences an escape from the grim realities of life in the 1930s.

By the end of the decade, the expansion of the New Deal had ended. Growing congressional opposition made it difficult for President Roosevelt to introduce additional new programs. At the same time, as the threat of war in Europe loomed, the president turned his attention away from domestic politics.

Technological advances of the decade included frozen foods, color sound movies, Airmail service across the Atlantic, Scotch Tape, and long-playing phonograph records, color film, nuclear fission, the Volkswagen Beetle, the chocolate chip cookie, FM radio, and the Bass guitar.

Some of the eras' best-selling books were "Grapes of Wrath," "Of Mice and Men," "The Good Earth," "Gone with the Wind," and "The Yearling."

In 1930, an average new house cost $3,845, the average salary was $1,970, a loaf of bread cost 9 cents and a gallon of gas was 10 cents, and the average cost of new car was $640.

Life expectancy for males was 58.1 years, and for females, it was 61.6 years. The US Population was 123,202,624.

There were 119 known lynchings of black people in 1930s.

Rona1d J. Gerhard

1930.1   MY PARENTS

The 1930 Federal Census shows my future father, age 24, living in a rented home with his widowed mother Estelle Tobias Gerhards and his older sister Beatrice Brite and her infant son Robert. They lived at 33 Sterling Place in Huntington, LI, NY. My father was single and the proprietor of a confections (candy) store. Ethel Newton, the woman my father would marry after he left my mother, was still living in Alabama at the time of the 1930 census.

My mother Pauline Mills, was living near Huntington at the time. She had left her home and family in Anson, NC after completing an advanced cooking course a few years earlier. We'll never know what may have motivated her to leave her family and travel a thousand miles to find work in a state hospital on rural Long Island. Was there a push to leave the socially limited and economically poor rural community or was it the pull of the urban area with its social diversity, employment opportunities and higher wages? Or perhaps the reasons were more personal, having more to do with her family or social life than with the enviroment in which she lived.

I have not been able to positively identify Mom in the 1930 census. However, I did find a Miss Mills, age 24, from North Carolina working on May 4th, 1930 as a waitress in Kings Park State Hospital which was 12 miles from Huntington.

(In the 1950's, I often visited to the taverns in the Kings Park area to meet the many young girls who worked and studied there. I didn't realize it at the time but it is likely that I was unknowingly following in my fathers footsteps.)

The photo is of my Mom in her early 20's sitting on a car fender and wearing a uniform like those worn by hospital waitresses. The photo also shows a barbed wire fence in the background like those surrounding the Kings Park State Hospital. Mom never learned to drive so the car belonged to someone else. She mentioned once that she never liked the name Pauline and rarely used it at work. Could Miss Mills be Pauline, there's no one left to ask and there are so many unspoken words and so many unanswered questions.

Mom retired from state hospital service as a nurses' aid in the early 1960's. She told me that she had once been enrolled in, but never graduated from, a state hospital school of nursing, like the one at Kings Park State Hospital. If the waitress in the census was Pauline, her first opportunity to enter nursing school would have been in Sep. 1931. My brother, Artie was born in Apr, 1932, perhaps it was his arrival that ended her professional nursing education.

1932.1   MY BROTHER ARTIE

My brother Arthur Gerhard Jr. was born on April 7th, 1932 at South Side Hospital in Bayshore Long Island, New York. I assume that my parents were living in Suffolk County, NY at the time, but I cannot find any records of them living together there or at any other site where I know they lived during their seven years together.

I never knew Artie to use the "junior" suffix after his name, perhaps because by the time I was old enough to be aware of his name there was no Arthur Gerhard "senior" in the family with whom he might be confused.

Although, Artie and I were never truly close, I've missed him for most of my life; during his frequent retreats to solitude when at home, during his many absents with friends in his adolescence, during his separation while away at college, the military, or work and finally when he left us all forever; five months after his 36th birthday.

1935.1   THE BEGINNING

 April 14 was the 104th day of 1935, but for much of the country it was called "Black Sunday." The worst dust storm that ever struck the farmlands in the Great Southwest Plains occurred on that day. The coal black ground-hugging cloud was the result of a prolonged drought and the removal of erosion-stopping sod and vegetation from the prairie through over-plowing. The dust storm's devastation forced hundreds of thousands of people to relocate. Their arduous westward journey, and their search for a new life is described in "The Grapes of Wrath," the Pulitzer Prize winning novel by Nobel Prize winning author John Steinbeck.

But as the Great Plains were clothed in darkness, I was freed from the darkness of the womb and bathed in light when at 4:20 that morning I was born at Van Cortland Park Sanatorium in the Bronx, NY. It was Palm Sunday there, and Christians were celebrating Christs' entry into the city of Jerusalem as the Gerhards were celebrating my entry into the city of New York.

My parents were Arthur Gerhard Sr. and Pauline Delphia Mills. At this writing, the Sanatorium where I was born has long since closed and I have not been able to find any information about it. I assume it was a private Tuberculosis or Psychiatric hospital. Perhaps my mother worked there as a nurse's aide; a career that she followed until her retirement in 1961. I believe that my parents were living in the Bronx near my father's family, as my mother once mentioned receiving frequent visits from her in-laws, Estelle and Albert Gerhards. Also, the 1940 census indicates that my father was living in one of the boroughs of New York City in 1935. Albert was the last of my ancestors to retain the "s" at the end of his name so Gerhards became Gerhard.

My parents gave me the name Ronald Gerhard, after Ronald Coleman an English actor, popular during the 1930s and 1940s. My middle name Joseph was added when I was confirmed before my wedding, as a member of the Roman Catholic Church, in 1960. Of course, I do not remember my birth, but I am as certain that I was there then, as I am that you are here now reading this account of my life.

1936.1   FAMILY-OF-FOUR

In the only memory, that I have about life before the age of four, I recall sitting terrified behind a row of vertical bars, with a large barking dog in front of me clawing at the bars and a woman standing to my left in front of a red wall. Years later, I mentioned the memory to my mother and she remembered the incident clearly, but was surprised that I could describe it in such detail. I was only eighteen months old in October of 1936 and our family-of-four was living in New Orleans, where, according to my mother, my father was working for the "Mob" fixing slot machines. My mother remembered that she was leaning out of the window, to my left, talking to a neighbor and hanging wash on the line strung between the red brick apartment buildings. The dog was our family pet, a large German shepherd who treated me as one of his pack. When I cried, he came to my aid, and would sometimes prevent my mother from changing my diaper unless he put his paws up on the changing table to supervise. On this day, I was crying and the dog was in frenzy because he could not get close to me because of the bars . . . on the crib.

Mom rarely spoke of her, or my, early life but what little she did say gave me the impression that this was a happy time for the four Gerhards. She did tell me that by the age of two I had been in 14 states. I suppose they were the places we passed though on the journeys from New York to New Orleans and on the return trip back to Maryland, and then back to New York.

1937.1   BALTIMORE

The Social Security Act was part of a series of economic programs that provided relief for the unemployed and poor, which President Franklyn Roosevelt created in response to the Great Depression. However, in 1937, unemployment remained high and by the summer, the economy took a sharp downturn. Perhaps that explains why we moved from Louisiana to Maryland and why on December 7, 1937, my father completed an application for a Social Security Card.

According to the application, he was living in Baltimore and working for the "Baltimore Vending Machine Company."

(The reference to the vending machine company is consistent with my mothers' comments that my father and his older brother Julius Gerhards were adept at electronics and worked at repairing gambling equipment. My brother Artie built his first radio in his early teens. My aptitude was more suited to mechanics and architecture.)

I assume that the entire family may have been living with him there at 4011 Fairview Ave., Baltimore, MD. In 2012, Google Earth showed 4011 Fairview as a two-story brick town house in a tree lined neighborhood.

1938.1   FAMILY-OF-THREE

I have no childhood memories of my father. I have a vague recollection of sitting in a small rowboat with my mother and a man. I imagine that the man was my father, but I try to resist the temptation of converting this imagination-enriched image into a memory. I believe that our minds can easily create "memories" that do not reflect history, but a reality of our own making. This is one reason why eyewitnesses provide a relatively weak form of evidence in court. Chief justice, Stuart J. Rabner, of the New Jersey Supreme Court, wrote . . . "Study after study revealed a troubling lack of reliability in eyewitness identifications . . . From social science research to the review of actual police lineups, from laboratory experiments to DNA exonerations . . . it is now widely known that eyewitness misidentification is the leading cause of wrongful convictions across the country."

I do not remember my father.

1938.2   A HOUSE DIVIDED

My mother told me that my father left our home when I was three years old.

The fact that the family stayed together for three years may have prevented my brother and me from developing Attachment Disorders. People with Attachment Disorders have difficulty forming lasting relationships and troubles with mood, and behavior, it is a serious condition. The lack of normal attachments to primary care givers between 6 months and three years of age may lead to the disorder. Problematic social relationships occurring after about age three may be distressing, but do not generally result in the more serious Attachment Disorder.

I suppose my parents were very unhappy in 1938. Unhappy parents may be one of the worst things that can happen in the life of a child. Not having them around eliminated that potential problem for me. My brother Artie was six when our father left, so he no doubt remembered our father, although he never spoke to me about him and sadly, I never thought to ask him until he too was gone. While Artie had been abandoned; I believe that my youth saved me from that psychic trauma. I suspect that this difference may have set Artie and me on quite distinct paths that likely played a role in determining how each of us would perceive and react to the experiences that followed.

It would be 25 years before I would see my father again … at my brother Artie's funeral in 1963.

The miracle isn't the life you missed; it's the life you have.
Beverly Lewis

1939.1   THE HAGG'S

When I was about four years old, Artie and I were placed in a foster home run by a German family on Suffolk Ave. near the border of Brentwood and Central Islip, L. I., NY; "The Haggs." I believe that we were there for about a year, and while I have several memories that indirectly involve Artie, I have no actual pictorial memories of his being there with me. Given all we went thought together it's amazing how few early memories I do have of him; it's almost as though each of us was an 'only child', living alone in the same places, like transient residents of a hotel, unknown and barely remembered. I do remember, however, roasted pigs hanging from the ceiling on the back porch, the smell of homemade sauerkraut drifting up from the basement. I remember that 'Uncle Otto' could eat a doughnut in a single bite (or was it two bites) and I remember almost choking tying to imitate him. My first memory that included Artie involved our goats. The Haggs' had several goats, one male the rest were female. My "job" was to feed and milk the females each morning. This was an easy and enjoyable chore even for a four-year-old, as the goats were friendly and freely roamed the large fields behind the two-story farmhouse. We would roll in the grass together; they were my pets and my primary playmates while Artie was away at school. A rope secured Arties' goat to a stake in the back yard. It had worn a circular path at the end of its rope. Artie fed him each day by placing a dish on the path. One day Artie was sick with the mumps and I was to feed all the goats. I fed my pets as usual. I took the dish to Arties' goat. He was across the circle from me as I walked into his ring. He seemed glad to see me as he ran headlong toward me across the grass. I walked closer; he ran faster … I awoke in bed with a pair of horn tracks from my groin to my chest. Artie had never mentioned why he always left the dish on the outer edge of goats' trodden path, but now whenever I hear that someone is at "the end of his rope" I think GOOD, if you need to be on a rope, the end, where there is no slack, is the safest place for you.

There were two other children living at the Haggs, a blond-haired boy, and his younger sister, both of whom were older than Artie and me. I remember little about them except a vague feeling of uneasiness associated with them. Data from the 1930 and 1940 Federal censuses implies that these children were just 'temps' like Artie and me for the Haggs had only one daughter who was much older than us and had long since moved out of the family home.

There was also a little girl, about my age, who arrived with 'Uncle Otto' and the donuts. I don't remember her name, or even what she looked like, but I remember that she evoked an unfamiliar feeling in me and I liked her. Whenever she left at the end of one the Hagg's frequent family backyard "pickniks," I would hide under the dining room table because I could not bear to say goodbye to the little golden haired girl.

For Christmas that year, Artie received a red fire truck. It was large enough to sit in and had peddles and a steering wheel. Artie drove up and down the sidewalk in his fire truck. I received a similar gift, but it was pink and shaped like a pig. Since I was three years younger and much shorter than Artie, I could not push the pedals far enough to make the pig move forward; I pushed just far enough to move the pig a few feet back and forth. I thought the problem was with the pig and wished I had a fire truck instead that could be driven the length of the sidewalk.

One day when Artie was at school, a man and a woman dressed in white found me in the back yard. They gave me a smallpox vaccination.

> *The smallpox vaccine isn't given as an injection or "shot." Instead, it's given with a needle that has two tiny prongs on the end. The needle was dipped into the green vaccine, and a small amount stuck between the prongs. The needle pricked my skin several times in upper part of my left arm. The scar on my arm took many years to fade. However, I still remember the warm spring day when two strangers assaulted me in the back yard; such was patient centered Health Care in the 1940's. (In 1980, the World Health Organization officially declared that Small Pox had been totally eradicated throughout the entire world.)*

I also remember a visit from my Mom near the end of our stay there. It was one of her rare visits and she had me lying across her lap as she used a bobby pin to clean my ears. It was quite painful. She was scolding Mrs. Hagg for not keeping my ears clean and for giving me chocolate, which she claimed made me constipated. Choosing sides here was a no-brainer; chocolate bars beat ear probing hands-down. The day ended in turmoil for Mrs. Hagg wanted to adopt me, but not my brother Artie. My mother said that she would kill us both before she would see us separated. I think I know how the Biblical Isaac might have felt as his father Abraham made his heroic stance before God, prepared to sacrifice his son Isaac to prove his own worth.

We left the Haggs' soon afterward, amidst a fury of words and angry faces, but no good byes to my friends the goats, to Otto the donut-eater or to the little blonde haired girl to whom I had never said good-bye. I guess that a part of life for second hand kids, like Artie and me, was learning to manage our disappointments. When Artie died by his own hand many years later, I realized that when pain can be endured, surviving the adversity can strengthen us, but when the pain is too great to be borne, it destroys us.

There came a moment in Artie's life, when his pain from the past met his fear of the future and before he died, his hope had predeceased him.

"To live without hope is to cease to live."
Fyodor Dostoyevsky

CHAPTER 2 *THE FORTIES*

The Second World War took place in the first half of the decade. It had a profound effect throughout the world and began when Germany invaded Poland in 1939. The United States entered World War II after the Japanese attacked Pearl Harbor on December 7, 1941. Over four hundred thousand (400,000) Americans lost their lives in that war.

Nazi Germany systematically killed six million Jewish men, women, and children during the war. The war ended a month after the United States atomic bombings of Hiroshima and Nagasaki in August 1945. The consequences of the war lingered well into the second half of the decade, with a war-weary Europe divided between the jostling spheres of influence of the West and the Soviet Union, which had lost 24 million people in the war. In total over 60 million people were killed, which was over 3% of the 1939 world population.

The post–World War II economic boom lasted well into the 1970s and encouraged decolonization and the emergence of new states and governments, with India, Pakistan, Vietnam, Iceland, Indonesia, Syria, Lebanon, and Burma and others declaring independence, rarely without bloodshed. Israel was established the Jewish people had a homeland again. However, the Palestinians who were displaced had lost their homeland. The ramifications of this conflict would affect world politics for decades. The United Nations and NATO were created to help prevent future wars.

The decade also witnessed the early beginnings of new technologies including computers, nuclear power, jet propulsion, radar, ballistic missiles, commercial television, the Slinky, the microwave oven, Velcro, Tupperware, the Frisbee, and radiocarbon dating.

In 1940, the U.S. Population was 132,164,569, 55% of US homes had indoor plumbing, and the life expectancy was 65.2 for women and 60.8 for men.

Best-selling books of the decade were: "How Green Was My Valley", "The Keys of the Kingdom", "The Song of Bernadette", "The Robe", "Forever Amber," and "The Miracle of the Bells.", the average cost of a loaf of bread was 10 cents, an average new house cost $3,920, the typical salary per year was $1,725, a gallon of gas was 11 cents, and the average cost of new car was $850.

There were 31 known lynchings of black people in the 1940s.

1940.1   SALT THEIR TAILS

My mother had attended a cooking school before leaving her home in North Carolina and was working as a private cook for a wealthy violinist, who lived on a large wooded estate in the north shore of Long Island. On one occasion, I was allowed to visit her at her work place. From the kitchen window, I saw deer grazing in among the trees. A man there told me that I could catch a deer if I put salt on its tail. Deer love salt and when it stopped and turned to lick the salt off its tail, I could catch it and bring it home. I grabbed the saltshaker and bolted into the back yard fully expected to go home with my own pet deer.

Years later, I tried unsuccessfully to find the name of a concert violinist who lived on the North Shore of Long Island at that time.

1940.2   SUMMER REUNION

For a few weeks during the summer of 1940 Grandma Hattie Mills, my Mother, her sister, Aunt Velma (aka Aunt Ann), Velma's daughter my cousin Joan, Artie, and I all lived together in a rented cottage in Central Islip. I'm the smaller child in the photo with my Mom and brother Artie. I remember playing in the adjacent field and being scolded for peeing behind a tree; the bathroom was usually occupied. One day Aunt Velma brought home a sailor she had met while on a trip to NYC. Mother was not amused. It would be many years before I would ever be surrounded by so many family members again. I have been unable to find my mother or Artie and myself in the 1940 Federal census. The entire block of Weeks Ave., where she lived seems to be missing from the Census data file.

1940.3   THE SECOND FAMILY

The 1940 Federal census shows my father living at 355 S. Union St. in Burlington, VT with his wife Ethel (nee Newton). He was working as a salesman of amusement machines. They lived there until my father enlisted in the Army Air Force on July 30, 1942. The stepmother, who I never met, was five years younger than my father was and came from Alabama. Years later, they were buried side by side in the town of her youth, Lanett, AL. Her two nieces Tressie and Nannette lived with my father and Ethel in Florida during their teens and it was them who provided me with much of the information needed to piece together some of my fathers' life after he and Mom separated. They loved my father, who they knew as Uncle Arthur, and they wanted me to know what a wonderful man he was. We traded information by phone, by letter, and by in person chats.

1941.1 & 1963   CHERAW, SC

When the summer ended, Velma, Artie, Joan, and I moved to live with our Grandmother Hattie Mills. Although Grandma's house was on the main street of Cheraw, SC, it was very quiet as there were few neighbors and fewer cars in pre-World War II rural South Carolina. As recently as the year 2,000, the population of Cheraw was only 5,500 people. It was a carefree time for me; there were few demands and fewer expectations. In the morning, I would step into the short pants that lay on floor besides the bed where I had stepped out of them the night before. I was dressed and ready for another day. Like the children of today, I played my way into the future.

We ran barefoot in the front yard. Aunt Velma would play the radio on the open front porch. I knew the words to "Mexicali Rose" and "You Belong to my Heart" and entertained Velma and Grandma by singing along in my Yankee accent with the radio.

> ♫ ♫ *You belong to my heart, now and forever,*
> *and our love had its start, not long ago.*
> *We were gathering stars,*
> *while a million guitars played our love song.*
> *When I said, "I love you," every beat of my heart said it, too. 'Twas a moment*
> *like this, do you remember?*
> *And your eyes threw a kiss, when they met mine.*
> *Now we own all the stars,*
> *and a million guitars are still playing*
> *Darling, you are the song,*
> *and you'll always belong to my heart.* ♫ ♫

One evening Artie made an airplane of folded paper and we took turns gliding it from the front stoop to see who could sail it the farthest. On his last toss, Artie's plane flew across the front yard, across the sidewalk, and landed in the tall grass in the area between the sidewalk and the road. He ran barefoot into the grass to retrieve the lost plane but soon returned screaming in pain. He had stepped on a broken bottle, hidden by the tall weeds. He left a bloody print of his foot as he ran to the house for help. I could see a large section of his big toe dangling below his foot as he shrieked in anguish.

(1963) When Artie died in September, I recalled his screams that day on the front lawn of our brief home in South Carolina. I remembered his bloody footprint on the sidewalk as I stood beside the blood-splattered car where his pain ended in Puyallup, WA. These two incidents were like bookends to a biography with many chapters of pain and disappointment. Now it seems as though I hardly knew him. I hadn't read the chapters of his life, even though I stood near his side as he wrote them, for I had lived in that inner world where we all dwell alone. Perhaps I was too busy writing my own chapters to take the time to read his.

If Artie were asked the question, "Who loved you as a child?" I believe that his answer might have been, "No one." If asked the same question at an early age, I might have answered, for reasons that remain obscure to me today, "Everyone." Was he simply more observant than me, or perhaps I was merely less judgmental than him? What's most impactful about life isn't necessarily what happens to us, but rather our perception of what has happened. Perhaps there are events or predilections that determine how we view our place in the world that ultimately determine the quality of our lives, for they determine how we assess our life and rate our satisfaction with it.

(1941) We had no phone so I don't know how it was arranged but soon "Uncle Buck," with one of the few automobiles in the area, arrived, and took Artie to be treated. Days later when I was riding in the same car, alone with "Uncle Buck" I asked him why he had only one arm. He told me that he had put his left arm out the window of this very car to signal for a left-hand turn when a big truck came by and cut it off and that was when he decided that it wasn't safe and that he would never signal for a turn again. I told him that I didn't believe him and that he couldn't signal even if he wanted to because he had no left arm. He told me that I was getting too big for my britches. At that point, I lost all faith in the man as my pants fit just fine. (The only male relative shown living near Cheraw in the 1940 Federal Census was grandma's nephew, Robert R. Mills living about 20 miles away, this may have been Uncle Buck.)

We ate fruits and vegetables that grew in the backyard and the chickens that roamed freely on the property gave us eggs in return for table scraps.

The well from which we drew our water was in the back yard. It was fun, but it was difficult to turn the crank and bring up the wooden bucket of cool water.

At that time, about 55% of U.S. homes have indoor plumbing, but grandma's house was not included among them. Her outhouse was in the backyard, perhaps too close to the well. It had two holes; I used the one on the left. There really was a Sears and Roebuck catalog on the bench between the holes. It was the only toilet paper available. Grandma didn't use the outhouse; she had a chamber pot in her bedroom. As the youngest kid, I had to empty it each morning.

Being the youngest also meant being the most naïve. Artie and Cousin Joan, who was a year younger than Artie, told me that Grandma would be glad to know that I thought she was a "real bitch." However, Grandma already "knew what she was" and to prove it she told me to take the butcher knife into the back yard and cut a switch so she could whip me. A simple definition of terms would have been sufficient for me, but Grandma had her own way of making a point. After the beating, Artie and Joan probably regretted what they did but they never mentioned it. Years later, I learned that Grandpa Mills, who I never met, left Hattie with three half-grown children still at home and I remembered her harshness and thought that perhaps he had good reason for leaving her, but I could never imagine leaving my own children.

Grandma had a cat that she treated as a barn animal, its' job was to catch mice. I considered the cat to be a furry replacement for the goats I had befriended earlier at my first foster home. It slept in my bed and we would spend at least part of each day together. One day a pack of dogs came into our yard. I heard the growls and screeches and ran outside calling to Grandma to come and help. Grandma didn't come; the dogs tore the cat to shreds.

Grandma's approach to raising animals was mainly an extension of her approach to child rearing, which in turn was an extension of the harshness of the lives of poor farmers and cotton mill workers in the rural Carolinas, where my Grandmother and her parents and grandparents for many generations had lived their lives. They were poor working class Scot-Irish people at a time when unseen forces maintained a social caste system from which few escaped. The social institutions that created the middle class were yet to be implemented. Many parents adopted the philosophy of child rearing based upon benign neglect. If the child survived, it would be strong. If not, it was clear that it would not have been able to cope with what lay ahead. There were no antibiotics to cure infections, there were no immunizations to prevent disease; no emergency rooms to treat injuries, the nearest hospital was hours away; and malnutrition was always close at hand especially during the spring when last falls' harvest was eaten and this year's early Winter Wheat and other crops were not yet in. The voice of the dead was a constant reminder of life's fragility. Life in the 1940's had improved substantially from the days of grandmother's youth in the late 1800s' and from the days when she raised her own children in the early 1900's, but the die had been cast. Grandma's attitudes were sculpted by time and "She knew what she was" and what life had to offer. The buried treasures lying in the graves of infants and children throughout the cemeteries of the Carolinas made it abundantly clear that one did not worry about a dying cat.

With breakfast, we had grits and potatoes were served with supper. While we were never malnourished, there were days when I left the table wishing for more to eat. I soon noticed that there were often leftovers put into the "icebox," even on evenings when I left the table hungry. When the 'family' retired to the front room or the front yard, I would make my way into the kitchen via the back door. A small potato would make an ample supplement to the scanty menu; a biscuit would make a happy stomach.

Sometime in the early spring, just as the flowers returned from their winter retreat, it snowed in South Carolina. Grandma, Velma and Joan were beside themselves with excitement. Artie and I couldn't believe that they considered this a major event. In New York, a snowfall of a quarter of an inch would have barely been noticed. Aunt

Velma used a large kitchen spoon to scoop up some snow into a mixing bowl before it melted in the spring heat. She added canned condensed milk, sugar, and vanilla extract to make something only vaguely resembling ice cream. It was terrible ice cream. However, it was fun to be part of a joyful family project.

1941.2   THE MORGAN'S

I don't remember the trip back from grandma's house in Cheraw, SC to Central Islip, L. I. NY. But I do remember arriving at the Morgan's house, late enough at night to be ushered directly to my room at the head of the stairs, overlooking the railroad tracks. Artie was down the hall on the left and the Morgan's were on the right, in the front bedroom, overlooking Brightside Ave. I had my own room with pale orange walls, a bare floor an overhead light, and no people. I felt abandoned. No one ever asked if I wanted to stay or go, if I was happy or sad, the reasons for change seemed quite unrelated to me and determined solely by the logic that only an adult could understand. Life was beginning to feel like being blindfolded in a room with an open trap door . . . you walk in, and then suddenly your life changes. When all in your life changes, do you become someone else; I wasn't sure.

But, life was generally good at the Morgans. The house was warm and so was Mrs. Morgan. I avoided Mr. Morgan whenever possible. But this was a buy one get one free arrangement; Mr. Morgan came with the deal whether you wanted him or not. Mr. Morgan's face was as rumpled as an unmade bed. He sat in the "Morris" chair in the living room; drank Ballantine ale, and yelled at Mrs. Morgan. Many years later, I learned that the Morris chair was not named for "himself," but actually a style of stuffed chair with wooden arms. He worked in the Central Islip firehouse, sitting at the desk waiting to blast the noon siren. I never knew why this happened but every day at noon; Mr. Morgan would blow the firehouse siren that was heard all over town, even in the school a mile away. He also had the important job of blowing the siren to call the volunteer firefighters when there was a fire in the village. Several times, he invited me to the firehouse to sit on the trucks and play with equipment. After 74 years, I still clearly remember the unique smell of the firehouse.

Windows enclosed the Morgan's front porch. There was a diamond shaped cardboard poster with one of the numbers 5, 10, 15, and 25 printed in each of the four corners. This was for the iceman.

Few people had refrigerators at that time and ice in the icebox had to be replenished every few days. Ice chopped in the winter months from the Hudson River near Albany was stored in large icehouses until needed, and then it was floated on barges to New York City and distributed throughout the region.

The numbers in the corners of the sign indicated the price of the piece of ice that was wanted. A 5-cent piece was about the size of a quart of milk; a 25-cent piece was about the size of a bushel basket. The rotation of the sign alerted the iceman how much was needed without first coming to the door to ask.

In the spring of 1942, a second item had appeared in the window; it indicated the number of family members in the armed services. It was a small white flag with a wide red boarder and it had two blue stars in the center, one for each of their two sons who I never met, John Jr. and Edward, who were drafted into military service. During the Second World War, most of the houses in town had stars in their windows; most of the stars were blue; some of the stars were gold for those who were not coming home. This was very sad, for those stars did not belong to borrowed families like mine, but real families who belonged together. The economic boom  that followed the Second World War would provide the refrigerators that would remove the ice signs and the return of the soldiers would remove the blue stars, but the gold stars were forever.

The American Gold Star Mothers Club was formed after World War I to provide support for mothers who lost sons or daughters in the war. On the last Sunday in September, Gold Star Mother's Day is observed in the U.S. in their honor. Now I wonder if there will ever be a Gold Star Fathers Club, if there is, I hope that no one in my family will ever have to join it.

The Morgan's back yard was large and covered with clover. On warm days, I would play with the cat in the clover, the blossoms were white, pink, and edible. One day a bee stung me as I played in the yard, I ran into the kitchen crying to Mrs. Morgan. She was disappointed that I cried and I tried to avoid doing that from then on.

Even though they didn't have a car, they did have a garage and a driveway with parallel furrows in the soil made by the car or cart of a former owner. Cinders, from the coal-burning furnace that heated the house, filled the ruts. In the winter, Mr. Morgan would keep the furnace burning and shovel the burnt cinders and ashes into a bucket next to the coal bin in the basement. On Saturday mornings, I would bring the bucket to the driveway and spread the ashes into the furrows. Sometimes there would be a clinker (a large cinder) in the bucket. These would have to be broken up into smaller pieces so that when Mr. Morgan eventually bought his car the sharp edges of the clinker wouldn't cut his tires.

The backyard ended near the railroad tracks. Often, I would stand by the edge of the tracks and wave at the speeding people going by in the coal fired, steam-powered train, and wonder if any of them were going to Cheraw. I never waved at one train, "the Five O'clock Flier."

This was a special military train from Camp Upton to New York City. Upton was a temporary Army camp created in Yaphank, Long Island, as part of the war effort, now it's the site of Brookhaven National Laboratory

The special high-speed train rushed non-stop for the fifty-mile trip. The houses along the route would shake and little boys would quiver as the train with its painted windows sped from town to town. Most people believed that the suction from the speeding train would pull you under the wheels. That was why I didn't stand near the edge of the tracks and wave.

It was a grand warm summer day when the cat finally had her four kittens. They lived in a cardboard box under the kitchen sink. I looked forward to playing with them in the back yard when their eyes opened. One morning Mrs. Morgan was sitting at the kitchen table when I came down for breakfast. She looked rather upset. We had coffee and hard rolls. (My coffee was a cup of warm milk with enough coffee to turn it light brown.) As I dunked the roll in the 'coffee' and watched the melted butter float around the rim of the cup, Mrs. Morgan told me that the kittens were gone. Later that morning I was at my station in the backyard when I noticed a bucket with a tin pie plate covering it. I lifted the plate and found the kittens, floating in the water-filled bucket. Mr. Morgan apparently had the same level of respect for cats as Grandma.

In spite of a few unpleasantries, life with the Morgan's was mostly good. Mrs. Morgan would sit with Artie and me around the kitchen table and talk about the old country (she was German), stories whose details have been long forgotten but still appreciated. And, occasionally we would walk downtown, sometimes in the morning to bring lunch to Mr. Morgan at the firehouse and sometimes in the evening to buy chocolate covered cherries at Hirschlein's Pharmacy. One day a very unusual looking bicycle appeared from the garage. It had once belonged to the Morgan brothers. It was small, oddly shaped and had solid rubber tires. The three houses to the east of the Morgan's each had metal fences that provided about 200 feet of handrail next to the sidewalk. I sat on the bike, held onto the fence with my left hand, and shoved off with series of grunts; a few huffs and puffs followed by a crash and a long moan. After a few days, I was riding and a new world that reached well beyond Brightside Ave. had opened to me. This was a new and exciting time.

1941.3   FIRST GRADE

While living with the Morgans on Brightside Ave. I entered first grade. Like most schools in that era, it had no kindergarten. The front of Mrs. Smith's first grade classroom contained the standard blackboards with the alphabet, printed in large letters, tacked overhead. I had never actually seen all fifty-two upper and lower case letters and ten numbers in one place before, and certainly never had any  idea that I was expected to learn how to draw them. I was in over my head. At that moment, I was certain that I would never be able to master this work. However, nine months later, with Mrs. Smith's gentle guidance, the material fell into place. In the photo, I'm in the middle row, five in from the left.

Mrs. Smith was a wonderful teacher. She helped shape the letters into words, the words into sentences, and the sentences into stories and songs. This too was a new and exciting time.

On the last day of school, I walked home with my closest friend Bob O'Donohue, who years later would be my tennis instructor and an usher in my wedding. He lived on Carlton Ave., which was the main street in town. We played tag as we approached his house. When we were adjacent to the spot where I would cross Carlton Ave. to go home I tagged Bob and darted across the street so he couldn't tag me back. I never saw or heard the car the car that hit me and I never made it across the street. I awoke on Mrs. Morgan's couch with a state trooper standing over me. When I could move all of my parts, the trooper left and I never saw a doctor. While this may sound bizarre, in those days few people ever visited a doctor. My first visit to a dentist was when I was in college.

1941.4 & 1945   SPECIAL CHRISTMAS

Christmas at the Morgans was like none other of my childhood. I received a gift that exceeded my expectations. It was a Gene Autry cowboy suit, complete with fur-covered chaps, twin holsters, two six-shooter cap guns, a leather vest, and a real cowboy hat. Gifting holidays before and after were generally barren events. I had no money to purchase gifts for the family and expected little in return. I was rarely disappointed. I was so excited I thought I would burst. I was soon dressed and 'armed.'

I 'moseyed' down Brightside Avenue, guns blazing. A neighbors' dog was the only other 'person' on the street. We were friends and I holstered my guns to pet him. He smelled the rabbit fur on my chaps, and chased me home yapping at my heels; another cowboy 'bit the dust.'

I spent a year or so with the Morgans in Central Islip, then a year in an orphanage in Sayville and from then until I left home at age 20, I lived with my mother and stepfather back in Central Islip. We spent our first year together in a rented bungalow on 3rd Ave. By the next year, Tony and Mom had saved enough to purchase a small house at 14 Pineview Boulevard. The daily walk to school from Pineview Blvd. took me past the Morgans' house on Brightside Avenue. I walked that route every school day for eight years, but I never saw the Morgans again. I wonder if Mrs. Morgan ever looked out of her window and saw me passing by. I looked at the house with the chipped asbestos shingles reminding me of the day that my neighborhood friend George C. threw a rock and missing me broke the shingle near the front door. The chip remained but the relationship was over. It had vanished as suddenly as it had appeared.

(1945) After the war, the Morgan's sons, like hundreds of thousands of others, were discharged from the Army. One son came to live at home and one went to live in a nearby Veterans Psychiatric Hospital; "Shell Shocked," as Post Traumatic Stress Disorder was called in those days. One night at home after his discharge from the hospital, he awoke in an apparent flashback to the horrors of war. He used a kitchen knife to repeatedly stab his father. Then he dragged the bleeding mans' body through the porch with the blue stars and the chipped shingle, to the downtown area, two blocks away, leaving a trail of blood along the sidewalk where I had learned to ride a bike a few years before.

(1941) I don't know why I never stopped in to say hello, I guess you don't have to be a soldier to get discharged, or perhaps Thomas Wolfe was right when he wrote, "You Can't Go Home Again." He said,

> *"You can't go back home to your family, back home to your childhood ... back home to a young man's dreams of glory and of fame ... back home to places in the country, back home to the old forms and systems of things which once seemed everlasting but which are changing all the time — back home to the escapes of Time and Memory."*

I guess this is true even if the home was only borrowed and "everlasting" was something hoped for but not really expected.

1942.1 & 2008   SECOND GRADE

At the end of the school year Artie and I left the Morgan's and were moved to an orphanage in Sayville, NY, called the Sayville Cottages of St. Ann or as the kids referred to it, "The Cottages." It was run by the Episcopal Church. During the lunch break on one of my first days at the new school, two boys who I remember as Queen and Fox attacked me. I think they liked to taunt the new kids from the orphanage. While the cottage kids lived in an invisible tent that only those of us on the inside could see, some outsiders could sense the self-imposed separation and often responded with hostility. I suppose they were seeking power or social recognition because they were social or academic failures. Perhaps their families did not provide warmth and love that I had found in the trek through my cascade of families. They chased me across the playground; I ran until I was completely out of breath. Then I stopped, turned, and put up my hand to protect myself. One of the boys ran headlong into my outstretched arm and landed at my feet with a bloody nose and crying in pain. The crowd assumed that I had punched him and knocked him to the ground; I never denied it, and they never bothered me again. A new school is like starting life over.

Not all of the "townies" were prejudiced again the cottage kids. One wintery day as I walked through town on Middle Road from the school to the cottage it began to sleet. The icy pellets tore my skin and the wind took my breath away. One of my classmates, whose father owned a stationary store, saw my plight and invited me in to the store. Her father served us ice cream sodas. It was the first time that I had ever eaten in a public place and it was my first ice cream soda. While I am not sure of her name, perhaps it was Judith, I have never forgotten her kindness as it helped my feelings slowly morph from rejection into acceptance.

Here I discovered books. There were books in the living room of the orphanage and books at school. While I don't believe, there were any books in any of the places where I had lived, I'm sure I must have seen books in the first grade, but I remember the second grade as the time that I eagerly began to read them. I remember "And to Think That I Saw It on Mulberry Street" Dr. Seuss' first book which greatly enriched my own strolls home from school each day. And there was "The Story About Ping" which I felt could have been written about me, as I often felt that my life was a misadventure. That year, as Christmas approached, I surprised my mother by asking her for a book as a Christmas present rather than for a toy.

> (2008) I marvel now at my granddaughter Emily, who began reading in kindergarten and writing in cursive in the first grade.

(1942) At school and at home in the "cottages" we were all very much aware of the war in Europe; it would be some time before the war in the Pacific would become as widely publicized. Many children of my age could identify the profiles of German and American airplanes. Our daily play included words like Carbine, Panzer, Jeep, and Medic. For the children of Sayville, the war was a real pastime, while the children of Europe passed their time in a real war.

I don't remember the second-grade teacher's name but I do remember that she continued to fan the flame that Mrs. Smith had lit. One of the class activities was a puppet show performed for students of other classes. Every member of my class had a role in the production; some built the stage, some made scenery, some built puppets, some performed with the puppets in the play while others, like me, constructed props. I made a papier-mâché tree stump. The play was about seven Chinese brothers who use their supernatural gifts to overpower a cruel emperor. The story shows how a family can survive seemly insurmountable problems by employing their individual talents, teamwork, and an indomitable spirit. Great idea, all I needed now was a family.

When the weather warmed one of the older boys took me outside to gather some pussy willows. I was disappointed to learn that these pussies were plants. The only animals at the cottages were the chickens who provided eggs which Mildred the cook turned into mouthwatering French toast. Months later, when the cottages began to close the chickens gradually disappeared into Mildred's soup.

1942.2 & 2010   THE SHEPARD

At Christmas, I played the shepherd boy in the annual Nativity Pageant at St Ann's Episcopal Church, which lies just across Middle St. from the orphanage. It was unbearably hot in my shepherds' robes, past my bedtime at the evening service and like most previous religious experiences not at all related to my life. I was leaning heavily upon my Shepherd's' staff and began to doze off. Giggles from the congregation woke me; I suppose it was cute seeing the little orphan shepherd losing the battle to keep his eyes open.

(2010) While my role was assigned, the older kids selected many of their roles; however, no one wanted to be the innkeeper. As told in those days the innkeeper was a less then admirable character. His dismissive "There's no room in the inn" was often presented as a value judgment about the late-arriving, unmarried, and pregnant 16-year-old girl rather than a simple statement about the occupancy rate.

Today I view the innkeeper's action to be a thoughtful response to a situation in which the privacy of the barn would be much preferred to a room shared with strangers, and being the last to arrive would assure that the beds would be occupied and a crowded and dirty floor would have been her "accommodation." Even in the eighteenth century when my sixth great-grandfather Garharth von Sweringen ran a public house (or Pub) in St. Mary's MD, public accommodations were shared by who ever happened to arrive that day and it was common for total strangers to share rooms or even beds.

1943.1 THIRD GRADE

The orphanage closed in the summer of 1943. One of the reasons was that much of the free government surplus food that we had been receiving was now needed to support the troops. We moved back to Central Islip to live with my mother and the man who I would eventually know as my stepfather and Mom's eventual husband, Anthony Thomas DeSant.

The third-grade teacher was Mrs. Mulvey; she also was the Assistant Principle of the Elementary school. She was stricter than her predecessors were, but fair and consistent. We learned the multiplication tables and had weekly drills in which Mrs. Mulvey would point to two or three digit columns of numbers she had written on the blackboard and the class would verbally add the columns in unison. I hated it and was sure that my answers were never loud enough to be heard. While I believe that I was one of only two members of the class of 1953 who would ever go on to take graduate level math courses, at this point they all seemed far more advanced than me. There were no ideas in the columns of numbers; they simply had to be memorized. I suspect that fear of failure kept me from mastering what most of my classmates seemed to think was an easy task.

Mr. Rude was the principal of the entire school. One of his two sons, Robert was in my class. He was always well groomed, well dressed, well behaved, and well respected. Being around him brought back the feelings I had in the orphanage that I did not really belong anywhere.

One day Mr. Rude came to our classroom and took four boys into the hall. Something had happened, I don't remember what, but we were the "usual suspects." He interrogated us for several minutes and when one of the boys gave an unsatisfactory answer Mr. Rude slapped him across the face with the back of his hand. He wore a college ring with a large gemstone insert: the ring cut the boys lip and we returned to the classroom. I had no idea what was going on, but it was apparent that Mr. Rude believed that I was likely to be guilty of whatever it was. As I reflected on what had just happened I began to feel that I was not the only one who thought I didn't belong there. A problem with feeling like you never fit in, is not being sure if you really are an outsider, or if you have simply set the bar too high, and expect more from society than it can deliver.

Blessed is he who expects nothing,
for he shall never be disappointed."

Alexander Pope.

1943.2   THE SUBWAY

On September 20 1943, long before I ever heard her name or even knew of her existence my father's mother, **E**stelle **T**obias **G**erhard died. I didn't know why we were visiting Aunt Bea on that Saturday morning in the fall of 1943. That realization would come 60 years later when the genealogy records of my ancestors began to reveal their secrets, including Estelle's death. Notice the initials on the Estelle's brooch in the photo.

Mom took Artie and me on the Long Island Railroad to Manhattan where we ate in a Chinese restaurant. I had never experienced either a restaurant or Chinese food until that day.

After lunch, we boarded a subway for the uptown trip to the Bronx where Aunt Bea and her son Robert lived in a walk-up apartment. I remember dark smelly staircases, straw colored subway seats, and swinging handrails. At one station, we had to change trains and I followed Mom and Artie as they stood up and walked toward the open subway door. But, before I reached the door, it slid shut with my mother and Artie outside on the platform and me still inside the car as the train pulled away from the station. I was terrified and forgetting Mrs. Morgan's admonition, I cried as Mom disappeared into the darkness of that frightful place. A woman seated nearby took my hand and told me that she would get me back to my mother. We got off at the next stop and walked across the bridge toward the trains going back to where I had last seen Mom. We were about to board the downtown train when I spotted my mother arriving on another uptown train. I could see her black and white dress through the windows of both trains. As Mom stepped off the train looking for me, I yelled to her before she reboarded to continue her frantic search. Like "Charlie" in the Kingston Trio song about the Boston M.B.T.A., I might still be riding the subway but for the intervention of that Good Samaritan. We spent the afternoon with Aunt Bea. Artie went off with our cousin Robert who was close to his age. I sat in the kitchen watching the people in elevated trains speed past the kitchen window.

The next time I would see Aunt Bea was at my wedding, she was the only member of my extended family to attend.

1943.3   ALONE

For the past few years, I had been sharing my bedroom first with three others children at the orphanage and then with my brother Artie on the porch of our rented cottage.

But when Mom and Tony bought our permanent home in Central Islip with its two second-floor hip roofed bedrooms, I had my own bedroom. It was quite big and largely unfurnished. The house was uninsulated so the second story was frigid in the winter and scorching hot in the summer. Mom worked evenings and Tony retired very early as he started work before dawn each morning. Artie was often away from home and my brother Richie slept in the downstairs bedroom with Mom and Tony. I was alone in the bedroom but it felt as if I was completely alone in this new house as well.

Psychologists claim that a stressful home life or major changes, such as a new baby, or moving to a new home, can cause bedwetting. I had a new house, a new brother, a new father, but no one to share them with; I was alone even as we lived together as a family for the first time in years. In a few months, my mattress was ruined and Mom bought me a new one. The bed-wetting stopped. I guess I didn't need much attention, just an acknowledgement that someone knew that I was there.

1944.1   FOURTH GRADE

Miss Rhode was new at the school. My first personal encounter with her occurred during the noon recess on one of the first days of the school year. The entire elementary school (about 150 children) was on the playground. The youngest kids played near the building and the older kids played farther away near the outer fence. A third grader came to the area where the fourth, fifth, and sixth graders were playing softball and he stole the ball. Miss Rhode came to see what was going on and I told her that the boy wasn't allowed in this area as he was in third grade. She told me that she made the rules and for me to mind my own business. In a brilliant move of diplomacy, I reminded her that she was new at the school and the rules had always limited access to the outer area to the three upper grades. She asked me if I would like to discuss it with the principal. Believing that he would clarify the rules for Miss Rhode I said, "Yes." I was shocked when she dug her fingernails into my left ear and pulled me across the playground to the office. I honestly believed that we were going to discuss the rules with the principal. Mr. Shertenlieb, the new principal, listened as Miss Rhode described my outlandish behavior. Then he lifted me by the hair, slapped me across the face, and sent me to detention: so much for the Socratic Method. Apparently, I had more to learn than the three the R's.

As Thanksgiving approached, our class put on a play for the school assembly. I suppose I was forgiven as I was assigned the lead role of "Squanto the Friendly Indian." (Tisquantum also known as Squanto was a member of the Patuxet tribe, part of the Wampanoag Confederacy who assisted the Pilgrims after their first winter. He was integral to their very survival.) The play told the story of how the Native Americans helped the Pilgrims survive and the first Thanksgiving. We all learned our lines and through many practice sessions, the play lasted about 20 minutes. However, on the day of the performance, one of the Pilgrims spoke the wrong line, and we all followed suit and the play was over in less than five minutes. We were very surprised, as it seemed so much longer during rehearsals. Miss Rhode, who seemed as bewildered as anyone else did, later figured out what had happened. I believe our record for the school's shortest play still stands.

1945.1   FIFTH GRADE

The attention that Mrs. McBreen showed to me, like all of the teachers I'd had before, spurred me on in ways that may not have been apparent at the time. I didn't become a conscientious student until college. Nevertheless, they planted something in me that changed the way I felt about myself and set the stage for future growth, much as the seeds of the Winter Wheat lie dormant awaiting their moment in the sun. Perhaps all students feel that way about their teachers or perhaps those students who receive less affirmation at home benefit more from the positive role of their teachers. I hope that Mrs. McBreen and all the others realize how important a role they play in the future lives of their students. I remember little about the content of the fifth grade, but I do remember that the context of classroom was very positive and welcoming for me.

In teaching, you cannot see the fruit of a day's work. It is invisible
and remains so, maybe for twenty years.
Jacques Barzun

1945.2   THE MARINE RETURNS

Uncle R.E. was stationed at Pearl Harbor when it was attacked at 7:48 a.m. on Dec. 7, 1941 by 353 Imperial Japanese fighter planes, bombers, and torpedo planes. They came in two waves, launched from six aircraft carriers. He was returning from breakfast when swarms of planes began strafing and bombing the installation. There was no radar or satellites in those days so he only knew that the Japanese were attacking when he saw the planes. He went onto the roof of a nearby building and manned a machine. Later he helped in the attempt to rescue sailors who were still in the oily water of the harbor.

He also participated in the military campaigns of Vella Lavella, Bougainville, and Guadalcanal, both in the Solomon Islands, and the five-week battle of Iwo Jima. When World War II ended my mother's only brother, Robert Edward Mills, Jr., visited us in Central Islip, NY. It was the first time I ever met him. As I came home for dinner from our nearby sand lot ball field, I saw him walking toward me in his green Marine uniform. I ran to greet him. I was so proud to be walking with him and believed that someday I too would be a Marine.

Many years later, we would meet again as Reg and I stopped to see him, his wife Mary and their daughter Robin in Darlington, SC. This time I would be in uniform, not as a Marine but as a Lieutenant in the Army. We arrived after dark and Robert, anxious to share a part of his life with me took me to the swamp to hunt frogs. My hero was playing the role of Red Neck for his New York nephew. We didn't catch any frogs, but I did ruin a pair of loafers in the muddy bog. It was good to be with Robert.

On one visit, R.E took me fishing on one of the many nearby small lakes. We were fishing for Brim, which is a type of Sunfish that live in the shallow waters of lakes and ponds, and along slow-moving areas of streams and small rivers. Of course, I had never heard of Brim much less seen one, so when I caught one which was just a slightly larger than my hand I threw back the little fish. Later I learned that I had thrown back the largest fish that either of us had caught that day. Fortunately, R.E.'s wife Mary had prepared another entre.

During later visits on our travel back and forth from Georgia, Uncle R.E told me many stories about the war, about the horrors, he witnessed, and about the injuries, he had received. He told me about his role in exchanging the small battle flag that was first raised on Mt. Suribachi, Iwo Jima for the much larger flag from a nearby Navy destroyer that appears in the famous photo. He also told of the American citizen of Japanese descent who was visiting relatives in Japan when the war started and he was drafted into the Japanese Army. On Iwo Jima, R.E. saw the Japanese soldier and wounded him with a rifle shot. Later when R.E. was injured, he met the man again as they both lay in the infirmary of a Navy ship. He told R.E. that if he had not shot and wounded him he would have died with the other 22,000 Japanese soldiers who were forbidden from surrendering.

Fortunately, I never had to go to war even though I was in the Army for six years. When he died his considerable collection of war memorabilia was donated to the local history museum in Darlington, NC.

A hero is someone who has given his or her life to something bigger than themself.

Joseph Campbell

1946.1   SIXTH GRADE

The post-World War II housing and population boom forced our school to reorganize as an increase in the enrollment of younger students stressed the existing structures. Historically, the sixth grade was part of the grade school and was housed in the 6-room elementary school building. Now for the first time the 6th grade was part of the Junior High and was moved into the high school building, as new construction began to house future classes. However, the town was still quite small with a population of about 2,500 people. I knew most of them, where they lived, and their pet's names. If someone at school had borrowed clothes from a friend, everyone knew where it came from.

Mrs. Burger was a very down to earth teacher who often surprised me by expecting me to do well. It reinforced a multiyear transformation that would change my perception of my abilities and myself.

My closest friend and I were both interested in one of the girls in our class. After several frustrating weeks, we decided to flip a coin to see which of us would pursue her. I won the coin toss and soon discovered that she wasn't interested in either of us. Perhaps we should have sought her council before deciding that a coin toss would solve our relationship problems. Women, who can understand them; certainly, not anyone like me who is naïve enough to believe that a coin toss can predict their hearts desire.

1946.2   BLUEBERRY HILL

One of my friends began the school year by bringing in a piece of petrified wood he obtained near the Yellowstone Petrified Forest in Wyoming. His family drove west during the summer vacation and saw many of our nations treasures. Many of my classmates were amazed by the beautiful rock and the interesting explanation that the teacher provided; I was amazed that a family all went somewhere together in a car.

I don't remember a single occasion when our entire family ever participated in any recreational or social activity. Life was about work, school, and home life. But on one occasion, Tony did take me out alone with him in the car to a wild blue berry patch on a hill several miles from home. We each had a kitchen pot and we walked slowly through the field searching for large ripe berries. Wild berries do taste better than berries found in berry farms but they are much harder to pick because the berries are smaller and sparse and the plants are scattered among undergrowth and shrubs. After an hour or so, I was hot, tired, and ready to go and was glad when we headed for the car. I suggested that I put my berries into Tony's pot. We both knew that I was feeling sheepish about having so few berries to bring home. Tony refused; I thought that if I were the Dad I would have let my son put his berries in my pot so we could both feel good about the bounty that Mom would soon bake into a pie. It's now 68 years later and I still remember that one trip with Tony, both its joys and its disappointments.

1947.1   JUNIOR HIGH

Mrs. Mulligan was the first teacher who ever insisted that I do homework and sent me to detention if I failed to produce. I had never done homework and never brought my books home from school. Staying awake in class was all that was necessary to get passing grades. I resisted for weeks and spent many hours writing with two pencils taped together to produce the required lines of "mea culpas." Eventually I succumbed and started doing homework for her social studies class. I still resisted working hard for other classes with mixed results. In later years, subjects like Geometry, where answers could be figured out based on a few principals I did fine. However, in classes like Chemistry, that required remembering many specific details, paying attention in class was not sufficient. Not studying beyond the classroom was beginning to take its toll.

1948.1   THE GROCER

Tony worked in Benstock's Grocery store for many years. It was one of four small owner operated food stores in town. One had a butcher shop attached while Benstock's had a hardware store attached. The owner Sid Benstock ran the hardware store and Tony ran the grocery store. As the town, expanded new stores were constructed and Sid built the first super market in the area. While small by today's standards, it was several times larger than any other store in town. Sid was to manage the store and Tony was to be in charge of fruits and vegetables. A few weeks prior to the opening of the new store, Tony suffered an inguinal hernia and he spent about a week in the hospital. When he recovered, and returned to work, Sid fired him as he had given Tony's job to his brother-in-law. Tony had no retirement plan and had to take a job as a cook in the local State Hospital. It was quite demoralizing for him but it saved our family from financial disaster. He was however able to work part time at Haliday's Grocery Store. Sam, the owner, and the butchers who worked across the aisle from the grocery liked Tony and they all seemed at ease and happy together in the store.

At the end of each year, Tony would bring home a box loaded with cans of food that had lost their labels. We would have potluck dinners for a few days, as we never knew what was going to be in the unmarked cans. Occasionally, I would slip down the aisle of the store to the canned fruit section and remove the label from a can of plums or cherries. We rarely had fruit except during the Holidays when we received Christmas presents of Oranges and Thanksgiving treats of Tangerines. There were few frozen foods at that time and fresh foods were only available during their peak domestic harvest season. A canned plum or cherry was an incredible treat.

1949.1   HIGH SCHOOL FRESHMAN YEAR

Freshmen could take one or two electives in addition to the required English, Social Studies, and General Science courses. Having absolutely no direction from my mother or stepfather, I signed up for the easiest courses offered: Art and Woodworking. As I walked the halls in the typical first day freshman daze trying to find the Art room, the math teacher, Mr. Jamison, interrupted the Introductory Algebra class he was teaching, when he saw me through the window in the classroom door. He took me by the arm and told me that I would not be taking Art and to take a seat in the Algebra class. Without his intervention, I would probably have continued to take the course of least resistance and graduated with the required 16 credits. However, because he had faith in me (possibly, because my brother Artie had won the math and science award the year before) I graduated with majors in math, science and woodworking, which I just couldn't give up, and received a Regents Diploma in addition to the School Diploma.

Mr. Markey, the Social Studies teacher and Junior Varsity baseball and basketball coach also helped me adjust to High School. One day during Social Studies class, he mentioned that the earth was closer to the sun when the northern hemisphere was experiencing winter than it was in the summer. I asked him why it was colder when the earth was closest to the sun. Not knowing the answer to my question, but obviously aware of the unplanned opportunity for a teachable moment he took me down the hall to the science lab. The science teacher explained about the earths tilt on it axis and its effect on solar absorption; but not until he made it very clear that he didn't appreciate being disturbed when he was teaching a class. I had several other adventures with Mr. Markey, who was a model train hobbyist, including a trip to Brooklyn to see a huge operating model train setup that took up the entire basement of a large apartment building. Years later, I would build my own model railroad in the basement of our first home. I don't know why he took an interest in me, but like many others in my early life, he contributed to my growth in ways that I cannot quantify. Simply being acknowledged is in itself a powerful form of affirmation.

The music teacher Mr. Mead asked me to join the marching band (again probably based on the achievements of my brother) and this lead not only my taking music lessons but also taking two courses in music rudiments and harmony. The classes required me to come to class an hour before school officially opened, because all of the classrooms in the small school were already in use during regular hours. The classes turned out to be more valuable to me than what little I may have learned about music theory. Mr. Mead gave me glimpses of the world beyond the little town where we lived. He opened my eyes and my mind to possibilities that were diametrically opposed to what my previous life experiences had taught me about the world and about my potential place in that world.

I hate to think what my life would have been if those three men (Mr. Jamison, Mr. Markey, and Mr. Mead) had not reached out to me or if Artie had not set the stage that provided the opportunities that I probably would not have discovered on my own.

1949.2   SAM THE BARBER

My barber was a first-generation Italian immigrant. When he left his home in Italy many years earlier, he brought a bare rooted sprig from his family's fig tree in his luggage. The tree produced fruit each year, however since it could not survive the cold winters on Long Island; he had to bury it each fall. He kept the tree pruned so it was small enough to be wrapped in newspaper and placed in a 2-foot deep trench. Sand substitutes for soil on Long Island, so it was easy to bury and replant the tree each year.

As fall approached in 1949, it became apparent to the aging barber that he could no longer bury the tree. As I was one of his only young customers, and since he knew that my stepfather was Italian, he offered me the tree. I accepted it and agreed to bury it each year as he had instructed. Apparently, I didn't bury the tree deep enough for in the spring when the flowers returned from their winter retreat the anticipated resurrection of the fig tree was replaced by a requiem. Sam never learned that the tree had died, as he had passed away a few months before the tree. I still feel guilty because I didn't keep my promise to the old man.

The best time to plant a tree was 20 years ago,
the second-best time is now.
Chinese Proverb

1949.3   SAND LOT BASEBALL GAME

It must have been a Monday because my mother, who worked six days a week, was home. It was a warm summer day and a pickup baseball game was scheduled that afternoon. I was planning to go and I hoped to try out my pitching skills in a nonleague game. I rarely had to babysit my brother Richie who had just turned 6, but on that day, my mother asked me to take him with me to the high school ball field. I put Richie in his red wagon and pulled him to the schoolyard about a mile away. He entertained himself as I proved to myself that I could never be a pitcher on the high school team. Soon it began to rain, everyone ran home, but I didn't want Richie to get wet, so I took him to the rear entrance of the school, which had a sheltered overhang. We waited until the rain stopped and then started for home, when it began to rain; again, we ducked into a store. Three times, we headed for home and three times, we got wet when the rain started up again. We were soaked by the time we got home. Mom was furious when she saw Richie dripping on the floor in the kitchen. She sent me to my room. A few minutes later, she charged up the stairs with the hose that we used to siphon water from the icebox. She screamed at me as she beat me with the hose. The feeling of injustice lasted much longer than the pain from the beating. I thought of running away from home, but I knew that I had already been there and it had nothing to offer.

Both Richie's age and the fact that he had slept in my parents' room until age seven when Artie left home in Sept. 1950 kept Richie separated from Artie and me. Artie and I had separate bedrooms on the second floor. I believe that Richie would have benefited from more contact with his older brothers, but our parents preferred as little contact as possible, they even kept their bedroom door locked when they were not at home. Richie was their son, and Artie and I were just part of the extended family from another time and place. Little changed after that day simply because there was little left to change, I already had little contact with my family. However, I did learn a lesson from my mother that day even though I'm not sure that she learned it as well.

At first I was reluctant to include this account in my memoir. But as I remembered the details I realized that only my mother could have offered the words of regret that would have provided the healing that I sought. However, that opportunity had long since passed and I would no longer remain the wounded victim. If the issue were ever to be put to rest I must personally take responsibility for the healing. Hearing the story actually spoken aloud in my own voice was the best therapy available; it provided sufficient comfort to allow me to finally put this incident to rest.

"Resentment is like taking poison and hoping the other person dies."
St. Augustine

1949.4 PREJUDICE

My mother grew up in rural North Carolina in the early 1900's. She often used the N word when referring to black people. To a casual observer my mother may have sounded like just another bigoted red neck. However, those who knew her would not accuse her of being prejudiced. In much of society the word nigger was first softened to nigra and then replaced with colored and then by black. Before the offensiveness of the insensitive terms became common knowledge, for those raised like my mother all the terms had the same meaning; black people. However, Mom had two distinct ways of using the word. One the straightforward descriptive term learned in her youth carried no intent to be offensive or to demean. Of course, her intent would be of no concern to any black person who might have heard her. The second use of the word was intended to be disrespectful. It was clear to me what Mom's intentions were by the way she spoke the word. Even when using the word in a hurtful way I never believed that Mom was actually bigoted against black people, any more than, if she had said "dumb blonde" or "fat jerk" would have been anything more than a personal insult aimed at a particular individual and not a sign of bigotry against all fair haired or overweight people. I thought Mom was insensitive and unconcerned about the feelings of others in general but not bigoted against black people in particular. At school, however, I did witness bigotry. The first black student arrived at our school as part of the mass migration of various minority groups from New York City after the Second World War. I saw him playing on various sport teams and he seemed to contribute to all of them. When I first overheard, his teammates making negative comments about him I thought that he had done something that negatively affected the team. I soon realized that the slurs were not about his performance but about him personally. As insensitive as my mother was, I had never heard her say anything suggesting that being black was a negative characteristic.

I remembered being jeered at school for living in an orphanage and thought that what the black boy was feeling was the same as what I had experienced. Later I realized that while the feeling may have been in some ways similar the causes were not at all alike. I would eventually be able to control where I lived and leave the orphanage behind, but the boy had no capacity to control the societal changes needed to leave the bigotry behind.

CHAPTER 3   *THE FIFTIES*

Clashes between communism and capitalism dominated the decade. The conflicts included the Korean War, and the beginning of the Space Race. The launch of Sputnik I, along with an increase in nuclear testing, created a politically conservative climate. The fear of communism was the prevailing sentiment in the United States throughout the decade; this led the country to intervene in the Korean and Vietnam Wars. Bomb shelter plans became widely available.

The Decolonization of European Colonial empires began, and many nations gained their independence from France, Belgium, and the United Kingdom.

The Arab–Israeli conflict escalated. Reconstruction continued in Japan, funded largely by the United States. Social changes included democratic elections and universal suffrage.

The Chinese invasion of Tibet and Korea caused years of hostility between China and the United States. The Chinese allied with the Soviet Union, which then provided considerable technical and economic aid. Mao Zedong (1893-1976) tried to rush the country's economic development with the creation of huge rural communes.

With the help of the Marshall Plan, post-war reconstruction succeeded, but Europe continued to be divided into Western and Soviet bloc countries. This division came to be called the Iron Curtain. It divided Germany into East and West Germany. The Soviet Union continued its domination of Eastern Europe. In 1953 Joseph Stalin, the leader of the Soviet Union, died. This led to a somewhat more liberal domestic and foreign policy, stressing peaceful competition with the West rather than overt hostility.

There were many new technologies in the fifties, including television, the first leak free ballpoint pen, and the first copy-machine. In 1953, the Chevrolet Corvette became the first car to have an all-fiberglass body. In 1954, Bell Telephone labs produced the first solar battery. Nineteen-fifty-five saw the invention of a solar-powered wristwatch. Jonas Salk created a polio vaccine. In 1958, the first plastic Coke bottle appeared and the United States conducted its first hydrogen bomb test. Passenger jets entered service. The double-helix structure of DNA was discovered, and the first successful use of ultrasound test of the heart activity was performed. The world's first nuclear power plant opened near Moscow, and the U.S. created NASA. President Harry S. Truman inaugurated transcontinental television service on September 4, 1951 when he made a nationwide speech viewed from the west coast to the east coast at the same time. Jackie Robinson became the first black person to play baseball in the major league. Doo Wop entered the pop music charts in the 1950s. Novelty songs came into popularity. In the mid-1950s, Elvis Presley was the leading figure of the newly popular sound of rock and the American folk music revival became a phenomenon in the 1950s to mid-1960s

Best-selling books were The Cardinal, From Here to Eternity, The Silver Chalice, The Robe, Not as a Stranger, Marjorie Morningstar, Don't Go Near the Water, By Love Possessed, Doctor Zhivago, and Exodus.

An average new house cost $8,450, the average salary per year was $3,210, a gallon of gas was 18 cents, a loaf of bread cost 12 cents, the average cost of new car was $1,510.

The U.S. Population was 150,697,361 and the life expectancy was 65.6 for men and 71.1 for women.

There were six known lynchings of black people in the 1950s.

1950.1 & 2013   HIGH SCHOOL SOPHOMORE YEAR

There weren't enough hours in the day to do everything that needed doing. As art is to the eye, and as music is to the ear, so ideas are to the mind. I was infatuated with ideas, all of them. At this point in my life, I rarely took the time to study a subject well enough to master it, there was always something new to discover. I was more curious than studious.

> (2013) One of my biggest concerns about modern secondary education is the size of the schools. When three small schools merge into one large central school, hundreds of opportunities are lost. There's only one student council, instead of three, one baseball team instead of three, one prom queen, instead of three, one valedictorian, instead of three, etc., etc. In addition to the reduction in the number of opportunities, there is a corresponding increase in the level of competition, as only the best at each activity can make the grade and late bloomers will have little opportunity to develop in the highly competitive environment.

(1950) Because I attended a small school, I was able to:
- Participate in varsity athletics even though I wasn't much of an athlete,
- Play in the marching band even though I wasn't a very able musician,
- Become something of a "nerd," even though I was a poor student,
- Become a school social and political leader even though I was relatively shy and socially inept.

This variety of activities was not unique; in a small school, it was easy and common for students to be active in many different activities. Once energized, I wanted to taste it all. My contribution to the various groups and activities that I was involved with was inconsequential, however their contribution to my development was substantial. Is it the responsibility of students to enhance the quality of the school or is it the role of the school to enhance the life of the student? How lucky I was to be in a small school, if I had to attend the high schools that my sons attended, I would have been lost in the cracks.

Artie left home after he graduated from High School in June 1950. He enlisted in the Air Force and soon left for Korea. Although we lived quite separate lives, at that point, I missed him and sometimes I went into his room to touch the personal memorabilia in his top dresser drawer. However, instead of making him feel closer, they only accentuated his absence. The trap door had sprung again.

1950.2   MY FIRST KISS

I had been walking Marlene home from school for a few weeks. On one warm spring day, her home was empty when we arrived and we went into the living room and sat on the couch. I leaned over and gave her a brief, ill-aimed kiss in the general vicinity of her upper lip. It was quite exciting. We dated for a month or so and on one occasion, her father took us for a ride in the rumble seat of his two-door car.

> *A rumble seat was an exterior seat, which hinged out from the rear deck of some pre-World War II automobiles. Models equipped with a rumble seat were sport coupes or sport roadsters. This type of seating became obsolete in the 1950s, possibly because cars became too fast for the comfort and safety of passengers.*

Since we were freezing in the open-air seat, we ducked down to avoid the wind. When her father could no longer see us in the rear-view mirror, he stopped the car and told us to stay in plain sight. I don't know what he thought we might possibly be doing in the back seat except holding on for dear life as he sped over bumpy roads with no seat belts or safety handles. We broke up soon after that: the reasons for the separation were as unknown to me as were the reasons for our having been together. It was fun, scary and a lot more, just part of growing up. Marlene gave me my first kiss, but she was not my first love; that would come later.

1950.3   A SELF-SUFFICIENT MAN

While it's hard to imagine today, but at the time it was not out of the ordinary for people to build their own homes with their own hands. In some cases, a family would live in a tent next to the construction site and then move into the basement, once it was capped and covered. The process could take several years and the family would gradually occupy the areas of their new home as they were completed.

A neighbor, who was planning to be married within the year, asked me to help him build a house for him and his future bride. He was a skilled worker in all of the construction trades and had no doubt that he could do the work. I was merely to be his helper. We started by excavating the hole for the basement. Charlie borrowed an old farm tractor with metal wheels. He created a large scoop by cutting the wheels and the front edge off of a wheelbarrow and attaching a chain that was then connected to the tractor. We would take turns driving the tractor and using the handles of the wheelbarrow to scoop up and spread a few cubic feet of soil with each rotation around the ever-deepening basement. When the excavation was done, cinder blocks were used to construct the cellar walls. The amount of work we could do weekend was limited by the amount of materials he could afford to purchase each week. When the shell of the house was completed and the roof was installed, Charlie hoped that the value of the semi-completed house would provide sufficient equity for a bank to lend him enough money to complete the installation of the expensive electrical, plumbing, and heating systems. The bank refused because the land on which the home was being build would likely be rezoned for commercial use, the house would be razed, and the equity would be lost.

As the wedding approached, Charlie asked me to join his future in-laws in a celebration of the engagement. As part of the family tradition, a goat was to be sacrificed for the feast. The family had raised the goat from a young kid and it had become a family pet, and they were unable to kill it. When they asked me if I would kill the goat, I assured them that I would. I knelt down pressing the goat to the ground as the father of the bride handed me the ceremonial knife. I looked into the eyes of the frightened goat and remembered the goats that I had played with years earlier in my first foster home, just a few miles from this very site, and I realized that I too was unable to kill the goat. The party proceeded with a delicious brisket and homemade wine.

Just before the wedding, Charlie sold the property with the half-completed hand built home and purchased a small house in one of the many development tracts that were springing up throughout the county as the post-war era's economic boon spread from city to the formerly rural areas of Long Island. The gains that the era provided were not without their losses. I never again saw a man create a home for his family with his own hands. Independence and handcraft was gradually being replaced by efficacy and mass production.

At the wedding, Charlie's nephew and I snuck into the kitchen and drank champagne. I got drunk for the first time, and was sick for two days. I never got that drunk again and rarely drank enough to feel the effects of alcohol.

1951.1 EBBETS FIELD

Near the end of sophomore year, the high school marching band was selected to play before the beginning of a Brooklyn Dodgers evening baseball game at Ebbets Field in Brooklyn. Although I was a Yankee fan, the thought of seeing my first major league baseball game was very exciting. However, as we marched onto the field, it began to rain and we marched off and went home. I never did get to see the Brooklyn Dodgers play.

> *The 1951 Brooklyn Dodgers led the National League for much of the season. However, a late season swoon and a hot streak by the New York Giants led to a classic three-game playoff series. Bobby Thomson's dramatic ninth-inning home run in the final game won the pennant for the Giants. The hit was immortalized as the Shot Heard 'Round the World.*

> *Six years later Ebbets Field was torn down when the Brooklyn Dodgers were moved to Los Angeles, California.*

1951.2 HIGH SCHOOL JUNIOR YEAR

In the summer between my sophomore and junior years my stepfather, Tony was still insisting on a 9 p.m. curfew. If I came home after curfew, I was grounded for a week. During one of my frequent groundings, while Tony was weeding the large vegetable garden in the back yard, I climbed out of a living room window and went downtown to meet my friends at the Skylark soda fountain, where I worked as a "soda jerk" on weekends. The next morning Tony told me that he was 'washing his hands of me' and that from now on I could do whatever I pleased. I felt so abandoned; all I wanted was a later curfew, not another lost family. It was like leaning against a familiar wall and having it collapse, no longer able to support my weight. The sought-after door to a place of greater independence and freedom was torn down with the wall. The new liberty was both freeing and frightening.

I know that you might learn from good examples, I guess you can also learn from bad examples, its' just more painful. I learned that fatherhood was more than just setting boundaries; it also was providing support, encouragement, security, and love.

I don't blame Tony for his limited view of fatherhood. His own father, a first-generation Italian immigrant, forced him to quit school at the age of 14 in order to go to work. He gave his salary to his father who in turn gave Tony a small weekly allowance. Tony grew up in a family where children were treated like chattel until they were married. Even after his first marriage, Tony and his first wife Marie as well as his brother and his family, rented their homes from Tony's father and lived in an enclave of Italian relatives.

At school, the courses were beginning to get harder but I had not yet begun studying and the only homework I did was what I could finish at school. For ten years, I was able get reasonable grades by paying attention in class, but now more was being required of me then I was prepared to give. No one at home ever asked me if I had homework to do or if I needed to study for an exam.

At that stage of my life, my plans for the future were little more than a blur; I didn't even know what it was possible to want. My vague dream was to be happy, secure, and successful but I had no idea what these things would look like having never witnessed any of them. I did know that college was the key to opening doors; even doors I didn't yet know existed. Eventually I would have to learn to study.

Looking for love but finding too many girls to love, I settled for a series of infatuations.

1951.3   FIRST LOVE

I first saw her at an evening Police Athletic League Teen get-together. The second story of the town firehouse was equipped with ping-pong tables and other activities and was opened for teens one evening a week during the summer. She was beautiful and had short blonde hair and blue eyes. I thought she was perfect even thought I had never spoken to her. I had never seen her in town before and asked who she was and was told that she attended a nearby co-ed Catholic School and that she would never go out with me. Shortly after that she transferred to the local public high school, she was one year behind me. We began dating and soon we were "going steady." We thought we were in love but we knew that we were not committed. After a few months, her family invited me to dinner. It was a disaster. The next day I called and she told me that it was over. I was so bereaved that I withdrew from most school activities.

I couldn't blame her parents for disapproving of me for I had no plans, no prospects, and no provisions for improving. If I had a daughter who was dating someone like me, I would have been terrified.

I was never quite sure if the anguish of losing her or the sting of the rejection was the most painful. However, it eventually passed and life returned to normal but the remnant of a lost dream remained until another dream, which had more substance replaced it. Part of growing up is the inevitable pain it brings.

> *". . . at some point you have to realize that some people can stay in your heart but not in your life..." Sandi Lynn*

The father of one of my neighborhood friends was a plumber. Occasionally he asked me to join them when they had large projects to complete. When my friend quit school, and took a full-time job with another firm, I became his father's assistant during school breaks. He was not an ambitious man. Often, I would wake him up in the morning and start his coffee. He often left me alone at job sites to complete installations. I learned a great deal about plumbing, including the fact that I never wanted to make a career of it. While I knew what I didn't want to do, I had no idea about what I would like to become.

> *We know what we are, but know not what we may be.*
> *William Shakespeare*

1951.4   KOSHER KITCHEN

✡ When I was about 16 years old, my mother told me a story about how she and my father would frantically prepare for visits from his mother. My grandmother, Estelle Tobias Gerhard, was Jewish and had raised her children to observe the tradition of maintaining a kosher kitchen. While my mother continued with the details of her story, my mind suddenly grasped the unstated implication of what she was saying, "I was partly Jewish." My mother rarely spoke about her past, especially about my father, so I didn't want to run the risk of ending the conversation by interrupting her with the dozens of questions that flooded my mind.

While we always had matzo in the spring, I had associated them with Easter rather than Passover. Several years later, I came to understand its' importance while working at a Jewish Hospital in New York City. While it was a surprise to hear of my heritage, it wasn't very important to me at the time. Since I had, no experience either of what it meant to be Jewish, personally or through hearing of the experience of others it had held no more importance to me than when I found out that my mother was raised Baptist and some of her grandparents were Methodists. Much later, I realized that being Jewish was for many people a key part of their identity and not simply about their religion. It was about their history, affiliations, and traditions. However, as I began to read and travel and more importantly think, the meaning of being a Jew began to take shape. My first experience was with a girl who was to become one of my best friends, Carol, who was Jewish. However, until she heard my news from her sister who was friends with my older brother, we had never discussed it. She asked me how

I felt about being Jewish. What I really felt was inadequate as it was obvious that this was important to her, and yet, at the time, it seemed inconsequential to me. Soon after that, her father offered me a job in the family variety store, which was one of the most prominent stores in town. Years later Carol revealed to me that her parents assumed that she and I would eventually be married, apparently either unaware or unbelieving that our relationship, by mutual agreement, would never be anything but platonic.

Although having 25% Jewish heritage never played a public role in my life, as time passed it did gradually come to be a more important, yet peripheral, part of my private identity.

1952.1   BEACH PARTY

The brilliant reflective light of the sun blanketed the sand dunes with a dazzling display of many shades of white and yellow. I walked the isolated beach of West Hampton with pretty but long forgotten girls, laughed with my friends and idled away much of the summer between my junior and senior years of high school. Two carloads of eager partygoers could spend an entire day and evening at the beach and never come across a person from another group. Some days we would go to one of the many quiet bays and coves that surround Long Island to gather clams for our beach parties. We tied burlap bags inside inflated inner tubes from old car tires. As we slowly walked across the cove with our gunnysacks floating beside us, we could feel the clams in the soft muddy bottom with our feet and place them in the bag. Some fresh picked corn and a watermelon would round out the feast for a small beach party. Today motels, summer homes, tourists, and municipal beaches compete for space at the shrinking seashore. The 1950's were a good time to live on Long Island. Unfortunately, there was no sun block and I would spend the next day (or two) in bed, beet red and aching. I now visit my dermatologist twice each year to have him remove the many cancerous and precancerous lesions that resulted from those carefree summer days at the beach in the blazing sun. As I write this, I am recovering from a skin graft on my nose that was needed to cover the wound created by the removal of my third squamous cell carcinoma.

1952.2   REBUILDING BILL'S CAR

Bill was my closest friend in high school. His life was so different from mine but we seemed to enjoy each other company. Bill worked part time at a local grocery store and saved his money to buy an old Ford sedan. In those days' cars needed to have their engines rebuilt after 70 or 80 thousand miles as the valves and piston rings would wear out and the engine would lose power and burn a lot of oil. Tires would only last for about 10 thousand miles. Bill's father and uncle knew a great deal about cars and had all of the tools and equipment needed to remove the engine, replace worn parts, and reinstall the engine. I spend several weekends at Bill's and helped him as he followed his fathers' instructions. His family was quite self-sufficient. Occasionally on Sundays, I would accompany the family to a small Lutheran Church with a largely German congregation. Since the family was also quite stoic I never knew if they approved of my attending their church or not. With the car repaired and running, Bill painted it gray and we spent many happy hours with friends some, going to destinations, and some just enjoying the ride. After high school, Bill joined the Air Force and I lost touch with him. Many years later we met again at school reunions and I could see that he was well liked by those who, like him, had remained or returned to the old hometown to raise their families. He was one of the few people that I have ever thought of as being a best friend. Now I have many associates and acquaintances but only one other person, beside him and Reg, had ever held the place in my life that Bill had once occupied . . . my best friend.

My best friend is the one who brings out the best in me.
Author Unknown

1952.3   WEDDING BUT NO MARRIAGE

That December day in 1952 stands out as one of the few truly celebratory occasions in our home on Pine View Blvd. It was the day that Tony and Mom were finally married, after learning that Tony's first wife Marie (nee Still) DeSant had died in Florida. It was the only time that I ever saw Mom drinking wine. I don't remember Mom and Tony ever going out to eat or to a movie or even to a friends' house for the evening.

According to the information on the marriage license application completed for Mom and Tony's marriage she and my biological father Arthur Gerhard Sr. had never married even though they lived together for about seven years from about 1931 to 1938. Although I had always thought of her as being rather prudish, all three of her sons were born out of wedlock.

I suspect that Mom stood apart from much of what society had to offer because she was afraid that her southern background and life style choices would prevent her from being fully accepted. She lived behind a door that few would enter. In her relative isolation, I suspect that she did not realize that the door was of her own construction and that only she had the key to open it.

"We have met the enemy and he is us"
Pogo

1952.4   HIGH SCHOOL SENIOR YEAR

The series of music courses I took with Mr. Meade included a field trip to Carnegie Hall. Leonard Bernstein directed an afternoon program for children and youth in which he led the philharmonic orchestra (or a portion of it) and provided his personal explanations and anecdotes. He was a brilliant teacher who used humor, demonstration, and explanation with equal ease. Although this was just a small slice from my four years in high school it remains today, almost 60 years later, as a cherished highlight.

The class of 1953 had worked for 4 years earning money for a one-week class trip to Washington, DC. We visited many of the tourist sites that I would be living near in the years to come.

I was asked to play the male lead in the annual senior play. Our Miss Brooks was well received and my friend Bob, who was generally considered quiet and reserved, excelled in his outgoing betrayal of the school principal.

King George VI of England died on 6 February 1952 and it was apparent that Princess Elizabeth would soon become Queen. As class president, I send a letter of condolences to the new Queen on behalf of the class of 1953. After her coronation on 2 June 1953, I received a black bordered reply from the Queen. While the letter has long since been misplaced, at this writing Elizabeth remains Queen.

I delivered the farewell address at the graduation ceremony. I guess it wasn't very impressive as not even I remember a single word of it.

1952.5   THE QUEST

As the uncertainty about my life after high school gradually stole into my life, I would sometimes lie in bed at night and think about my future. I would imagine that I was a Psychologist living and working in upstate New York. Of course, at that time to a boy on Long Island, upstate New York meant Yonkers not Albany. I wasn't quite sure what Psychologists were or what they did; but I did know that I couldn't stay in the small rural town where I grew up and where the opportunities that I saw around me looked more like disillusionments than dreams. The Quest that took years to fulfill had begun.

"Everything you possess of skill, and wealth, and handicraft, wasn't it first merely a thought and a quest?"

Rumi

1953.1   GRADUATION

I don't know if the hardest thing about leaving high school was that I didn't know how to take the next steps or that, I had no idea where the next steps might lead so of course I didn't know which steps were worth taking. At any rate, graduation was like being evicted from life. The photo is a reproduction of a sketch that I drew in June of 1953, showing the long sought-after diploma turning on me in a totally unwarranted attack and kicking me into the abyss called "Real Life."

Although I never expected either my mother or stepfather to attend any of my dozens of band recitals, track meets, baseball, basketball, or soccer games, I was disappointed that neither could attend the senior play in which I had the male lead, or graduation where as class president I gave the student address. They had no idea what I had achieved in high school and offered no guidance about what should happen afterward. Tony's only visible sign of concern was that I begin paying room and board now that my education was behind me.

1953.2   LEARNING TO DRIVE

Many of my friends learned to drive in their family's car, taught by their parents or by the newly initiated and costly driver-training program at the high school. Tony did not allow me to drive his car and I could not have afforded to take the driver-training course. When I went out to bars or parties with my friends who had their own or their family's car, I would not drink. When it was time to go home, I was often the only sober one in the crowd. Therefore, I learned to drive by becoming the default-designated driver long before the phase became popular. This did require my acquiring a second set of friends as my friends from school would rarely go to bars or over-drink at parties. Fortunately, there was little traffic in the early morning hours of rural Long Island in the nineteen fifties and I always managed to get everyone home safely.

1953.3   FIRST STEPS INTO THE REAL WORLD

Artie had joined the Air Force immediately after graduation three years earlier, but I wanted to go to college. But, there were a few obstacles to overcome, I didn't know how to get into them, and I had no money to pay for tuition even if I should ever find an open door.

The Korean War was almost over, but the cold war that caused it was still in full swing, and the military defense industry on Long Island was thriving. I soon obtained a job on the evening shift at Republic Aviation in Farmingdale, L. I. NY. We were building the F-84F Thunderstreak and RF-84F Thunderflash (a recognizance version of the fighter plane.) NATO and U.S. Air National Guard units used the planes, which were too slow to compete with the Russian planes used in Korea.

We worked in two person teams; my team's job was to install two stainless steel braces near the rear of the fuselage that secured the huge exhaust pipe. The space that we worked in was a little over 3 feet in diameter. It was hot, cramped, and smelly as my partner rarely bathed. So, when he called in sick one evening I gladly installed the units by myself. Since this cut the cost in half, the supervisor was interested to know if I could keep up the pace. I assured him that I could and would actually enjoy the fresh air. In a few weeks, I cut the costs in half again by reducing the time it took to install the units in the two airplanes we were expected to complete each evening. This left me with four hours each night with nothing to do. Often, I would get a blue print from the stock clerk and walk around the factory trying to look like I was on a mission to prevent being stopped for being in the wrong sector. I soon gained a general overview of how the entire plane was assembled. One evening I accidently walked into a restricted area where a sleek new swept wing plane was being housed, possibly the prototype of an F-105 Thunderchief. Several security guards immediately stopped me; and it took some taking to convince them that I had simply taken a wrong turn.

Whenever someone in my section called in sick, I was available to help for half of the shift. I soon became proficient at every job in our section, which installed parts in the rear (aft) portion of the fuselage. After several months, I was promoted to assistant to the most senior mechanic in the section. Frank's job was to repair damaged components. The engineers would design a repair and Frank and I would make the necessary repairs. It was great work compared to sitting inside the tail pipe. And Frank was not only an excellent mechanic, but also a great teacher who helped me develop the confidence I would need in the future.

The Korean War, or Korean police action as the politicians called it, ended on July 27, 1953. Artie came home in September and joined me working at Republic.

However, in 1954, the world's need for jet aircraft fell off sharply. After a year of working from 6 p.m. to 2:42 a.m. with several thousand dollars in the bank and correspondence courses in college Physics and Trigonometry under my belt, I left Republic Aviation as the layoffs were beginning and enrolled for the fall semester at Farmingdale A. & T.

1954.1 FARMINGDALE A & T

My work at Republic had spiked my interest in airplanes, so when I started college, I decided to major in Aircraft Operations. This general program surveyed many aspects of the aircraft industry including aerodynamics, aircraft design, airport management, aircraft maintenance, and repair. I hoped to finish the two-year program and go on to a four-year program in Aeronautical Engineering. One of my classmates had been flying for years and had an instructor's license. The instructor, two other students, and I would occasionally rent a four seat Cessna at a local private airport. Two students would sit in the back as observers and one would sit in the front. Only the student in the front seat could get credit for flight training. I believe that 20 hours of in-flight instruction were required to obtain a pilot's license at that time. I only had four hours when I left school. Before I finished the second semester, my savings were gone and I had to withdraw. My original plan of pursuing a career in Aeronautical Engineering was derailed when the money that had taken me two years to accumulate ran out. I had hoped for it to last two years; however, when my stepfather, Tony, decided to charge me rent for living at home as I commuted daily to college, the money lasted only one year.

1955.1   THE AIR CADETS

Between the classes and the flying lessons, my interests in airplanes and flying had increased greatly while at college. So, in May 1955, having exhausted my funds I left college and applied to the Air Force's Air Cadet Program. Prior to the graduation of the first class from the Air Force Academy in 1959, the Air Cadet Program was the only training program available to become an Air Force pilot. Entrance required passing an eight-day battery of physical, mental, and psychological tests at Hancock Field, located near Syracuse, New York. Several months passed since the notification arrived that I had passed the tests, and I had no word from the Air Force. I called my contact at Hancock Field and he told me that members of the Air National Guard filled the classes and they only called civilians if there were not enough Guard members to fill each class and that they hadn't called civilians in many months. I had to join the Air National Guard if I was ever to become a jet pilot.

The only Air National Guard Unit on Long Island was located at Floyd Bennet Field. The field served as a base for units of the New York Air National Guard from 1947 to 1970 and was located in a remote section of Brooklyn, which required my getting up at 4 a.m., taking a train to Jamaica, Queens then a subway to the end of the line in Brooklyn, then a bus that passed the field. Unfortunately, the bus did not pass the front entrance so I had the bus driver let me out on the road near the end of the runway. (A second bus taking an additional half hour could complete the trip to the front gate.) After the five-hour trip, a climb over an 8-foot cyclone fence and a half-mile dash to the barracks area, I would arrive 15 minutes late for our 9 a.m. roll call. The sergeant was just thrilled with my late arrival and I think that he never believed that it was impossible for me to arrive earlier as all of the other guardsmen were able to make it on time. Of course, they all lived in Brooklyn not two counties away. They tolerated my tardiness because the Guard was not interested in me as a basic airman; my signing obligated me to become a pilot in the Air National Guard when my training and other active duty military obligations were over. While I was waiting, I worked one weekend a month as an airplane mechanic's helper. Mostly I cleaned parts and checked brakes.

The New York State Air National Guard 102 Bombardment Squadron was equipped with B-26 Invader light bombers and B-25s. Lt. Col. James Doolittle's used similar planes for his flight of sixteen B-25's from the navy carrier, U.S.S. Hornet, on April 18, 1942 to bomb Japan in retaliation for that country's attack on Pearl Harbor on December 7, 1941

For two weeks during the summer of 1955, the entire unit traveled to Camp Drum (now Fort Drum) in Jefferson County, near the Canadian border in upstate New York. The post had served as a prisoner of war camp for captured Italian and German troops in World War II. During and after the Korean War many units trained at Drum to take advantage of the terrain and climate.

I was never issued a uniform, as it was anticipated that I wouldn't be around long enough to need it, and the pilot training program had a distinct uniform. So, I purchased some olive-green pants from the local Army-Navy Store and left on a bus for Camp Drum. I worked on the flight line performing pre-and post-flight checks on the aging aircraft. Near the end of our stay, a General came to inspect the troops. Since my clothes only remotely resembling an actual military uniform, they assigned me to "emergency rescue duty" during the General's visit. This sounded more important than it really was; I sat in a jeep at the end of the runway where the General couldn't see me. I was losing my enthusiasm for a military career. It was also becoming apparent that the end of the Korean War not only reduced the need for airplanes but also the need for pilots. I would have to find a new career. Fortunately, the National Guard was willing to find a way to give me a discharge as their funding was being reduced. Therefore, even though I had long since passed the eight-day battery of tests, I signed a statement indicating that my release was because I failed to qualify for pilot training. This was not the last time that a sergeant, who knew how to use the regulations to get things done, would help me negotiate the military red tape.

1955.2   CENTRAL ISLIP STATE HOSPITAL

While waiting for the call into the pilot training program, I had taken a job as an attendant in the local psychiatric hospital, Central Islip State Hospital. Long Island contained three major mental hospitals within a radius of twenty miles, Central Islip, Kings Park, and Pilgrim State; together they housed more than twenty-eight thousand patients in the 1950's.

The hospital was the main industry of the village and had over 10,000 patients, only a small percentage of whom actually needed hospitalization and even a smaller percent benefited from their stay. In those days, state mental hospitals housed the elderly, the indigent, the homeless, and others who lived on the margins of society. There were few treatment options available so the primary role of the institution was to provide tutelary care.

The institution was amazingly self-sustaining. It contained more than two thousand acres with farms, cattle, cows, pigs, mattress and broom factories, and dietary and laundry services for staff and patients. Like the cotton plantations' use of slaves, the hospitals survived because unpaid workers performed much of the work: the patients. Within a few years, I would play a role in eliminating this form of forced labor.

The hospital employed thousands of people including physicians and other health care staff from many specialties as well as firefighters, police officers, maintenance workers, tradesmen, and laborers. Many of the early employees were recruited from Ireland and migrated to the U.S. in the 1880's, to join relatives who migrated a generation before them to escape the potato famine.

I met many patients during my time there; two remain clear in my memory.

"Andrew the Poet"

Andrew was from Chicago and suffered from alcoholism. He had been hospitalized many times in a variety of treatment facilities. He now had no hope of ever being released from the institution, as he had nowhere to go, no resources, no family, or friends to provide support in the community and a long history of failure. The mental health system had not adopted the role of providing the level of services and supports that would allow marginally able people to live outside of an institutional setting. Andrew lived in one of the oldest and most remote areas of the hospital and was one of the few truly lucid patients on the ward. With little to do on the back wards but wait for the next meal, I found talking with Andrew to be a welcome relief to the boredom of the daily routine. Most of the other attendants spent their time playing cards or watching television. Andrew kept a note book in which he had recorded dozens of his poems. The book was filled and he needed a new notebook. When I gave him a new lined notebook, he gave me the old one; I was stunned. This was his only possession and it took him months to create it; I never thought he would want to part with it. As I look back on it now I imagine he was eager to have someone see him as an individual and not just another link in the almost endless chain of anonymous faces that comprised the bulk of the institutions population. A few years later when I was working as a nurse on the surgical ward of the same hospital, I met Andrew again. He was unconscious and had broken his hip, and it soon became apparent that the doctors would not repair the fracture. He died a few days later of pneumonia, never knowing that his old friend was there to care for him. I kept his book for years, hoping one day to put it to some useful purpose; however, on our move back from Georgia to New

York in 1979 the book was lost together with several other keepsake items. I'm sorry Andrew, I lost your poetry, but I do remember you, the poet.

"Christian the Instructor"

The 100-year-old building that housed Andrew closed and I was transferred to another building. Here I met Christian. I noticed that he had scratched a large arrow in the floor next to his bed. I asked him what it was and he told me that it indicated, "True north." I brought a compass from home and found the line perfectly aligned with north on the compass. When questioned about how he was able to determine the direction with such accuracy without equipment he proudly showed me his notebook. Unlike Andrew's notebook, which consisted totally of rhyme, Chris' contained only reason in the form of pages and pages of arithmetical computations. Chris explained his methodology and complained the process took much longer than necessary because he didn't know how to use logarithms and did not have access to the requisite log tables. Since starting work at the hospital, I had been trying to teach myself German from an old textbook I had found. Chris was German. We agreed that I would teach him how to use logarithms and provide copies of the log tables and in return, he would teach me German. We spent two hours each day with our mutual tutoring sessions. Although it was obvious to all that Chris was seriously mentally ill, he was a great student and a good teacher. I tried to ignore the fact that he believed himself to be Christ rather than Chris. He was soon showing me how he could use logs in his never-ending calculations, the meanings of which only rarely related to the world that others shared. I was not as adept at learning German; I learned a few words or phrases each week.

I was playing semi-pro soccer at the time with a nearby soccer club that had several German born players. At a bar after one of the games, I tried out my new language skills. My teammates stared at me in disbelief. I was talking gibberish; they thought I was deliberately making fun of their accents by making sounds that sounded like German but had no meaning. I explained that I truly believed that the words were German and I was not trying to insult them. Later I confronted Chris. He explained with crystal clear logic how the German language had become corrupted over the centuries, so he created a new purer version which he believed would replace the old German once people saw its' virtues. Psychiatrists call this phenomenon "neo-linguism." I had heard the term before but had no idea that the delusional system that supported it could be so extensive. I still cannot speak but a few words of German. Chris died one weekend while I was off. I never believed the official explanation about his fall down the cellar stairs, for I knew his condition included a morbid fear of the basement and he would never have voluntarily ventured down the stairs. I'm sorry Christian.

1956.1   SEMIPRO SOCCER

Downing Stadium was on Randall's Island in the East River between Manhattan and Brooklyn and was in use between 1934 and 2002. It served as home base for professional football and soccer teams, as well as Olympic Trials and a plethora of music concerts. Soccer star Pele made his American debut for the New York Cosmos at Downing in 1975. Although any similarity between Pele's skill and my own is too absurd to consider, I did play at the famed stadium in a semipro soccer game in 1955. At that time, there were no professional soccer teams in the USA. I played for a team from Lindenhurst, NY, one of many teams struggling to get enough support for Association Soccer teams to start professional leagues. There were few fans at our games and it would take years for professional soccer to become a reality. We often referred to ourselves as a semipro team, but we never received any money for playing; it was part of the strategy to elevate the level of the sport in America. We played all year round, in blizzards when it was snowing so hard you could not see the goal posts from midfield. We played one game when it was raining so hard that the entire field turned into a sea of mud. The newly created field lied atop an old landfill. As the mud deepened, the debris, which had been just below a thin layer of top soil, began to rise. After the game in the shower, we all began to feel stinging pains where the shards of glass and metal had torn our legs beneath the encrusted layers of mud.

While the injuries were rarely as serious as those experienced by football players were, I did receive injuries to my knees and back, which I believe contributed to problems that required surgery on both later in my life.

Since we had won the Long Island Soccer League championship that year, we were to play the Austria national football team in Yankee stadium. It must have been a major disappointment for them as there were only a few thousand fans in the stadium. Two years earlier, they had played in the 1954 FIFA World Cup finals in Switzerland where tens of thousands of people watched every match. They came in third. The Austrians were touring America and playing exhibition games. We lost. It was the most humiliating day of my brief sports career. America had a long way to go, the level of play in the "Fédération Internationale de Football Association" (FIFA) was far superior to anything that we could offer. While I was clearly the weakest player on the team, I am sure that even the best players we had would not have been able to earn a starting position on the Austrian team, and they were only the third best in the world that year.

1956.2   BACK TO COLLEGE

The local state hospital had a school of nursing, which had recently changed its three-year curriculum and was then sending its' students to Adelphi University in Garden City, NY for the first two semesters and a summer session. While the courses were not in the engineering field that I desired, they were mostly science and humanities courses that I had hoped would serve as electives when I reentered an engineering program. The program's state funds provided free tuition, free room, board, laundry, and transportation. I decided to apply for admission and even though I did not really want to become a nurse, I knew I could resign after the first year at college.

When the first year ended, the only prospect I had was a small scholarship offer from the head of the Psychology Department at Adelphi. The only Engineering options required moving to a new city, finding a part-time job, and gaining admission. With no guidance counselor at my former high school and no guidance from my parents, the dream of engineering school faded like my bank account.

During our first year of nursing training, we spent Wednesdays at Central Islip State Hospital and on the other four workdays we attended college. Wednesday's courses were a complete bore. Which I satirically describe as Fundamentals of Nursing (i.e. how to make a bed) History of Nursing (i.e. who made the first bed) and Philosophy of Nursing (i.e. why make a bed.) The four days at Adelphi were wonderful, we studied Human Anatomy and Physiology (eight credit hours), Chemistry, Inorganic and Organic (8 credit hours), Microbiology (4 credits), Psychology (3 credits), Nutrition (4 credits), English, (6 credits), Physical Education (1 credit), and Child Growth and Development (5 credits which included a summer internship at a New York City day care program.)

I did reasonably well in everything but Psychology where I excelled. After one semester, the head of the Psychology Department, Dr. Iverson, offered me a small scholarship based on my performance in his class. Like most college classes, this one was marked on a curve. If my marks were included in the curve, all of the other 100 or so students in this required class would have failed. I received an "A" and the rest of the class was graded on a curve that excluded me. Unfortunately, the small department could not offer enough to allow me to accept it and transfer from the nursing program.

Reg was a student in my class and we soon became friends together with a small group of six or so including Mike and Jo with whom we maintained contact for many years. We studied, played, and matured together. A psychiatrist who lived in my dorm helped me learn to use hypnosis. I entertained some of my classmates by creating post hypnotic suggestions. On one occasion, I suggested to a student that the roses in the tapestry wall hanging had the most beautiful aroma, for days afterward she would turn and stare at the tapestry every time she passed it and comment that the woven roses seemed to have a real odor.

The Nursing Program also provided a $30 a month stipend for incidentals. However, since I was a state employee prior to entering the program, I was required to continue my membership in the retirement program. So, the stipend yielded only $8 in disposable income after deductions for taxes and retirement contributions. When Reg and I began dating, we spent much of our time walking and talking. A closed chamber inside me was opening. We would walk to the Villa Contento to share a single slice of pizza, on special occasions, we would walk to town to see a movie, but most often, we would walk on the hospital golf course, which was free and in the evening after the sprinklers had watered the greens it was cool. There were no air conditioners. After more than 55 years together, we still like to walk alone and plan our future, just as we did in that spring of 1957.

Reg's dominant characteristic is her beautiful spirit. I believe that spiritually mature people, ideas, events, and actions are Good (as in high quality) True, (as in proper) Beautiful, (as in elegant) and Loving (as in caring). Reg meets all of those criteria. Today she wears her lines of aging as a mask veiling but not obscuring the eternal beauty that now lies just below her surface, and she remains the spiritually mature person who is Good, True, Beautiful, and Loving.

1957.1 HARLEM DAY CARE

During the summer between our freshman and sophomore years, we took a 5-credit course in Developmental Psychology at Adelphi University. We spent 8 hours each Friday in class at the college. The other four days of the week, we each worked at different NYC Day Care programs. We lived at Creedmoor State Hospital, in Queens Village and traveled by public transportation to Manhattan from Monday to Thursday. On Friday, we would travel by car to Adelphi, in Garden City and after class on to Central Islip until Sunday night when we would return to Creedmoor.

The Day Care Center where I worked was located on Second Ave in East Harlem near Metropolitan Hospital. There were about 15 preschool age children, 2 teachers, and myself. Two children stand out in my memory. Ramon was the leader of the group. He used his charisma and physical strength with equal skill to maintain his influence and control over the other children. Juan was quiet and shy but had  an IQ known to be well above average. Juan's father, a house painter, took Juan on many field trips around the city. One Monday morning Juan came to school very excited to show his classmates what he had learned over the weekend. His father had taken him to the Tri-borough Bridge and he was anxious to show his classmates what he had learned. He started to build a bridge with large cardboard blocks. First, he laid a foundation across the room. Since it looked more like a road than a bridge, the other children began to lose interest. Next, he started to place vertical supports at strategic locations along the length of the foundation. It was obvious that Juan had a much broader view of bridge construction than the other kids, who were looking to see simple row of three block arches. Already upset at being usurped as the center of attention, Ramon taking advantage of the groups' unrest mocked Juan and destroyed the construction. Later Juan explained to me what he was planning to do; it would have been beautiful.

A few days later, we were playing outside when Ramon, anxious to show what he had learned in church the week before, suggested that we play Joan-of-Arc. I went along with the game and let the kids tie me to a jungle gym, but I had to escape when Ramon produced a pack of matches and I fully believed that he would have set me on fire if given the opportunity.

I can only imagine what might have become of Juan whose environment could punish him because of his mild manner and intelligence, or of Ramon, whose environment could reward him because of his gregariousness and aggressiveness. I can only hope that they each found ways to use their individual gifts that were constructive and wholesome.

1957.2   MANHATTAN, NY

We spent our sophomore year at Mount Sinai Hospital on Fifth Ave. in Manhattan. It was a wonderful time to be in New York City with many opportunities provided by the hospital in the form of free tickets to off-Broadway shows and a whole city to explore. The hospital is one of the finest in the country and offered a teaching experience that Long Island could not match.

One Sunday afternoon Reg and I went for a walk in Central Park, which lies directly across the street from the hospital. Since I was still living on only $8 of disposable each month, the expenses for our date consisted solely of purchasing a bag of peanuts that we shared with the squirrels. We held hands and strolled through the Park tossing peanuts to the occasional squirrel. Soon the number of squirrels began to increase and as the peanuts ran out, we were surrounded by hungry critters. Reg never liked squirrels and claimed that they are just rats in cuter outfits. She panicked and began running; she was last seen running over a grassy knoll followed by a herd of well-dressed rodents. Eventually Reg forgave me for laughing at her obvious distress.

Our most expensive date started with a walk from Fifth Ave. and 98th St. to Lexington Ave. and 96th Street. There we would take the subway to the South Ferry station at the lower end of Manhattan (cost $0.50 apiece). We would purchase a bunch of grapes from a street vendor (cost $0.25) and take the Ferry to Staten Island (cost $0.05

apiece). The ride took us past the Statue of Liberty and offered a great view of New York harbor and the Manhattan skyline. When we reached Staten Island, we remained on the ferry and returned to South Ferry (cost $0.00). The trip home on the subway ended our adventure (cost $0.50 apiece.) The total cost for an evening out was $2.35. In the retelling, its sounds like we spent our time counting our pocket change, but we hardly noticed. We had a wonderful time because we were together.

Even though I grew up on Long Island surrounded by water, I never learned to swim as a child. I don't recall my parents EVER engaging in any form of recreation, athletics, or entertainment outside of the home. That plus a near drowning experience at the Sayville Orphanage left me with a real fear of the water. The Mount Sinai Hospital had made arrangement with a hotel on the west side of Central Park that allowed students to swim, without charge, in the hotel pool. For a few weeks in the winter, several of us would walk across the Park and while the others swam at the deep end of the pool, I practiced the moves that my friend Mike suggested. I was soon able to swim across the pool either above or below the water. And, while I never really enjoyed it, I did enjoy the fact that I could make some progress in an area that had once seemed impossible. Thank you, Mike, you were one of a small number of people that I ever thought of as a best friend.

We spent our year at the hospital rotating through the various departments. One of the jobs in the Obstetrics delivery room was to write the baby's gender on the numbered identification bracelets placed on the wrists of the mother and baby. On one occasion, I wrote the wrong information. I don't remember if the baby was a boy and I wrote girl or visa versa. But I image that the mother who had to deal with my mistake will always remember the details. After the mistake was discovered, I tried to reassure her that the only mistake was in what I had written, and that the integrity of the matching number identification bracelets had not been comprised. Despite that terrible mistake, each new birth was a profound experience of wonderment. Later as an anesthetist, I would see more births, mostly as C-sections. When asked what, she felt about reincarnation Eleanor Roosevelt implied that being born the first time was the real miracle. How could I not agree?

The most talked about incident occurred in the operating room. The interns also rotated through the various services so there was always at least one physician in the room with no experience, no authority, and little practical knowledge of surgery. Their role was often limited to cutting the ends of sutures after the surgeon had tied them. On one occasion, the surgeon told the intern that he was cutting the sutures too short and mercilessly berated him. The following day the surgeon told same intern that he was cutting the sutures too long, followed by more humiliation. On day three, as the intern took up the scissors he asked the surgeon, "How do you want your sutures today, too long or too short." The surgeon was not amused and the intern was thrown out of the O.R. Physicians in training had to put in long hours and put up with abuse from their mentors. A lot of this has changed over the years, I think for the better, as I never believed that humiliation was the shortest route to real confidence and was more likely to lead to a defensive form of arrogance.

1957.3   TELL THEM MIKE SENT YOU

I needed a new suit to wear at an upcoming event and my friend Mike told me where I could buy a high-quality suit at a reduced price at a location on lower Broadway. On the block where I expected to find the store, the buildings on my side of the street didn't have street numbers. I could see the numbers on buildings on the other side and estimated where my building would likely be located. However, the streets in lower Manhattan make many turns so the street numbers one side of the street don't always matchup closely with those on the opposite side of the street. I went in the only available entrance. It lead into a windowless hall with another door at the far end. The solid door had a doorbell and a peephole. I rang the bell, eventually the peephole open, a face appeared, but it said nothing. I told him Mike M. sent me. He looked puzzled, and repeated Mike's last name, but with a significantly different pronunciation. I nodded; the face disappeared. I few moments later, the door opened. I walked into a large room filled with hundreds of suits hanging on iron pipes. They were organized into two groups. I was told to pick any suit from the group on the right for $100 or any suit from the group on the left for $200. I selected a suit from the $100 group, paid up and left. Later that night back at the dorm, I showed Mike the light blue suit that I had purchased. He told me that next time I bought a suit he was coming with me because this suit was terrible. I told him that there were many to select from at the warehouse he sent me to in lower Manhattan. He didn't know what I was talking about; he had directed me to a famous low overhead Men's Clothing Store where he knew one of the salesmen. Apparently, the street numbers were farther off than I thought and the clothing store was on the next block. The warehouse I went to was probably a fly-by-night operation that sold suits that "fell off the truck," (i.e. acquired illegally.) Mike's last name just happened to sound like the name of one of people with access to the hot merchandise. I can only image what might have happened if they discovered that I didn't know their Mike, after I was admitted and seen the display.

1957.4   THE COLD WAR

The Sputnik crisis was a turning point of the Cold War that began on October 4, 1957 when the Soviet Union launched the Sputnik 1 satellite. The United States had believed itself to be the world leader in space technology and thus the leader in missile development. Sputnik's appearance rattled the United States. The people found themselves lost in a sense of fear and wonder. President Dwight D. Eisenhower called the countrywide shock the "Sputnik Crisis" because of the looming threat of the Soviet Union. During the Cold War, America was in a constant state of fear from the Soviet Union. Once they started to launch objects into space, even a satellite harmless to the U.S., the country went into a panic. If the USSR could launch a harmless satellite, they could also launch a nuclear warhead that would be able to travel intercontinental distances. After this initial public shock, the Space Race began leading up to the first human being launched in space, the Project Apollo, and the moon landings in 1969. In the 1950's and 60's we lived in fear that nuclear war was not only possible but also likely. I wonder what life choices were made by people who believed that they would never live to their grandchildren.

1958.1   HELEN HAYES

n my senior year of Nurses Training, I was elected to the Board of Directors of the New York State Association of Student Nurses. My position was Director of Public Relations, which included publishing the quarterly newsletter with a circulation of 60,000. The other responsibilities were rather vague and I could find little that was done in prior years. At one of the regular meetings, the Board agreed to produce a half hour documentary film to show to high school students to promote an interest in the nursing profession. A student from Bellevue Hospital in NYC was president of the association and wrote the script for the film. I found a NYC-based Film Company and arranged for them to do the filming and the postproduction work needed to complete the film. However, we needed a narrator for the film who lived in or near New York City and had name recognition. Helen Hayes, the First Lady of American Theater, lived nearby in Nyack, NY. Much to my surprise, she accepted my invitation to narrate the film and told me when she would be in NYC. At the scheduled time and date, she arrived in front of the studio in her chauffeured limousine. After giving the chauffeur instructions about where to bring her overcoat to have a button replaced, we went into the building. The audio engineer, who had placed the double spaced 30-minute script in plastic film so the paper would not rustle when the pages were turned, suggested that Miss Hayes read the script to get familiar with the phrasing. She agreed and read the script aloud. When she finished, the engineer left the control room and told her that he had recorded her reading and it was perfect. I accompanied Miss Hayes to the curb where her chauffeur was waiting. After thanking her for her help, I returned to an astonished engineer. While I assumed that I had witnessed an ordinary session, the engineer was prepared to spend most of the day recording multiple attempts to get a usable sound track. He had never seen someone read an unrehearsed script perfectly on the first attempt. The film was well received.

I have recently checked the Helen Hayes web site to see if the documentary film was included among her many credits. It wasn't there; however, she did perform in three plays, two television shows and received a Tony Award and an honorary degree from Brown University that year. Ms. Hayes died in 1993 at the age of 92.

1959.1 SWIFT CREEK

Reg's father, Bill Straub, was an award-winning angler who spent many hours fishing in the Great South Bay off the southern shore of Long Island. I on the other hand had never rowed a boat, baited a hook, or caught a fish. In an effort to show him that I was not a complete nerd prior to marring his daughter, I planned a day on the water with Reg. We rented a rowboat at Slim's Bait Shack, where Bill always bought his bait. I rowed out through a channel that led to the Bay. It was easy; too easy, I soon realized where Swift Creek got its name. The outgoing tide and the local topography directed water through the channel and it would be many hours before the tide would turn and make it possible to row back to Slims. I could only imagine what Bill would think of his future son-in-law if I didn't get Reg back in time for dinner. I tried to row against the tide, but it was hopeless, each time I would lift the oars to take the next stroke the tide would push us further out. I noticed that the anchor had a very long line attached. I stood in the front of the boat and hurled the anchor as far as I could. When it landed in the shallow mud near the edge of the channel, I pulled the boat forward. Each time I repeated the process we would move about 20 feet forward. However, as I retrieved the anchor and threw it forward we would be carried back about 15 feet. Gaining only 5 feet with each throw, it took over an hour to get out of Swift Creek where I could row, arms aching, back to Slims. We made it back to Reg's home in nearby Richmond Hill in time for super with her family. I told Bill that we had rented a boat from Slim's and gone for a ride; I may not have mentioned all of the details of exactly what had transpired.

1959.2 THE RELUCTANT NURSE

In September 1959 after graduating from the Central Islip State Hospital School of Nursing and passing the State licensing examination I became a Registered Nurse. A psychiatric hospital, which shared the name of the village of Central Islip, dominated the local economy. Male nurses were common and since most of the hospitals' employees were attendants or nurses' aides, nursing was a relatively high status position. However, outside of my hometown in the world beyond where I assumed I would spend my life, male nurses were still an oddity. Sadly, I shared many of the prejudices and stereotypes about the career, which I had just entered. I spent the next ten years of my life trying to move beyond the profession that had provided me with what I believed to be the only available flight from a stifling life of mediocrity. However, while I was a nurse, I did try, perhaps not always successfully, to be competent and caring.

1959.3 VETERANS HOSPITAL BROOKLYN, NY

After graduation, in September 1959, I worked for a few months on the surgical ward of Central Islip State Hospital. However, I found the environment depressing, the hospital underfunded, and the town where I lived for most of my life no longer felt like home. And since Reg had moved back to her family home in Richmond Hill, NYC and was working in Queens General Hospital I was ready to relocate to be further from the village and its occupants whose history were permanently etched on my soul.

I worked on the psychiatric ward of the veterans' hospital in Brooklyn and found an apartment a few blocks away. I rented what had been the master bedroom suite of a one family home. The owners, an elderly Greek couple lived in the rest of the one-story house. The apartment in the finished basement was also rented to a Veterans Hospital employee.

The patients on the 16th floor where I worked were all former service men some of whom were suffering from posttraumatic stress disorder (PTSD.) An anxiety disorder associated with serious traumatic events and characterized by such symptoms as survivor guilt, reliving the trauma in dreams, numbness, and lack of involvement with reality, or recurrent thoughts and images. Others suffered depression or the various forms of schizophrenia that tend to occur in early adulthood. On one occasion, a police officer arrived on the ward and asked me to come to the parking lot where a recently discharged former patient, committed suicide in his car. He left a note in which he reminded the staff that he had insisted that he wasn't ready to leave their care.

In a few months, after taking the driver's exam and test drive in Brooklyn, I bought my first car, a Green and Cream colored 1955 two-door Ford sedan. For the first time, I didn't have to play designated driver in order to drive a car. As with most used cars of that era, it burnt a lot of oil and gas; had no seat belts, almost bald tires, but I loved it.

CHAPTER 4 *THE SIXTIES*

The year was 1960 and the U.S. and Russia were in a "space race." An outgrowth of the Cold War, the two super powers had already sent up satellites, and plans were underway to send men into space, and eventually to land on the moon. From our honeymoon beach on Bermuda, we could see the Russian "Sputnik" satellite's blinking lights streaking across the Caribbean sky. Nine years later on July 20, 1969, Apollo 11 carrying Neil Armstrong and Buzz Aldrin, landed on the moon.

The first weather satellite, Tiros I, was launched on April 1, 1960 and changed weather forecasting forever. Nine more satellites followed giving meteorologists a view of the cloud cover around the world. The addition of infrared sensors would allow for the tracking of temperatures around the globe.

Television, which began when I was in High School during the early 1950's, was now in the mainstream of American life with nearly 90 percent of U.S. households owning a television set. Fifteen years prior, there were fewer than 10,000 sets in the U.S. Viewers watched new television shows hitting the airwaves such as The Flintstones, the Andy Griffith Show, and the Bugs Bunny Show. While Bugs had been around for many years, he was first on primetime TV in 1960. On weekends during the early 50's we would gather around the TV's of a few friends who had sets and watch Milton Berle and Sid Caesar.

The Civil Rights movement was taking shape and in Greensboro, North Carolina, where four black students staged a sit-in at a Woolworth's lunch counter. The students sat at the lunch counter until the store closed, but were never served. The next day they returned with more students and the peaceful protest called a "sit-in" began. They were joined by other black students in the following days and the protest soon spread to other cities.

Across the South, peaceful sit-ins by students took place in more than 100 cities in 1960. Although the protesters were beaten, and sometimes sent to jail, they continued to peacefully sit-in until they achieved their goals - desegregation of places of public accommodation.

In 1961, African-Americans were still sitting in the back of public buses in the South and were not permitted to use "whites only" restroom facilities in the terminals even though the Supreme Court had outlawed segregation on interstate buses in 1946. In May 1961, the first group of 13 Freedom Riders, white and black ranging in age from college students to a 60-year-old professor and his wife, left Washington, DC, on their way to Louisiana. They went in two buses. Riders in the first bus were attacked in both

Anniston and Birmingham, Alabama. Men with pipes beat the Freedom Riders on this bus. The second bus was firebombed just outside of Anniston, Alabama. At the same time as the sit-ins and Freedom Rides, other protesters demonstrated against segregation in other facilities.

Martin Luther King, representing the Southern Christian Leadership Conference, was among the leaders of the civil rights organizations who were instrumental in the organization of the March on Washington for Jobs and Freedom, which took place on August 28, 1963. Other leaders were Roy Wilkins from the National Association for the Advancement of Colored People; Whitney Young, National Urban League; A. Philip Randolph, Brotherhood of Sleeping Car Porters; John Lewis, Student Nonviolent Coordinating Committee; and James L. Farmer, Jr. of the Congress of Racial Equality. President Kennedy was concerned the turnout would be less than 100,000. Therefore, he enlisted the aid of additional church leaders and the UAW union to help mobilize demonstrators for the cause.

Originally, the march was to dramatize the desperate condition of blacks in the southern U.S. Organizers intended to denounce the federal government for its failure to safeguard the civil rights and physical safety of civil rights workers and blacks. However, the group acquiesced to presidential pressure and influence, and the event ultimately took on a far less strident tone.

The march did, however, make specific demands: an end to racial segregation in public schools; meaningful civil rights legislation, including a law prohibiting racial discrimination in employment; protection of civil rights workers from police brutality; a $2 minimum wage for all workers; and self-government for Washington, D.C. Despite tensions, the march was a resounding success. More than a quarter of a million-people attended the event, sprawling from the steps of the Lincoln Memorial onto the National Mall and around the reflecting pool. At the time, it was the largest gathering of protesters in Washington, D.C.'s history.

Martin Luther King is most famous for his "I Have a Dream" speech, given in front of the Lincoln Memorial during the 1963 March.

> *". . . I say to you today, my friends, so even though we face the difficulties of today and tomorrow, I still have a dream. It is a dream deeply rooted in the American dream. I have a dream that one day this nation will rise up and live out the true meaning of its creed: 'We hold these truths to be self-evident: that all men are created equal.' I have a dream that one day on the red hills of Georgia the sons of former slaves and the sons of former slave owners will be able to sit down together at the table of brotherhood. I have a dream that one day even the state of Mississippi, a state sweltering with the heat of injustice,*

sweltering with the heat of oppression, will be transformed into an oasis of freedom and justice. I have a dream that my four little children will one day live in a nation where they will not be judged by the color of their skin but by the content of their character. I have a dream today. I have a dream that one day, down in Alabama, with its vicious racists, with its governor having his lips dripping with the words of interposition and nullification; one day right there in Alabama, little black boys and black girls will be able to join hands with little white boys and white girls as sisters and brothers.

I have a dream today.

"I Have a Dream" is regarded as one of the finest speeches in the history of American oratory. The March, and King's speech, helped put civil rights at the top of the liberal political agenda and facilitated passage of the Civil Rights Act of 1964.

Title III of the Civil Rights Act of 1964 prohibits discrimination in public facilities because of race, color, religion, or national origin.

In September of 1960, Hurricane Donna struck Florida and continued with hurricane strength winds all the way up the eastern coast of the U.S. to New England. The storm claimed fifty lives and caused $387 million in damages

Technological advances of the '60s included: halogen lamps, Valium, non-dairy creamer, audio cassettes, fiber-tip pens, Spacewar, the first computer video game, silicone breast implants, video disks, Acrylic paint, Permanent-press fabric. Also BASIC (an early computer language), Astroturf, Soft contact lenses, artificial sweetener, compact disks, Kevlar, Electronic Fuel injection engines, handheld calculators, the computer mouse, computers with integrated circuits, random access memory, The arpanet, (first internet), artificial hearts, ATMs and bar-code scanners.

Best-selling books of the decade were Advise and Consent, The Broad Highway, The Agony and the Ecstasy, Ship of Fools, The Spy Who Came in from the Cold, The Source, Valley of the Dolls, The Arrangement, Airport, and Portnoy's Complaint,

Rachael Carson influenced the environmental movement as no one had since the 19th century's most celebrated hermit, Henry David Thoreau, wrote about Walden Pond. Her book, "Silent Spring" presented a view of nature compromised by synthetic pesticides. Once pesticides enter the biosphere they not only kill insects but also make their way up the food chain to threaten bird and fish populations and could eventually sicken children. Much of the data that Carson drew from existed for some time, but Carson was the first to put them all together and to draw stark and far-reaching conclusions. Carson, the citizen-scientist, spawned a revolution.

The average new house cost $12,700., the average salary was $5,315., a gallon of gas was $0.25, a new car was $2,600, and the average cost loaf of bread 22 cents

In 1960, the US population was 179,323,175 and the life expectancy for men was 66.6 years, and 73.1 for women.

There were 3 known lynchings of black people in the 1960s.

1960.1 & 1959 & 1980   THE RINGS

We loved our new rings. In the winter of 1960, we bought them in anticipation of our August wedding. We walked along Liberty Avenue near Lefferts Boulevard in Richmond Hill, Queens, N.Y. This was Reg's neighborhood. It was so different from the small town where I grew up. The 'A' train on its elevated platform was noisy and the streets were crowded, dirty, and cold. I thought about that August day a year earlier, when I had purchased the engagement ring that Reg had accepted just six months earlier.

> (1959) I had walked alone along Suffolk Ave. in Central Islip, NY. It was quiet, clean, and warm. But not warm enough to dispel the chill of separation that I felt. Reg, about to graduate from Nursing School at the local hospital, was soon to leave town. The thought of her leaving filled my mind with concern and my heart with loneliness. I did not want her to leave before I had a chance to secure our future together. And, so with the money that had been accumulating in my New York State retirement account, I entered the town's only jewelry store and found the engagement ring that Reg has worn all these years. This was the most expensive purchase that I had ever made. I knew nothing of diamonds or of gold. I had to trust the honesty of the jeweler and hope that he would not take advantage of my obvious inexperience. The rural community was both isolating and insulating and on this day, I was glad to be shopping in a small town.

> We had discussed rings and this one matched my understanding of Reg's' description of what she liked in an engagement ring. The few women I knew who actually owned engagement rings all seemed equally pleased, even though their rings did not seem all equally pleasing. I knew that Reg would never complain if it were not exactly what she wanted. So, I listened carefully on the rare occasions when she spoke of material things. A few days before she was to leave for her new job at Queens General Hospital in New York City, we celebrated at what was to become the last gathering of our small clan of college classmates. I offered her the ring in the parking lot of "Scots Bar and Grill" where we had often danced and shared our student lives with our closest friends, Mike and Jo and several others. The sounds from the jukebox

could be heard in the background; Johnny Mathis was singing, "Chances Are." Reg seemed pleased with the ring. She accepted it to encircle her finger, and she accepted me as well, to encircle her life as we promised ourselves to each other forever. I promised to share my life with Reg so that she would not be alone; but also, to bear witness to her life so that she would never be forgotten.

(1960) But today, with the shadow of the 'El' above darkening the storefronts on Liberty Avenue, we strolled from store to store in search of the rings that would seal our promise. We had been looking for a few days for rings that were a little unique but not faddish, as we fully expected to have them for a lifetime and did not want them to become outdated. When we saw them in the jewelers' window, we both knew that our search was over. Unlike most rings, with their convex outer surfaces these had concave florentined surfaces. The parallel edges were faceted and it has brushed concave surfaces. While they had style, each aspect was muted, so the overall effect was conservative.

We put the rings on during the wedding ceremony on August 13, 1960 in the church that Reg's immigrant grandfather, Florian Straub, had help to build, St. Benedict Joseph Labre Roman Catholic in Richmond Hill, Queens, NY. At the wedding reception, we danced to the song "True Love" from the movie "High Society" starring Bing Crosby, Grace Kelly, Frank Sinatra, and Louis Armstrong. Its words seemed to sum up our feelings for each other and our hopes for the future.

(1980) About 20 years later, we were still wearing the rings and the rings were wearing thin. The heavier we got, the thinner the rings became, as we had them stretched to keep pace with our spreading physiques. In a last-ditch effort to regain my former athletic body, I had lost about 20 pounds and was drying my hands in the men's room at 44 Holland Ave., Albany, NY, where I was working as Associate Commissioner in the New York State Office of Mental Health. I had an uneasy feeling that something was wrong. It was the familiar subtle uneasiness that I could so easily ignore and so often later regret. And, the kind of feeling I usually vowed never to ignore again, after discovering the cause too late to correct the problem. My ring was gone. As I undressed that evening, I realized that the ring was not on my finger. Instantly I recalled the uneasy feeling in the men's room that afternoon. The ring was gone, in a moment, in a paper towel, in the trash. How could I have ignored the uneasy feeling? I vowed never to ignore those feelings again. But as Leo Durocher once said, "I never make the same mistake once."

I went without my ring for some time, and had become accustomed, but not contented at not having it. On our 30th wedding anniversary, Reg gave me a ring. As I opened the box, I thought to myself that this was a nice gesture but it would never be the same. In fact, it was better. Reg's' ring was very wide, almost twice as wide as mine had been. She had taken her ring to the local jeweler in Delmar, NY and had it cut in half vertically. We had two rings again. Of course, they were only whole when we were together. That seemed quite appropriate, especially for me, as  I never felt quite complete when separated from Reg. I felt that the world would be flat again if she should die before me. (In the photo above we can see the two separate rings that Reg's created in 1990, by having hers sliced in half vertically.)

Reg's act was at the same time both a simple practical solution to a commonplace problem and a powerful symbol of our lives together. She gives to me that which I lack, that which I need, and that which makes me whole. In our early years, together, I loved Reg because I needed her, now I need her because I love her and I realize that the center of my life no longer resides within me.

Love is not who you can see yourself with.
It is whom you can't see yourself without.
Author Unknown

1960.2   THE DRAFT

In April 1960, just four months before our scheduled wedding, I received a notice from the Selective Service Board ordering me to report for examinations in preparation to being drafted into the U.S. Army.

The draft began on May 18, 1917 in preparation for World War I. Men were inducted into the armed forces, which could not be filled voluntarily. The draft ended in 1973 when the U.S. moved to an all-volunteer military. However, the Selective Service System remains in place as a contingency plan; men between the ages of 18 and 25 are still required to register.

The inspection and induction process was designed for efficiency. It began on the top floor of the examination building on Whitehall Street in lower Manhattan. Then it spiraled down floor by floor to each of the various exam stations. By late afternoon inductees have had every part of their body examined, every paper stamped and every hope destroyed of not being on the bus waiting at the back door to take them to the Army induction center at Fort Dix, NJ. As a Registered Nurse, I was eligible to become an officer so when I received my draft notice immediately applied for a commission. But I had to delay both the induction and the commission processes for four months if I were to be available for the August 13 wedding, which had already been paid for by Reg's father. I was lucky to be able to drag the medical examination process through five separate visits to specialists at Whitehall. The residual effects from soccer injuries, a sore jaw, limited availability of needed MD specialist, broken X-Ray equipment, and scheduling problems all worked in my favor for three months. But in July 1960 with all potential health issued properly dismissed I stood by the back door and could hear the bus idling as my cohorts climbed onboard. Sergeant Jackson sat at the last station between me and Fort Dix and a postponed wedding. He asked me if I had ever been in the military before and if I had an honorable discharge. I had my discharge paper from the Air Nation Guard in a folder under my arm. I asked him what would happen if I didn't have the documents. He told me that I couldn't be drafted until I could prove that I wasn't dishonorably discharged. At that point, I told him the whole story about the delays with the commission and the imminent wedding. He told me to put my folder under my shirt and go home. He would request a copy of my discharge papers. (See 1966.1 for the conclusion to the draft story.) While I was now reassured that I would not be drafted prior to the wedding there was still my application for a commission to deal with. During the three months that I was trying to delay the being drafting, I was also trying to get my application approved while hoping that it wouldn't call me to active duty before the wedding. The FBI needed my fingerprints as part of the vetting process. However, five sets of prints, taken at various federal installations in the area and they were all rejected. Finally, I asked Reg's uncle, a detective in the Nassau County Police department to look at my prints. He noticed a pair of parallel lines on my left thumbprint that looked like an artifact or imperfection, which would void the prints. However, when he looked at my thumb he saw the same lines. They were scars from a pipe thread I received several years earlier while working as a part time plumber's helper. He marked the print indicating that the lines were scars not imperfections. The FBI accepted the prints and I could then receive a Commission as a Second Lieutenant in the United States Army.

1960.3   SILVER TREADS AMONG THE GOLD

One afternoon as Reg rode home on the city bus from her job at a local hospital in Queens, NY, she noticed that her gold engagement ring no longer looked gold, but silver. When I arrived at her parents' home for dinner later that evening, she was distraught because the ring that she loved and which meant so much to her seemed to be fading. I was hurt because I felt that her sadness suggested that I gave her an imitation gold ring. Perhaps I had, I didn't know, and I remembered how insecure I felt when I purchased it several months earlier. My insecurity suggested that Reg's agitation might reflect a lack of trust. I left in a huff and sat in a local bar to cool down. As I considered what could have happened, I remembered caring for patients in the past whose treatments required the use of gastric tubes filled with mercury because it provided stabilizing weight while remaining flexible. I also remembered that when a metal is exposed to mercury it would become totally coated by the stuff; there is a reason that the metals nickname is "quick silver." I called her and asked if she had been handling mercury that day, she had; problem solved. I returned and we rubbed the mercury off the ring and she reassured me that she had lost faith in the ring not in me. I think she always had more faith in me than I did.

Mercury is no longer used routinely in hospitals and dental care. Mercury poisoning is caused by exposure to mercury and produces toxicity or death by blocking blood vessels which leads to damage to the brain, kidneys, and lungs resulting in sensory impairment, and a lack of coordination. Mercury was widely used in many products such as dental fillings, florescent bulbs, thermometers, blood-pressure gauges, thermostats, toys, silent light switches and in medicines such as Mercurochrome, an antiseptic that was banned in 1998. A 1990 FDA regulation, put mercury on a list of toxic pollutants that need to be controlled to the greatest possible extent.

Today we laugh as we remember the incident and the ring remains golden as we passed our golden wedding anniversary.

> ♪*Darling, I am growing old*
> *Silver threads among the gold*
> *Shine upon my brow*
> *Today life is fading fast away.*
> ♪*But, my darling, you will be always young and fair to me*
> *Yes, my darling, you will be always young and fair to me.*
> *Lyrics by Eben E. Rexford,*

1960.4   THE WEDDING

With the Army crisis on hold, the wedding took place as planned on August 13, 1960 in St Benedict Joseph Labre Roman Catholic Church. Saint Benny's, as the family referred to, is an historic Roman Catholic parish church complex at 94-40 118th Street in Richmond Hill, Queens, New York. Completed in 1919 the church is the only one in the world placed under the patronage of Saint Benedict Joseph Labre, the Beggar Saint. Reg's grandfather was one of the many Irish and German immigrants who helped construct the church and its many adjoining buildings. Reg and her three siblings attended school there and it was the center of religious and social life in Richmond Hill for decades.

Monsignor Thomas Swarbrick provided the Pre-Cana training, my second baptism, my confirmation, which I shared with Reg's younger brother Gerry, and the wedding ceremony. Reg had attended many family gatherings like our reception, and insisted that the guests would have to go to the bar to get their drinks refilled. As planned, there was none of the over drinking that had ruined some earlier family weddings. Reg's father paid to have the band stay for an extra hour and before the last dance, Reg and I took a taxi to the hotel near Kennedy Airport where we would be departing for Bermuda in the morning. Reg's father was visibly shaken when Reg and I got into the taxi; his "toots" was really leaving home forever and with someone he had not yet learned to fully trust. Our opening chapter was the close of an important chapter in  his life. Reg was part of the glue that held his family together; soon she would begin to play that role for me and for the family that we would create together. He had taught her well.

There is no more lovely, friendly and charming relationship, communion or company than a good marriage.
Martin Luther

1960.5   HONEY MOON, BERMUDA

We arrived at the small Bermuda airport and began rushing to find a cab. The porter smiled and told us, "Maan, no one rushes in Bermuda." We followed his lead and soon we could feel the pressure of the past few months fade away as we melted into each other's life. We danced under the moon light to the strains of "♪Yellow Bird♪," strolled along the pink-sand beaches, rode motor bikes among shaded lanes to secluded hideaways, ate at wonderful outdoor seaside restaurants. We visited the Crystal Cave and many other beautiful natural sites and tourist attractions.

We chose Bermuda because it was possible that a telegraph would arrive any day telling me to report for military duty. We felt that it would be safe to be out of the country and unavailable until we returned.

When we first arrived in our economy suite, we found two single beds separated by a large floor model electric fan. I imagined the nightly trauma that might result from that configuration and we promptly upgraded to a room with a queen size bed and an air conditioner. We met a few other couples but didn't spend much time with them; we were complete and wanted for nothing. It rained almost every afternoon for about half an hour. We escorted one forlorn and soaked new bride back to her groom who had sped off in the rain and was too skittish to turn around while riding and look back to see that his bride couldn't get her motor bike started. We found her crying hysterically outside of the restaurant "abandoned by her lover."

When our stay was over, we wired home for more of our wedding money and extended our stay for a few more days. On our last night in Bermuda, I went out for sandwiches with a neighbor and Reg stayed at the hotel with his wife. The separation although brief was much too long for either of us.

We had nothing to do at home but wait for the military call-up to begin the next phase of our life. While we were away Reg's Mom found us a month-to-month rental apartment just a few miles from her home. She was a great help to us both.

1960.6   MEDICAL MIRACLE

When we returned from our Honeymoon, we rented an apartment on 115 St, in South Ozone Park, Queens, NY, where we lived for 3 weeks waiting for my orders to report to Fort Sam Houston for Officers Training. While we waited, I worked as a private duty nurse at various hospitals throughout New York City. One of the cases was at St. Barnabas Hospital in the Bronx. In the 1950s, Dr. Cooper reported an accidental finding while removing a brain polyp from a patient with Parkinson disease. Dr. Cooper cut off the blood supply to a portion of the brain, and observed a reduction in tremors and rigidity without the loss of motor strength. He was now experimenting with surgery that permanently destroyed nerves and tissue in the Globus Pallidus. My patient was a 60+ year old man whose tremors were so strong that it was difficult to steady him on the operating room table. Dr. Cooper used a fluoroscope to guide the insertion a thin needle deep into the patient brain. When it was properly located, he injected alcohol through the needle and killed the cells around the Basal Ganglia. Instantly the tremors on the left side of his body stopped. The patient was awake throughout the procedure and felt no pain or side effects.

Later, as his wife entered his private room, obviously anxious to see her husband after the experimental brain surgery, he raised his hand, slowly, the tremor gone and waved as he said "Hi Honey." Tears washed the anxiety away; this was the most amazing thing I had ever witnessed.

This and similar surgeries have all had problems and have been largely replaced with the less destructive deep brain stimulation which has helped to reduce many of the symptoms of Parkinsonism.

1960.7   FORT SAM HOUSTON

A week after returning from our Honeymoon in Bermuda, the commission that I had applied for In April finally arrived. Two weeks later, we flew to San Antonio, TX to begin the three-month officer-training program.

I learned how to dress, march, shoot, survive, and act like an Army officer. At home in the evenings I would show Reg what I had learned which would frequently result in my marching her toward the bedroom.

We spent some time in the field learning how to handle gas masks, field equipment, and weapons; although no one in the Medical branches were required to qualify in the use of any weapon. We did have to become familiar with the 45-caliber pistol and the carbine rifle. I found it virtually impossible to hit anything with the pistol but the rifle seemed to aim itself at what target I pointed it at.

There was some training in emergency medical care in which I murdered my goat when an instrument I was using to create an air way slipped and punctured the poor animals' carotid artery.

During one of the frequent inspections a Lt. Colonel, asked me if I had polished back of my brass belt buckle. Without thinking I glibly responded, "No, and I hadn't polished the soles of my shoes either." I immediately regretted the statement, which was totally uncalled for and disrespectful. I wanted to apologize, but the Colonel walked away in disbelief. Who knows what could have happened to me if he had pressed the issue. I regret not seeking him out later and apologizing to him in person.

Reg's father wrote letters every week about the daily lives of those we had left behind. I know he was worried about his daughter who had chosen a path so foreign to the close-knit family in which he was raised. I still have those letters in my genealogy files.

We visited Austin, TX on a weekend and were stunned to see a "White Only" water fountain in the state capital building. While segregation was apparent in many ways in 1960, this sign, in this place, struck us both as being especially egregious. Perhaps it was just that much of what black people experienced on a daily basis was hidden from view from those of us not personality involved. This was not subtle; it was blatant bigotry that could not be ignored. It brought to our consciousness that which we ignored so easily in the more insidious signs of bigotry that surrounded us at home. Our attitudes were not so much being changed as they were being newly formed.

Reg worked as a nurse at Santa Rosa Hospital near the Alamo and learned a new Spanish word each day. We lived near the gate to the Army post so I was able to walk to work and Reg drove our new white 1960 Ford Falcon to work.

The San Antonio River Walk was just a muddy path when we strolled along the San Antonio River on our days off in 1960. However, since its renovation in 1968 the picturesque walkway has become the number one tourist attraction in Texas, with holiday watercraft and sidewalk artisans selling handmade jewelry, pottery, or fine art beside sidewalk cafes and upscale shops.

We took a day trip to Nuevo Laredo, Mexico, to see a bull fight. We were shocked by both the poverty of the small city and by the brutality of the bullfight. I wondered why this city was so poor when it lies just a few miles from incredible wealth.

We also took a trip to one of the Air Force Bases located near San Antonio. The Officers Club there held a Casino Night and we decided to try our luck. We didn't have much luck but I did learn that I really didn't enjoy gambling. Reg on the other hand found it to be fun and exciting.

When I graduated from the training program in November, we packed our Falcon and headed for home. We stopped in Huston, TX the first night and decided to stay at a five-star hotel to celebrate. I was searching through the household items that filled the trunk looking for our suitcase. I was still in uniform and holding a large cast iron frying pan when Bob Hope approached me shook my free hand and thanked me for my service. He was performing in Huston and staying at the hotel. He had devoted much of his career visiting and supporting service men and women.

Because I was transferred to the Inactive Reserves after leaving the Air National Guard in 1956, I had accrued several years of Military service, which raised my pay to the level of a Captain even, though I was only a Second Lieutenant.

1961.1   FORT DIX, N.J.

At Fort Dix, we lived in a small rented apartment for a few weeks until a house became available on the Army post. My brother Artie visited us there. It was his only visit with us, as his work took him far from our various homes.

We soon moved into a 2-bedroom ranch style home furnished mostly with Army furniture. We gradually replaced many of the items and at this writing; we still use the bedroom set that we purchased in our first year together. We had a cat named Princess who stood upright on our bed and caught the socks I tossed to her each evening. We planted a small garden and enjoyed many visits from Reg's family and our old friends; life was good.

Lulled by predictions of a mild winter, New York was ill prepared for the 20-hour snowstorm that poured down nearly two feet in Jan 1961. I was on a Holiday leave from Fort Dix, NJ, and Reg and I were visiting her parents in Richmond Hill, NY. Reg's cousin Virginia Straub and Fred Sender were getting married on the weekend while we were home. We loaded Reg's Mom and Dad into the Ford Falcon and set off for the wedding in the middle of a blizzard. We drove for over an hour trying to find a passable road that would lead to the wedding. Like most of the other invited guests, we never made it.

Despite the ban on traffic on city roads, I had to return to Fort Dix. Traffic jams and snowdrifts forced all schools and services to close. I wore my uniform hoping that I would be able to drive through New York City. Remarkably, we were the only car in view, as we drove on the Long Island Expressway and through the Queens Mid-Town Tunnel. At each check point police officers waved us through. The city was almost deserted except for trucks and tractors moving snow to the rivers. When we went through the Lincoln Tunnel, we saw that thousands of stalled commuters stretching for miles on all three northbound lanes of the New Jersey Turnpike waiting to enter or merely pass by the city.

While working at Walton Army Hospital I applied for admission into the Anesthesia Training Program at Walter Reed. Reg worked in a near-by civilian hospital in the open-heart recovery room. Deborah Heart and Lung Center is the only hospital in the region that focuses exclusively on cardiac, vascular, and lung disease. It has been named "the place to get the best cardiac care" and is ranked among the top hospitals in the country for patient satisfaction by independent research companies, national consumer magazines, and the federal government. While Reg may not have been personally responsible for all those accolades her work was up to their high standards and as expected, she made many friends there.

On one occasion, we went to Monmouth Park Racetrack and we won the daily double, we spent the money going to our first Broadway play and had dinner at the Cattleman, a well know NYC restaurant at that time.

1961.2   CUBAN BAY OF PIGS

On April 17, 1961, 1,400 Cuban exiles launched what became a botched invasion of Cuba. The CIA-sponsored paramilitary group Brigade 2506 undertook the Bay of Pigs Invasion. A counter-revolutionary military, trained and funded by the United States Government's Central Intelligence Agency, Brigade 2506 intended to overthrow the revolutionary left wing government of Fidel Castro. Launched from Guatemala, the invading force was defeated within three days by the Cuban armed forces, under the direct command of Prime Minister Fidel Castro. It would be 55 years before relations with Cuba would begin to thaw. While this crisis was short lived, it was just the first of several international incidents that erupted during my military career that caused me to pack my duffel bag and be ready for reassignment to a Mobile Army Surgical Hospital (MASH.)

1962.1 & 1942 WALTER REED ARMY MEDICAL CENTER

The School of Anesthesiology, at Walter Reed Army Medical Center in Washington, D.C., seemed to hold the perfect solution to the career dilemma I was facing. Anesthesia with its high degree of technical skill and greater autonomy and respect, seemed to me to be a reasonable avenue to escape the stigma that I felt about being a male nurse. It was soon apparent that I was well suited for the job and was often among the first in my small class of five Army Officers to be given new responsibilities. An important milestone in the training was the first time I was to use general anesthesia on a young child. The technique used was quite primitive even by the standards of 1962. It was taught in military hospitals because it required little by way of special equipment and could be used in certain isolated situations. Ether was dropped on a curved screen placed over the patients' mouth and nose. Ricky lay on the operating room table, barely aware of where he was, because of the medications he had received before coming to the operating room. This step was not merely a comfort to the patient, but also an important safety precaution, as the first stage of anesthesia is one of excitement. The Adrenaline rush from the excitement combined with the anesthetic agents can produce heart failure. I had spent the prior evening in our Washington, DC apartment reviewing the technique, the signs of each of the stages of unconsciousness and all of the things that might go wrong, and how to respond to each. As I opened the can of ether that morning, the pungent fumes filled my nostrils.

> (1942) I tried to scream but I couldn't catch my breath, I punched and kicked at the arms and straps that held me down. The smell grew stronger, my mouth and nose were on fire; I was dying and I had to escape. Later my mother, who had taken Artie and me to Dr. Kings' Hospital in Bay Shore, LI., NY said that everyone in the waiting room could hear my terrifying screams. Artie and I received the pre-anesthesia medications in the waiting room. However, I went into the O.R. before they took effect. By the time Artie was called he was already half asleep and had a much easier time of it.

> Later, that day we went back to Mrs. Morgan's to recover and for the long-promised ice cream; a rare treat in those days. Mrs. Morgan had failed to mention that my throat would be too sore after a tonsillectomy to eat ice cream or anything else.

(1962) Ricky was soon unconscious. There was no screaming, kicking, or punching from him or any of the hundreds of patients I would serve during my remaining four years in the Army.

Among those patients were many wives and children of soldiers and since the war in Vietnam was not yet in full force, the only battle-wounded soldiers I would serve were those hurt in training exercises or accidents. Among them was George, a badly burned helicopter pilot whose airship had crashed. He was in Walter Reed long before I got there and he was there when I left. I gave George anesthesia for two of his many surgeries, which consists mainly of skin grafts. The surgeons would partially lift a flap of viable skin from an unburned area and attach the lifted end to another part of his body. When the blood supply grew between the flap and new site, the flap was moved from the original donor site. Sometimes a skin flap would have to be moved from the body to an arm and weeks later moved from the arm to another location. The agonizingly slow process often required George to be placed in body casts as the skin flaps were gradually moved in leapfrog faction to the burnt areas of his body. While I didn't really know George very well, I never heard him complain and I wondered if my earlier dream of becoming a pilot had come true and if I were wounded would I have been able to endure the pain, the disfigurement, and the loss of a career with such dignity and bravery.

I almost met President Kennedy while working at Walter Reed. All surgery patients were anesthetized in an Induction Room at the end of the long hall of operating rooms. Once asleep, they were wheeled down the hall to the appropriate OR. The transfer included a sharp turn past the entrance to the VIP suite of the hospital. Just as two Army Corpsman and I were moving, my patient around the tight turn, President Kennedy and two Secret Service Agents came through the door from the VIP suite. As the heavy steel table was about to smash into the Presidents legs the agents lunged in front of him. He smiled, the agents frowned, I nodded, and the patient dozed. Later in the day when my work was done and the President was leaving the hospital, he stopped on the outside stairs, turned, and waved as I looked out of the window. I doubt that he knew that he was waving at the person who almost extended his hospital stay. Although he looked healthy and had an athletic build, President Kennedy suffered from several serious medical conditions and made many visits to Walter Reed during his all too brief 3-year term in office.

1962.2 UNIVERSITY OF MARYLAND

While I had accumulated many college credits, I did not have a bachelor's degree since the credits were in different fields and from different schools. I decided to take evening courses from the nearby University of Maryland to continue to move closer to obtaining a degree. I completed a course in American History during the fall semester and enrolled in another course for the spring semester, which I could have completed prior to finishing the Anesthesia program. However, one of the instructors at Walter Reed overheard a conversation and learned about my enrollment in College. She insisted that I drop the college course. I tried to explain that unlike some of my classmates, I had no children, which took up much more time than one evening course, and unlike others, I didn't belong to a bowling league or have any hobbies or outside interests that occupy the time of many students. However, she insisted that I drop the course because it was competing with my studies at Walter Reed even though I had just completed the fall semester at the head of my class. I considered her attitude to be very rigid, provincial, and typical of other nursing instructors I had known earlier; yet another reason to seek another profession.

1962.3   CIRCULAR SLIDE RULE #1

In the spring of 1962, I invented a circular slide rule with the Gerhard Blood Volume Estimator on the obverse, which calculated patient blood volume based on weight and height. The reverse contained an adaptation of the Radford nomogram, which helped determine the necessary tidal volume for artificial respiration based on respiratory rate, body weight, and gender.

A Nomogram is a graph with three lines graduated so that a straight line intersecting any two of the lines at their known values intersects the third at the value of the related variable. Prior to my invention anesthetists had to juggle the graph and a ruler to determine the needed values. The circular slide rule could be operated with one hand. When I left the Army in 1966, the slide rule was in use in Army Hospitals.

Founded in 1862, The Armed Forces Institute of Pathology was on the grounds of the Walter Reed Army Medical Center. It provided diagnostic consultations on pathologic specimens and had a large staff of graphic artists. I got permission to work with their staff to mass produce plastic copies of the original cardboard slide rule I created on our kitchen table. The Army owns all rights to the invention.

1962.4 & 1942   A REAL ORPHAN

Later in the spring of 1962, Barnum and Bailey's Greatest Show on Earth came to the nations' capital. Still childless, Reg and I decided to take a child from a Washington area orphanage on an outing to the circus. The nuns matched us with a young boy of about eight or nine. Sadly, I have forgotten the boys' name and have lost his photo so he remains forever anonymous in my memory.

He enjoyed the circus, and Reg and I delighted in watching his excitement. When we brought him to his home later that evening we made plans for another outing, the following weekend.

The following Saturday was a warm sunny day and we headed out on our adventure. As we drove down one of Washington's many grand boulevards in our new blue Oldsmobile convertible, he suggested that since he had no mother and father and since we had no children that we should adopt him and become a family. Reg and I were shocked by both the fact that we were not ready to adopt and by the recognition that what we had intended to be a happy respite for the boy was about to turn into a painful rejection.

(1942) Many of the kids at the Sayville Cottages, even those like Artie and me who were not actually orphans, were unable to separate our feelings about our dysfunctional situation from our feelings about ourselves. Some felt guilty, some confused, some angry; but most felt vaguely at odds with the world and the kids at public school who had parents who weren't paid to love them. I heard the stories from kids who were desperate to have someone know that it wasn't their fault and that inside they were just like the other kids. Many hoped for someone to come and revitalize their life with a sense of dignity, others fearing rejection, had stopped hoping. Artie and I just waited for the trap door to open again.

(1962) Reg and I wondered how badly we had hurt this boy in our back seat as we explained that I was soon to be transferred to another Army Post and would not be able to see him again. At the end of our outing we brought him home and said goodbye for the last time and I remembered the stories that I had heard and the feeling that I had when it was me rather than a stranger who was living as an orphan. The next time we would visit an orphanage, in 1965, our intentions would be clearer.

1962.5   CUBAN MISSILE CRISIS

For thirteen days in October 1962, the world waited—seemingly on the brink of nuclear war—and hoped for a peaceful resolution to the Cuban Missile Crisis, which began when an American plane secretly discovered nuclear missile sites under construction by the Soviet Union on the island of Cuba. Because he did not want Cuba and the Soviet Union to know that he had discovered the missiles, Kennedy met in secret with his advisors for several days to discuss the problem. After many long and difficult meetings, Kennedy decided to place a naval blockade, around Cuba to prevent the Soviets from bringing in more military supplies, and demanded the removal of the missiles already there and the destruction of the sites.

The Soviet Union, installed nuclear missiles in Cuba in an attempt to create a balance with the U.S.'s ability to reach any site in the Soviet Union from its' Turkey-based nuclear missiles. The world had come so close to nuclear war that the threat of total annihilation was palpable throughout the country. As a member of the U.S. Army, I was at a high level of readiness, with a duffel bag packed at all times.

When President Kennedy spoke to the nation about the crisis in a televised address Reg and I were glued to the TV, as our future and the future of human kind seemed to hang in the balance. At that time, the crisis was generally regarded as the moment in which the Cold War came closest to a nuclear war.

Fortunately, both Soviet Premier Nikita Khrushchev and U.S. President John Kennedy ignored their more militant advisors and found a diplomatic solution. The Soviets removed the missiles from Cuba and later the U.S. quietly removed its missiles from Turkey.

1962.6   THE MATTHIESENS

I had met Jerry Matthiesen at Fort Sam Huston in 1960. He was a member of my Officer Training class. His wife, Carol, was expecting their first child at the time and she did not accompany him to Texas. It was a welcome surprise to find him in the Anesthesia Program at Walter Reed. Reg and I would spend many evenings and weekend days with Jerry, Carol and their daughter Desiree. They taught us to eat tacos, play canasta, and watch speedboat racing on the Potomac River. When their second daughter, Michon, was born the spring of 1962, they asked Reg and me to be her God Parents. We would see Michon again many years later and establish a close relationship with her as an adult.

In 1966 when Jerry and Carol were returning from a tour of duty in Germany they, now with three daughters, visited us in Ithaca. While our lives were now quite different, we each were satisfied that, we had chosen the right path. Jerry retired from the Army in 1980 as a Lieutenant Colonel; he died a few years later.

1963.1   ROCK CREEK PARK

Rock Creek Park is a gem in our nation's capital. Reg and I spent many hours there allowing the fresh air, majestic trees, wild animals, and the ebb and flow of the creek to soothe our spirits. We followed in the wake of thousands of years of human history. American Indians made tools from its rocks, fished the creek, and hunted wild game. Then Europeans grew tobacco there and when tobacco exhausted the soil, they switched to wheat and corn and gristmills were constructed to convert the grain into flour. The area was deforested during the U.S. Civil War to make a secret Confederate march through the valley impossible. In 1890, the 1,700-acre Rock Creek Park became one of the first federally managed parks.

In the evenings, we would slowly drive through the tree-lined lanes with the car top down and our spirits up. On weekends, we would sit near the banks of the creek in the day and visit the Carter Barron Amphitheatre in the evening. We saw the "King and I" there and it remains one of our favorite musicals.

We took some of our frequent visitors to the park, but with so much to see in Washington, D.C., much of our time together with friends and family was spent visiting historic sites and memorials. We became quite knowledgeable about the city and entertained our guests by filling the time with facts and stories to supplement the sights.

1963.2   FORT BENNING, GEORGIA

In May of 1963, with more confidence than experience, I began my career as an anesthetist at Martin Army Hospital, at Ft. Benning, GA. There were five of us on staff, two physician anesthesiologists, and three nurse anesthetists. We shared the on-call duty and the MDs were excellent teachers. Gradually I earned the trust of my collegues and the surgeons. The program at Walter Reed had prepared me well.

On one occassion I was called in to assist one of the anesthetists who was having difficulty intubating a new born infant. There was concern that contuined probing would result in inflamation of the treachea and significant breathing problems post-op, so I was asked to try to intubate the child. I knew the importance of succeeding on the first attempt, failure might have required the child to have a second operation to insert a breathing tube in his trachia. As I took up the needed equipment I could feel the room and the staff fade from my consciousness: I was alone with the baby. I saw the endotracheal tube slide into the trachea between the vocal cords and the child breathed easily. After giving the anesthesia equipment back to the anesthetist who had called me, I left the room. I was very impressed that the anesthetist was able to put aside personal feelings of pride and ask for help. I hoped that I would be as professional and mature if I were ever faced with a similar decision. This was an important lesson for me and it added a valuable tool to my tool box, "The call for help."

When I answered the phone on nights when I was on call, I would listen to the discription of the patient's problem. Then during the ten minute ride from our apartment to the hospital I would imagine everything that might go wrong and how I would respond, and how I would respond if the solution didn't work. I would remenber the aphorism, "When you hear hoof beats, think horses not zebras." It helped me to stay focused on the reality of the situation. While studying and being prepared in case a zebra actually showed up was also important, first I had to weigh the evidence at hand. The excitement of being called to assisst with life saving surgery was the most rewarding part of the job.

Many of the late night calls involved automobile accidents involving young men and alcohol. One accident didn't involve autos, alcohol, or after-hours activity. Fort Benning was among other things a training site for paratroopers. One day, corpsmen rushed a young soldier into the operating room with massive head wounds. After his landing, a gust of wind caught his parachute and dragged him on the ground, and his head crashed into a large rock. We all knew that this was a catastrophic injury. I stood ready to give anesthesia in the unlikely event that it was needed. The tension was palpable as the surgeon cut into the shaved scalp. The soldier's gray brain tissue flowed slowly into the basin below. Someone remarked, "There goes 1947, 1948 . . . " We all faked a muffled laugh at the sorely need tension breaker. To an outsider, a joke at that time would have seemed unbelievably crass and insensitive, but we all knew that it prevented the room from breaking down in tears. It was over.

Wages were very low in the South at that time, especially for Black women. Although we weren't sure if we were helping a person in need or taking advantage of another's' difficulties, on the recommendation of neighboring officers' wife, we hired a house cleaner. She came once a week and helped with the cleaning. Gradually we got to know her and planted morning glories on a trellis as she suggested. We were shocked to hear that her home had a dirt floor. We raised her wages and when we left, we offered her a large nylon carpet to cover her floor. She accepted and husband came took it home.

I took several night courses at the local American University campus.

Reg took a nursing position at the local hospital in Columbus, GA. She found the attitude there so unwelcoming of Yankees and so disrespectful of their Black patients that she decided to leave after a month.

We both took up golf and played at the officer's club. Neither of us was very good and neither really enjoyed the game. We carried our clubs from home to home for many years before finally disposing of them at a garage sale. During one of our telephone conversations with Reg's parents, we mentioned that we had taken up golf. Her father asked me what I went around in, I replied, "Bermuda Shorts." It was only after we hung up that I realized that he was asking about my score. No wonder he had concerns for his "Toots."

I had little in common with my neighbors at the Army Officers housing area where we lived; they were Army Rangers, Helicopter Pilots, and Special Forces Instructors. However, Reg and I did get to know many of them and enjoyed many evening get-to-getters where we learned to drink Martinis. I hoped that I would never have to meet them at work, for their work was war and my work was caring for the wounded.

1963.3   ARTHUR GERHARD JR.

Artie called me at our home in Fort Benning, Ga. in Mid-August, his life finally seemed to be providing him with some of the joy that most of us take for granted, but which he rarely experienced. His new job at the Sales Training Institute in Seattle was going well, he had an apartment in an upscale neighborhood in nearby Puyallup WA, a new luxury car, and most importantly, he had a relationship with a woman, with two young children, who all seemed to love him. I did not know at that time that his joy was based on his expectations of a committed relationship with someone who was not yet ready for a second marriage. I will never know for sure, but I now believe that it's possible that Artie called me to say goodbye.

Artie's dream like mine was to have a 'normal' family of his own. However, I believe that his private feelings of inadequacy carried with it a fear of failure, especially the fear of passing his assumed inadequacy along to any children he might father. This 'ready-made' family with two 'normal' children allowed Artie's dream to soar. However, when his proposal was rejected the wings of his dream were clipped and with them his hope for finally overcoming the melancholy of his childhood. I believe this to be true for I shared some of the same feelings and I suppose that many of the children raised in dysfunctional or socially marginal families assume that they are somehow defective because of their negative experiences or possibly even the cause of the family's  problems. The walls we build to protect ourselves from pain may also shield us from joy.

Seeing my children soar ranks as my greatest joy in life. No matter what happens in my life to clip the wings of my own private dreams, I know that they are safe . . . they are normal . . . they will not pass on this "Mark of Cain" to the next generation. They will no doubt face their own trials, disappointments, and failures, but they will face the circumstances and decisions of their own lives and not the haunting of ghosts from lives past. The cycle has been broken.

Two weeks later Mom called to tell me that Artie had committed suicide and the familiar clouds of Artie's past loneliness and isolation gathered in my head.

I flew to Seattle and met with Artie's friend and former boss, Donald. He took me to Arties' apartment. I lived there among my brothers' things for the next week as I gathered the facts about his life and death and met the people who had known him. I searched in vain through his files, records, and old receipts for some insight into this man who I had only known as a boy. I touched his clothes, and ate from his dishes, but it was too late, I should have tried to know him sooner, but then I did not know that our time was so limited. I know now that we all have limited allotments of time, and I try to know those who matter to me. Sometimes I succeed, but not always. It's hard to change who you are, even when you know that change is needed. We have very few unique or original thoughts and spend much of our lives replaying them repeatedly in our minds, like a prisoner locked in a cell with a single book to reread because it is the only one available. One of the challenges of life is to find another story to read or to write and not let ourselves to become imprisoned by our past.

In the end, I arranged to have Artie's body sent to Ocala, Florida. Mom buried him between the graves of his grandmother Hattie Mills and the future gravesite of his mother and stepfather.

Donald and I visited the isolated dirt road in the woods where his body was found, still sitting behind the wheel of the lime green 1962 Cadillac sedan in which he shot himself in the heart to end his pain. At the coroner's office, I had the option of seeing photos of the body; I declined and later regretted the decision. The police had his two guns, the shotgun that he had used to kill himself and a high-powered rifle with a hand-carved stock, a detachable sight, and a fur lined carrying case. I gave the shotgun, still stained with Arties' blood and tissue, to Don who was a hunter and who told me that he would cherish the gun. I had the rifle shipped home with a few other personnel items, and later sold it to an Air Borne Ranger who lived next door to us at Ft. Benning, GA. I never owned another gun.

I visited the auto repair shop where the police had impounded Artie's car. The seat and ceiling were splattered with parts of my brother. The smell of death was carried on the wings of the hundreds of flies swarming inside. My chest was so heavy that I could barely breathe. I tried to imagine what Artie was feeling as he sat in the car alone orphaning himself, hopeless and despondent. It was hard to believe that what I was witnessing was the solution to a problem. Grief came over me like the waves at the beach. I was drowning again.

Near the end of my stay, Don and I went to visit Arties' former girlfriend. She lived in Bellevue, a suburb of Seattle, with her two young children. She was recently divorced. Apparently, Artie had assumed or hoped that with her divorce finalized, they would be married. She, however, was not ready to recommit; the rejection tore the scab from the aging wound. For Artie, love was like a mirage, always in sight, but never within reach. Her rejection changed the melody of his life into a requiem hymn. Grief is the price he paid for love.

Artie had kept many of his personal items at her house including his prized leather-bound book collection and the shells for his shotgun. She heard him in the basement the night before he disappeared; she thought he was gathering some personnel items. He was. He took the shells for the gun from their hiding place among the floor joists in the basement. Several days later a young couple looking for a place to be alone in the isolated wooded area, found his body.

Before he died, Artie had changed the beneficiary of his $10,000 G.I. life insurance policy from Mom to his girlfriend. I think Artie wanted to leave her a message that would remind her that he loved her and that she had made a mistake. I tried to read the two-page suicide note that he left. Between his 'physician-like' handwriting and the tears in my eyes, I know that I missed much of Arties' last message, another regret.

I visited Arties' gravesite each time Reg and I visited Mom and Tony in Ocala, FL. While Artie rested secure at last in the warmth of the valley of death, I stood alone in the shadow of the valley, which provided no warmth, no rest, and no security. On each visit, my chest responded with the familiar heaviness that took my breath, but how could I express emotions to others when they felt so foreign to me. Grief was more like a distant ache, a dreamy disbelief that reminded me of all that was lost, and how little I had done for my brother. It reminded me of the many occasions for affirmation and support, sorely needed, but selfishly withheld. I also knew that someday I would stand there and those feelings too would be gone.

Many years later I stood there for the last time and I knew that something was lost that could never be recovered. I felt somehow diminished by the loss, for the pain of grieving was all that had remained of my brother, and now that too was gone. It was like losing him again. On that last visit to his gravesite it seemed that the only thing that mattered about Artie was the fact that he was dead. It wasn't just the memory that had faded; it was me.

Our dead are never dead to us, until we have forgotten them.

George Eliot

1963.4   JOHN F. KENNEDY

Eighty days after Artie died I was again working, as an anesthetist, at Martin Army Hospital in Fort Benning, GA. After returning to the operating suite from the recovery room where I had left my last patient, I entered the doctors' lounge for a quick lunch and a cigarette before my next case.

It was immediately apparent that something was very wrong; the tension in the room was palatable. The room was full and the television was on. Since my arrival from Walter Reed Army Medical Center six months earlier, I had never before seen more than two or three people in the lounge at one time and the television was rarely on.

One of the anesthesiologists said, "Kennedy has been shot." The impact was as immediate and as dramatic as the explosions often heard from the training areas of the Fort where the real soldiers were taught how to kill and how to stay alive. It was instant and empty. The intensity lasted for days as the drama played itself out on black and white television screens around the world. However, the sorrow lasted for years, the office would be refilled, but the man would never be replaced. No one has ever stirred my spirit like JFK.

What John Kennedy did for the country (and for me) was to give us confidence; confidence, not only that our strength would ensure that we would do well, (well, as in amply) but also the confidence that our ideals could ensure that we will do well as in proper.

In his inaugural address, President Kennedy declared that "a new generation of Americans" had taken over leadership of the country. He said Americans would "... pay any price, bear any burden, meet any hardship, support any friend, and oppose any foe to assure the survival and the success of liberty." He told Americans, "Ask not what your country can do for you, -ask what you can do for your country." We believed him and were glad to be part of that new generation. But neither he, nor we, could know that his life would be the price that would be paid for a few brief years of optimism and that the next decade would be viewed through the prism of grief. JFK's death redefined tragedy as the difference between what is and what might have been.

At this writing, it has been over 50 years since his assassination, and time has dulled the intensity of the grief of that day, but periodic TV documentaries still recast its haunting shadow of disappointment. And the shadow morphs from disappointment to disillusionment by the 'rein of error' carried on by so many of his successors who were untethered by talent and who speak of values to lure supporter, while their actions reveal their self-serving motivations.

1964.1 & 1963   MEETING MY FATHER

In June 1964, after completing my internship at Fort Benning I was reassigned to the Army Hospital at the West Point Military Academy. We decided to take a week in Florida to see Mom and Tony and to spend a few days relaxing on the beach.

> (1963) Only my mother, my half-brother Richie, Reg and myself were present at the funeral home when Artie's closed casket was placed in the viewing room. However, the next day at the cemetery about a dozen people showed up for the brief graveside service. Mom, Tony, Grandma Mills, Mom's sister Esma Overcash, and her daughter Diane, Mom's brother Robert Mills and his wife Mary, a neighbor of Mom's from Ocala, Reg, a few others, and me.

> After the ceremony, Mom, Reg and I walked toward my car, which was parked on a nearby driveway. As we approached the car, Mom turned to a far-off couple who were walking toward a distant roadway. I hadn't noticed them before, as they arrived after we sat down in the front row, and left before we turned to leave. Mom said, "See that man walking over there. He is your father. But please don't try to speak to him as Grandma would be furious if she knew he was here." The seed was planted

(1964) While at the beachfront motel, I recalled the figure of my father walking away from Artie's grave. I remembered that he lived in Ft. Lauderdale, which "coincidentally" was the site of our motel, and I found his address in the phone book. A local map, and a short drive later we were parked in front of his small neatly trimmed ranch-style home. I recognized the car parked in front from the cemetery six months earlier. I had not planned to go in, merely to see where he lived, but on an impulse, I knocked on the front door, as Reg waited in the car. "Hello, I'm your son, Ronald."

He invited Reg and me in and we spoke for about an hour as his wife, Ethel stayed out of sight. Later the three of us went out to dinner. He was a very congenial man and seemed genuinely interested in us, and I was very glad to have finally met the man who was my biological father. We never discussed his reasons for leaving. Some questions are better left unasked and many remain unanswered. The next morning, he called us at the motel and made it clear that he too was glad for the long-postponed reunion and that he wanted to stay in touch. We never met again, but for about 30 years we exchanged cards and I sent him photos of his grandchildren as they progressed. One year the Post Office returned the Christmas card. We assumed that he had died. Thirty-eight years would pass before I would finally learn the details about the end of his life, about his wife Ethel Newton, and about several members of Ethel's family who had known and loved the father that I had only met but once.

1965.1 & 1504   DAVID ARTHUR

After five years of marriage with no effort to prevent pregnancy, Reg and I were each examined to determine why we remained childless. The analysis showed that It was likely that Reg may have had some very early miscarriages and that my sperm were less than vigorous. I remembered a very painful soccer injury several years earlier and wondered if it contributed to my problem. We decided to visit the local adoption agency in Goshen, NY. We had an initial visit where we filled out forms, learned some of the details of the adoption process, and scheduled a second appointment. As we prepared to leave for the second appointment, Reg became too ill to make the journey over the mountains from West Point to Goshen. We rescheduled. Reg was sick the next morning and every morning for the next week until her obstetrician prescribed medication to relieve the morning sickness produced by her pregnancy.

On December 23, after forty-five hours of labor, David arrived. As I saw him for the first time I couldn't decide if I should laugh or cry . . . so I did both. Reg was remarkable and was out of bed a few hours later. We enjoyed Christmas dinner in the hospital where David was born and where I worked and were soon home in our apartment next to the hospital. When the sun rose, I would awake and wait impatiently for David to let me know he was ready to eat. I resisted the temptation to wake him so I could be with him. I remember sitting in our gold colored chair with the early morning sun pouring in over my shoulder and thinking that the happiness of these quiet moments together could never be duplicated for I had fallen in love again. I was wrong. To my great relief, I discovered that the births of Brian and Greg also gave birth to a previously unknown wellspring of love and happiness.

(1504) David was named for the statue of King David, which was created 461 years earlier by Michelangelo. I had just learned the story of this remarkable feat when I read "The Agony and the Ecstasy," Michelangelo's biography. The piece of Carrara marble that Michelangelo used had laid discarded for many years because it had a flaw that ran through its entire length. Michelangelo's genius allowed him to visualize David standing with his hand on his hip with his torso slightly turned so his body avoided the defect. It wasn't that I thought a statue was a worthy namesake for my son. Instead, it was the idea that something so perfect as David could be created from something so imperfect and discarded like me that struck a chord in me, which I had never played before. David's middle name, Arthur, was after my father, not because I was close to my father, but because I appreciated the long missing sense of continuity that it added to our family.

1965.2 CAT IN A TENT

Our third-floor apartment at West Point overlooked the Hudson River and had a small balcony, which opened off the master bedroom. It was barely wide enough for a beach chair and we rarely used it until I noticed a very old, damaged, and unusable oxygen tent in a storage closet at the hospital where I worked. Instead of throwing it out, I cut the clear plastic tent down to size so it would serve as a shelter for the kitty litter box, which we placed on the balcony. It was low enough that it could not be seen from the ground, and of course, "Dixie" had a privy with a great view and we got the litter box out of the apartment.

1965.3 AUTO SAFETY

One of our neighbors in our apartment building at West Point lost their young daughter in an automobile accident. While seat belts were available, in most cars, since the late 1950's few people used them and there were no child safety seats available. The young girl was sitting in the front seat of the car when her mother had to jam on the brakes. The girls' head hit the windshield and she died.

Before David was born, I created a safety harness that attached to the back of the car seat that would prevent him and eventually his brothers from being thrown around inside the car. All three boys used these harnesses and when they grew large enough to want to see out of the windows, I built padded bolster seats that were used with the harnesses.

While these devices were primitive compared to modern safety seats, I believe that they did provide some degree of safety.

1965.4   ORANGE COUNTY COMMUNITY COLLEGE

While working at West Point I continued to take college courses at night in hope of eventually obtaining a Bachelor's degree. The only college with commuting distance was Orange County Community College, located in Middletown about 35 miles away. When I arrived at West Point, I had 147 college credits, and while this was more than the 120 needed for most bachelor's degrees, I needed to obtain the last 30 credits from the degree granting institution. That was going to be difficult because of the frequent transfers while in the Army. I took 21 additional credits at Orange County during my two years at the Military Academy.

One foggy evening on a mountainous hairpin turn while returning home from class, I came face to face with a huge stag; he stood frozen five feet from the car in the oncoming lane. I stopped the car and opened the window. I could almost reach his antlers. Eventually I became concerned that if a car came from behind me, it would not be able to stop on this hairpin curve in time to avoid a crash and I drove home. He was magnificent and I felt so blessed to be able to be so close to him.

> *Nature holds the key to our aesthetic, intellectual, cognitive*
>
> *and even spiritual satisfaction.*
>
> *E. O. Wilson*

I spent most of my evening drives home listening to Jean Shepherd on the radio. He was a writer, humorist, satirist, actor, radio raconteur. He was a master storyteller in the league of Mark Twain. Sometimes I would slow down to hear the end of one of his great stories before I entered the mountains where reception was poor. Today he's best known as the narrator of the movie, "The Christmas Story."

1966.1   LEAVING WEST POINT

One of the last surgical cases I had before leaving the Army in 1966 was another young boy. Paul had a ruptured appendix. The O.R. called in the middle of the night and when I arrived at the hospital, the surgeons were anxious to begin before the purulent material, spilling from his bowels, would develop into a massive (and possibly fatal) infection if not treated. But, the pre-operative medications had not yet had time to take full effect. As I took the boy on the elevator to operating room, I let him hold the oxygen mask that I had brought with me just for that purpose. As the elevator started its rise, I began the role-playing. We were astronauts going up in the gantry elevator to enter the space ship. I reminded him that astronauts lie on their backs during blast off. After we entered the flight deck (the O.R.), the surgeons, and nurses were waiting and quickly joined in the game. I showed him the control center (the anesthesia machine) with its many knobs and dials, and asked him to move onto the cockpit and strap himself into his recliner in preparation for take-off. One of the nurses offered to help with the straps and showed him how quickly they fall away after launch. The surgeon added background chatter from Houston Mission Control. With the preparations completed, I handed him the mask, now attached to the anesthesia machine, and asked him to put it on and prepare for lift off. We all counted 10, 9, 8, 7 … as I slowly added Nitrous Oxide and Halothane to the Oxygen already flowing into his mask. The drug smelled faintly sweet and easily shrouded by the smell of the rubber mask. As the boy counted, he drifted off. Again, there were no punches, no kicks, and no screams.

When I left West Point and the Army, I also ended my career as an anesthetist. There were many other, changes as well. It was the last time that Reg and I would be the youngest members of our social circle, the last time our friends would come primarily from the medical field and the last time that foreign policy would play such an important role in our daily lives. The week before we left, the physicians at the Hospital offered me either an Army Commendation Medal or a Plaque from the Medical Staff. Having a closer allegiance to the hospital staff than to the Army in general, I chose the plague. Now, whenever I look at the plaque, I remember the physicians, surgeons, and nurses with whom we shared a portion of our lives and I remember Paul, who had become a symbol of the many soldiers and family members that I had served.

The only military medal that I received was the National Defense Medal. I believe that everyone who served in the armed forces and was not dishonorably discharged received this metal. While I am technically a Vietnam Era veteran, I never refer to myself that way because I never went to Vietnam and I do not consider myself a veteran of the war. Rather I am a veteran of the peace whose only relationship to the combat soldiers of our many wars is to reap the benefits of their service and to try to live a life worthy of their sacrifices, especially those who will remain forever young.

I did receive a Citation from the Commandant of the U.S. Military Academy and five Letters of Commendation for the contributions I made. These included several inventions and a circular slide rule used to estimate the tidal volume of respirations. This helps hospital staff regulate the breathing apparatus. The back of the slide rule is used to determine a patient's blood volume, which helps determine when transfusions are needed.

My request for release from active duty was delayed for five months. A physician who I never met was suing the Army claiming that he had a contract that allowed him to exit the Army when he paid back the time he had spent receiving training. The Army claimed that in a time of war they could keep officers for the duration, regardless of their previous conditions of employment. The physician won his case and hundreds of medical professions seeking discharge, including me, obtained release from duty. On appeal, the decision was reversed and he had to remain in the Army, however those of us who were released were not recalled. Had the physician lost the original case, I would not have been discharged and I may have decided to stay in the Army rather than to go to graduate school. That one event divided my life forever and allowed me to select a path of my own choosing rather than simply following the one that circumstances had laid before me.

A few months prior to my leaving the Army, the documents that Sergeant Jackson had requested in 1960 from the Air National Guard arrived. After serving over five years in the Army, my local draft board now deemed me eligible to join the military. Thank you, Sergeant Jackson, you made it possible for me to attend my wedding and enter the Army as an Officer rather than a private: another life-changing event.

"And that is how change happens, one gesture, one person, and one moment at a time."
Libba Bray

1966.2 & 1943   OMAHA

We packed our belongings into the Maroon 1965 Pontiac Tempest, into the U-Haul trailer, and into the attic of Reg's parents. After almost six years in the army, we were leaving the Military Academy at West Point, NY for the University of Nebraska at Omaha where I would finally complete my Bachelor's Degree. We drove off early in the morning, Reg, five months pregnant with Brian, and our new baby, David, aged seven months and me. This was a new and exciting time.

(1943) The back seat of the 1930's Plymouth was gray and the heat made the horsehair fabric feel very scratchy. Tony and Artie were in the front seat as we drove for the last time down the long driveway of the orphanage that had been our home for the past year.

The rumors that the "cottage" was closing became a reality as one by one the kids left for parts unknown. Some kids left for new lives with old families, but some were merely "left" behind for social workers to find a home. Artie and I were among the last to leave. The buildings were later converted into administrative offices for the Episcopal Church, which had operated the orphanage for many years. Before that morning, I had no idea when we would leave, where we would go, or whom we would live with. Tony, who I had never seen before, arrived on a Sunday morning. He introduced himself and told us that he was going to take us to our mother. Artie and I each packed all of our belongings into a pair of cardboard boxes and left with him. It was later during the half-hour drive from Sayville to Central Islip that we learned that he was going to be part of our latest "family" … he and our new one-month-old baby half-brother, Richie. Later that evening the four members of this newly forged family sat in the living of our small bungalow. I sat on the arm of the Tony's lounge chair and ran my fingers through his thinning hair. Who could have known that it would only take one day to be transported from the dormitory in an orphanage to living room in a family home? This too was a new and exciting time.

(1966) The temperature was in the 90's when the highway traffic backed up. The Pontiac soon overheated. We had just passed the last available exit on the Pennsylvania Turnpike when the radio news repeated the warning to travelers that a fire in the westbound tunnel of the Turnpike had backed up traffic for 30 miles in both directions. Parked and mostly overheated cars filled both shoulders of the highway. Our engine was overheating, but there was no room to pull off the road. I turned on the car heater to draw heat from the engine. It worked, the thermostat gradually dropped below the danger level, and the temperature inside the car grew even hotter than the 95 degree July day. Reg had packed bottled water so we wouldn't have to rely on the quality of the roadside water supplies. Dave sat between us haltered in his car seat and finished his last available bottle. Reg filled the thermos cup with water. Dave had never drunk from a cup before, but he learned quickly that day. He gulped down the water, and never used the bottle again.

(1943) I grew to love Tony and Richie, who Mom referred to as my half-brother (I thought that was because he was so much smaller than I was.) Artie, who never seemed quite at peace with life, resented Tony taking on the role of father. Being three years older than me, Artie, remembered life before our "real" father left for greener pastures. My youth protected me from that conflict of allegiance. I was a fish, born to the sea of darkness, and quite happy with it. My previous experiences had defined normalcy as that which I saw around me, and now, each home I entered was a new and exciting time. This was normal.

Our bedroom was the enclosed front porch of the small 3rd Avenue bungalow; windowed on three sides and about a foot wider than the two side-by-side cots Mom had prepared for our reunion.

I was an adult long before I asked myself, "How long were Mom and Tony living together before Artie and I were invited to join them?" Or "Why Artie and I lived in an orphanage with a family of strangers in Sayville when we had a mother and a new 'father' in Central Islip," or "How long we might have stayed in the orphanage if church finances didn't dictate its closing?" At the orphanage, I felt like a bit player in other peoples' tragedy, and it didn't occur to me that being immune to tragedy might mean that I could be immune to love as well. Those fears would come later. For kids living in institutions, life is like being a second stringer on a ball team, waiting on the bench and taking what comes your way. They are accustomed to being treated as interchangeable parts and rarely ask why.

(1966) The state police alternated the eastbound and westbound traffic through the one lane eastbound tunnel through the Allegany Mountains. In a few hours, we were in Ohio. Passing through that tunnel was like being born again, waiting, and waiting, then passing through the long dark tunnel, and finally the light. The air never seemed so fresh and the light so clear. We were on our way again.

The heavy-laden U-Haul trailer was clamped to the rear bumper of our '65 Tempest and with every jolt; the bumper was pulled farther from the frame of the car. A few days later, when we arrived in Omaha, Nebraska, our car had gained five inches in length.

Later that afternoon I met with a Real Estate agent to find a rental apartment and drove off on a clear sunny day, leaving Reg and David in the Motel. A few hours later while returning from the apartment that would be our home for the next year; I had to pull off the road because I could not see. It had turned dark as night and the rain was so heavy that the windshield wiper could not clear the window. This was not the last time we would see how fast the weather on the Mid-West open plains could change or how violent the storms could be. I often watched black storms race across the flatlands and disappear into the horizon as I sat in class. Reg was very frightened back at the motel as she not only had the storm to deal with but also the fact that she was left alone in a strange city and had no idea where I was.

Fortunately, I was eligible for the G.I Bill that helped pay the college tuition because I was unable to find a job as an anesthetist and took a much lower paying job in the business office of Bergen Mercy Hospital. I worked four hours each afternoon in the admitting office on days when I had college classes. On weekends, I worked eight hours on the evening shift as both the admitting clerk and the hospital cashier. This was many more hours than I would have had to work as an anesthetist and it was hard on Reg with David less than a year old and Brian on the way.

We spoke to Reg's Dad who worked at the stock market on Wall Street and told him that Omaha had its' own stock market but it didn't sell securities, it sold beef and hog bellies.

We spent two summer sessions and the fall semester at The University of Nebraska, and I graduated in the spring of 1967 and began interviewing at graduate schools around the country. As usual, I had no idea where our next home would be.

1966.3   BRIAN THOMAS

After waiting five years for David to make his appearance we were both surprised and thrilled to hear that Brian was scheduled to arrive just eleven months later. I was working in the business office of the hospital where he was born on the day that he arrived. When I went upstairs to the nursery, and I saw him, the fear that I could never love another child as much as I loved David vanished, never to return. When he came home from the hospital, he contracted a serious intestinal infection caused by an Echovirus. He was in pain that was only relieved by being held upright so his abdomen was supported against my chest. I loved holding him. David walked along and we chatted as I walked the floor with Brian in my arms for hours. My schoolwork was put on the back burner until he recovered. I was unconcerned; the bond that would dominate much of my adult life was set. These boys and the brother who would come later were the focus of my life. I recall one of the few occasions when Reg was able to get a break and go out alone, sitting with David and Brian in our rented basement apartment on Taylor Circle in Omaha and feeling such joy at my good fortune; I wanted for nothing.

Brian's middle name was in honor of Tony, my stepfather, whose middle name was Thomas. While Tony and I had many differences, I know he made many sacrifices for Artie and me and was much more a part of my life than my biological father was.

> *"It is not joy that makes us grateful;*
> *it is gratitude that makes us joyful."*
> *Brother David Steindl-Rast*

1967.1   BACCALAUREATE

Finally, with 189 credits from eight different institutions I received a Bachelor's Degree from the University of Nebraska. I had three concentrations: Business, Psychology, and Nursing. The Omaha campus program served Military personnel who, like me were transferred from post to post before they were able to accumulate the 30 in-residence credits required by most colleges. Their program required only 21 in residence credits, which I completed in two sessions in one summer and one fall semester. I was admitted to the Honors Program in Psychology, and at the end of the semester, the professor asked me if he could publish my term paper on the use of feedback systems to personalize education curriculums. Carelessly, I failed to ask him for a copy of the published version.

While the course work was not difficult, finding the time to complete the requirements was difficult because I was working full time in the business office at a local hospital. My original plan was to find a job as an anesthetist so I would only have had to work part time, but there were no such positions available. Reg was busy as well, David had been born the previous December and Brian was born the following November, a month before the end of the semester.

After the January graduation, I continued to work at the hospital until May when we decided which graduate school I would attend the following fall. We left Omaha towing a U-Haul trailer with our Pontiac Tempest packed with babies and high expectations for the future.

1967.2 PH.T.

Reg also received a diploma from the University of Omaha, now the University of Nebraska Omaha. The honorary degree was in recognition of her Feeding, Caring, and Coddling of a UNO student and for having retained her physical fortitude in the patient and diligent discharge of her duty. The P.H.T. or Putting Hubby Through degree was awarded on January 28, 1967. If ever anyone earned the degree it was Reg as she not only cared for me but also nurtured one-year-old David and gave birth to our second son Brian. What a year she had, she was also the MVP (Most Valuable Parent.)

1967.3 FLAT TIRE SCAM

On our way to our next home and adventure in Ithaca, NY, we stopped for gas somewhere on I-80 in Indiana. Because we were towing a trailer, I had large mirrors attached to the front fenders of the car and I could clearly see the gas station attendant go behind the car and briefly disappear. When he reappeared, he told me that there was something wrong with my right rear tire. I was the perfect sucker, because I was so grateful that they found the defect and had a replacement tire in stock. With my entire family in the car, the idea of having a blowout at 65 miles an hour was terrifying. We drove on feeling very secure with our newly replaced tire. It was many months later that I remembered how the attendant briefly disappeared from view and how perfectly smooth the cut in the tire was and how the small gas station luckily had just the right size tire for our car. This is now a well know swindle and I no longer sit in the car on those rare occasions when an attendant approaches to fill the tank.

1967.4 OVID, NY

We arrived in Ithaca, NY in May of 1967. What work that was available in town was already being performed by the thousands of Cornell and Ithaca College students who live in Ithaca. The local hospital had no opening for an anesthetist. I was however able to find a full-time summer job as a nurse at Willard State Hospital, about 30 miles away. There was practically nothing for a nurse to do where I worked on the back wards with chronically ill ambulatory mental patients. I spent my days waiting for a need to arise. I soon realized that the nurse's aides who staffed most of the hospital had little or no training cardiopulmonary resuscitation or in the safe use and handling of oxygen. I proposed to the hospital director that I set up a schedule of classes for the many hundreds of workers at the hospital. For the remainder of the summer I taught two classes a day. In that way, I would train every nurse's aide at the hospital. During one of the last classes, a student reported that one of aides had used her new skills to help save the life of a patient who had aspirated food in the dining hall. Just before classes began the anesthetist, who worked at the State Hospital and at a local general hospital, asked me if I would take his on-call duties while he went on vacation. I was glad for the chance to work at the career that I thought would support me while in college. I was called only once to a hospital about 45 miles away in Seneca Falls, a young boy with appendicitis. This was my last case and the only case I ever had as a civilian.

When school started, I found a part time job in town working for a collection agency. It was a terrible job trying to squeeze nickels and dimes from people who obliviously couldn't afford to pay their long overdue bills. As the course work increased I had to give up the job to keep up the workload.

1967.5   CORNELL

It had been almost a year since I had left the Army and my career as an anesthetist. Reg and I had just arrived in Ithaca after finishing the final year of my Bachelor's Degree from the University of Nebraska. I went to Malott Hall on the Cornell Campus. The Sloan Institute of Health Care Administration, where I would be studying for my Master's Degree, was very impressive and intimidating with its teak paneling, thick carpeting, and expensive furniture. It was late on a Friday afternoon and the building was empty. On the table outside the glass-enclosed entrance to the Institute was a term paper that was thicker than the rug. The title page listed the course, professor, title, and students' name. The grade was scribbled in red, 'B.' I read a few random passages and my heart sank; I was in over my head. The paper was filled with dozens of references, detailed analysis, comparisons of alternatives, and economic and social implications. I felt that I should have selected an easier school. I was accepted at all the graduate schools to which I had applied and selected Cornell because I thought it would help overcome my patchwork bachelor's degree which was pieced together from eight different colleges of varying reputations and because of Reg's encouragement. She always wanted the best for me. At that moment, I was certain that I would never be able to master this work. But with Dr. Roger Battistella's guidance, the material gradually fell into place.

Most of the other students in Sloan program and the Business School in general were much younger than I was. Many were from wealthy families and recent graduates of other Ivy League schools to which I could never have gained admission. But the Cornell program leveled the playing field and here performance was the only measure of success. I was working in a local loan office when school started but I had to resign to devote more time to studying the difficult quantitatively orientated program. A Kellogg Loan, a full fellowship and a Research Assistantship in Operations Research during the second year helped pay the bills.

Two and a half years later I looked around Malott Hall for the last time and it no longer looked very intimidating, and yet it hadn't changed at all, perhaps I had. When I stepped out of Malott Hall that day, I stepped into my new self.

I returned to Cornell for many years after graduation giving lectures and colloquiums for new students.

> *You must do the things you think you cannot do.*
> *Eleanor Roosevelt*

1967.6   KATZENJAMMER KIDS

The Katzenjammer Kids is an American comic strip about two creative brothers Hans and Fritz, who are constantly getting into trouble. It was the first cartoon to express dialogue in comics using speech balloons.

The ages of two and three were especially creative for David and Brian. David would routinely climb from his crib across the dresser top to play with Brian in Brian's crib. On one occasion, they found a bottle of India ink in my office. Their hands were black from the spilled ink and their carpet was red from the quart of fabric softener they poured to clean the ink off their hands; all this while Reg and I were still asleep in the next room. On another early morning adventure, the artists found a box of colored marking pens and turned one of the kitchen walls into a giant abstract mural. I punished them for this misadventure by making them join me in repainting the wall. It was great fun.

> *Creativity is allowing yourself to make mistakes.*
> *Art is knowing which ones to keep.*
> *Scott Adams*

On one fall afternoon walk on the path in the woods behind our apartment, Reg met a friend coming from the opposite direction. Reg thought that she seemed uneasy about something but she said nothing. As she walked away, Reg looked down to find a dozen Woolly Bears crawling up her jacket; the boys were starting a caterpillar collection in her jacket pocket and the spiny larva were running for dear life as fast as their 14 legs would carry them. Most escaped to go about their business. Soon it would be the end for the caterpillars, but what a caterpillar sees as the end, the rest of the world sees as a butterfly.

> *The Banded Woolly Bear larva emerges from the egg in the fall and overwinters in caterpillar form, where it survives being frozen by producing cryoprotectant tissue. In the spring, it thaws and emerges to pupate. Once it emerges from its pupa as a Tiger Moth it has only days to find a mate.*

Even when they were alone, they could often find some mischief to occupy their time: like the time David removed the pin from the neighbor's screen door as she and Reg stood by the door talking when it went half off its hinge as Dave walked away smiling while slipping the hinge pin into his pocket.

The missing gold fish story followed Brian for years until I finally broke down told the family the truth that he didn't actually eat the fish, he merely played with it for a while until the poor hypoxic fish became bored and died.

> *"Boredom is a pleasing antidote for fear"*
> *Daphne du Maurier*

Brian could often be seen wearing his red boots and carrying his Mighty Mack truck while trying to keep up with his fleet footed older brother. Our neighbor had a daughter about Brian's age, and while she suffered from serious chronic disease, she was quite able to play outside with the boys. When she and Brian drove out of sight on their trikes to see what lay over the knoll in our apartment complex, the entire complex was in a panic searching for the two youngsters who had disappeared without a trace. Upon their return the little girl was spanked and warned never to leave again. Brian was hugged and told to tell us when he was leaving and to always return.

The little girl's father was studying for a Ph.D. in Math Education. Not only did he understand the level of math that I was about to face, but he loved finding ways to ensure that students with various levels of aptitude would learn the material. Soon after we arrived in Ithaca he set up a black board in my study and helped me begin the process of catching up on college level math courses which were never included in any of my previous majors. When our respective classes began in the fall our time together ended, but I always appreciated his help and my good fortune of having him as a neighbor.

> *How often we fail to realize our good fortune in living in a country where happiness is more than a lack of tragedy.*
> *Paul Sweeney*

1968.1   STUDENTS FOR A DEMOCRATIC SOCIETY

Before beginning a summer internship between my first and second year at Cornell, I spent a few days in Manhattan working with members of the "Students for a Democratic Society (SDS)." It was the largest and most influential radical student organization of the 1960s. It was inspired by the civil rights movement and initially concerned with equality, economic justice, peace, and participatory democracy. With the escalation of the Vietnam War, SDS grew rapidly as young people protested the destruction wrought by the war. Polite protests later turned into stronger and more determined resistance as rage and frustration increased all across the country.

But our concern that week was not with the war but with the lack of Health Care Services for the poor of New York City. We had obtained a list of schoolchildren who were examined by school physicians and were found to have serious health problems. The schools gave the students notes that described the health problems to bring home to their parents. But no actual services were provided, no referrals were made, and no follow-up was ever made by the school to see if the parents had acted. Our goal was to find as many of these children as possible and help the parents make appointments at city run or funded clinics. My co-worker, a young black woman who knew the Harlem neighbor where we worked, lead the way as we knocked on tenement doors only to find that most parents had never received the notices that were intended to warn them about their children's potentially serious health problems. We had little success in making the needed appointments as we faced unanswered doorbells and families struggling with other issues. I never followed up to see if we did succeed in alerting the schools and the city administration about the absurdity of their short-sighted practice. I like to think that somewhere there is at least one person whose life was prolonged or improved by our effort, but I will never know. Doing what seems right at the time guarantees neither success nor recognition.

Not being able to do everything is no excuse for not doing everything
you can.
A. Brilliant

1968.2   SUMMER INTERNSHIP

The Master's program at Cornell included a two-month long summer internship. Because I had received a fellowship from the New York State Department of Mental Hygiene, my internship was done at one of their facilities. Suffolk State School (later called the Long Island Developmental Center,) which closed in 1993 was located near Melville Long Island. Reg and I found an apartment in a one family home in nearby East Meadow close to Eisenhower Park where we took the boys on weekend get-a-ways. The Institution had been built to replace some of the older institutions, which were notorious for their poor care. Although the facility was only partially occupied, it was already apparent that it would offer little improvement over the programs it was designed to replace. I wrote a paper that utilized some of the Operations Research techniques that I had learned at Cornell to help organize the expansion of the facility. The administration ignored my plan. Later I would come to believe that it is not possible to provide a quality life style in an institution designed to segregate its residents from the very resources, people, and opportunities that enrich the lives of other people. I met Rich Dorgan while working at the state school in Melville. Rich and I were appalled at the conditions at the institution and how little was being done to improve them. My second paper, which Rich and I wrote together and was published in the British Journal of Social Psychiatry, described a process in which one well-organized unit of the institution would be established and the staff of the other units would rotate through it and receive training. It was hoped that since all of the staff throughout the entire institution would share the same experience, the culture of the institution might improve and enable other changes to occur. This was the first of many collaborative articles I would write with Rich. The school never implemented the reforms.

One evening David fell and cut his lip, the cut crossed the vermillion (the red moist portion) of the lip. It was important that it be sutured perfectly so when it healed, the lip would not be deformed. We took him to a plastic surgeon; I sat at the head of the operating table, held David's head, and softly reassured him. The surgeon realigned the severed lip as David lay quietly in my hands. He was so brave, and we were so proud and relieved that he would be left with only a minor scar rather than a misshapen lip. This was the first of many visits to surgeons and pediatricians we would take to have our three sons repaired or restored.

While on Long Island, we visited Reg's family often. My family had all long since moved to Ocala, FL.

I took a Speed Reading course in the evenings because the reading lists for the second year at Cornell were going be burdensome. While I may have improved my reading speed somewhat, the results fell far short of the promises in the ads. My efforts also fell far short of what was needed to succeed fully.

I took a speed reading course and read 'War and Peace' in twenty minutes.
It involves Russia.
Woody Allen

1968.3   SMOKERS

The 1964 Surgeon General's report about the health effects of smoking was being to get the attention of the general public. Public service ads with dire warnings were beginning to appear on television. One particular ad showed a father and his young son sitting on the bank of a stream fishing. Each move the father made to attach the reel, bait the hook, cast the line etc. was repeated by the son with a voice over saying, "Like father like son." Then the father reached into his breast pocket and withdrew a pack of cigarettes as the lad watched and imitated his father's action. Again, "Like father like son" sent the impelling message. I had to quit smoking. It took many attempts and about five years but eventually I was able stop smoking. It's no accident that it is so difficult to stop. The addictive drug nicotine prompts the release of dopamine, a chemical produced by the adrenal glands which effects the brain by increasing the sense of pleasure and arousal. Manufacturers deliberately add other drugs such as pyrazines to increase nicotine's potency making it more difficult for smokers to quit. It's all quite legal. Apparently, the phrases "Land of the Free" has been expanded by corporate lobbyists to include the notion that companies are free to kill citizens so long as they tell you how they're going to do it and "Home of the Brave" now redefines bravery as being able to look death in the straight eye through the blue haze of a drug induced euphoria and bravely take the drug that's killing you.

1969.1   MASTERS

> *Cornell is a private Ivy League university located in Ithaca, NY. Founded in 1865, it's organized into seven undergraduate colleges and seven graduate divisions. The student body consists of nearly 14,000 undergraduate and 7,000 graduate students from 50 states and 122 countries. It counts more than 245,000 living alumni, and as of this writing, it includes me. I am very proud to be a Cornell alumni, I never dreamed that I would ever attend an Ivy League School. I never would have if Reg hadn't encouraged me to select Cornell over the other three graduate schools that had accepted me. She always provided good council.*

The Graduate School of Business and Public Administration offered a Master's either in Business Administration (MBA) or in Public Administration (MPA). The only difference in the curriculum was one finance course. I elected the MPA because I was going to work in the Public Sector. I later regretted that decision when I learned that some MPA programs were not up to the standards of many MBA schools. The Sloan Program in Health Administration, was a subset of the graduate school, and provided a Graduate Certificate in Health Care Administration in addition to the degree. The combined 2½-year program has since been transferred from the Business School to the School of Human Ecology.

I found the course work so demanding that I was not able to work full time and part time jobs were in scarce supply. Fortunately, I was able to obtain a Research Assistantship in Operations Research. This involved searching the literature for articles that demonstrated the use of Operations Research techniques in the health field. (Operations Research is a discipline that deals with the application of advanced analytical and mathematical methods to help make better decisions.) I reviewed and summarized hundreds of articles on 5" by 8" cards because personal computers were not yet available. I learned more about the use of mathematics for analysis and modeling during the literature reviews than I did in any of the management classes. Knowledge that I would be able to use years later. In the second year, I also received a Kellogg Foundation Loan, and a New York State Dept. of Mental Hygiene Fellowship. The fellowship required me to work for the Dept. of Mental Hygiene for two years. It was the beginning of a 22-year career.

Dr. Roger Battistella was my muse and the source of my inspiration long after I left Cornell. During my career in Mental Health Administration, I could often hear his voice, "Ron, think about this." I know I was an unremarkable student but Cornell and Roger Battistella changed my worldview. My experience at Cornell opened a door for me and I found my life waiting on the other side. This too, was a new and exciting time.

1969.2 UNIVERSITIES UNDER THE GUN

My second year at Cornell ended a month earlier than planned when classes were cancelled after 11 fire alarms rang out across the Cornell campus early in the morning of Parents' Weekend, April 18, 1969. At 3 a.m., a burning cross was discovered outside Wari House, a cooperative for black women students. Afro-American Society (AAS) occupied Willard Straight Hall to protest Cornell's perceived racism, its judicial system, and its slow progress in establishing a black studies program.

In an attempt to reclaim the building back, Delta Upsilon fraternity brothers entered Willard Straight Hall and fought with AAS students before being ejected. Fearing further attacks, the black students brought guns into the Straight to defend themselves.

On the evening of April 19, in freezing rain, a rookie Cornell police officer, George Taber, patrolled the perimeter of the occupied Willard Straight Hall unarmed. Members of Students for a Democratic Society, students far to the left of many of the black students inside, formed a ring around the Straight to lend support.

On Sunday afternoon, following negotiations with Cornell officials, the AAS students emerged from the Straight carrying rifles and wearing bandoleers. Their image, captured in a Pulitzer Prize-winning photo, appeared in newspapers across the country and on the cover of Newsweek magazine under the headline, "Universities under the Gun."

Five days later a counter protest occurred when 16 professors decided not to teach unless order at Cornell was restored.

Although physical disaster was averted, deep psychological scars burned into the minds of many on campus. The university as a bastion of reasoned argument, thoughtful debate, and academic freedom seemed to be under siege. An atmosphere of pervasive fear and anxiety gripped the campus and the nation. Within Cornell, the takeover was seen as an event that gave birth to enormous social, governance, and ideological change. The events lead to weeks of consciousness-raising and decades of social, cultural, and political change at Cornell and across much of America.

1969.3   MR. RALPH'S HOUSE

I had accepted a position as a Budget Analyst with the Office of Mental Hygiene in Albany, NY and we planned to move as soon as school ended. A few weeks before we moved, Reg and I drove to Long Island, left David, and Brian with Reg's parents, and drove to Albany to find an apartment. I had studied a map of the Albany area and thought that Delmar would be a good place to settle because of proximity to Albany and its small-town milieu. We found several apartments listed in the local paper; all were disappointing. We also found a house for rent on the main street, Delaware Ave. We called for an appointment and met with Mr. and Mrs. Vitello. The aging couple was downsizing and had built a new home behind the brick house that "Mr. Ralph" had built with his own hands many years before. After a brief tour and chat, Mrs. Vitello told Reg "I think I `lika' you." We agreed that we liked her, her husband and the home they were renting as well. We decided to rent the house. They told us that they were going to paint all the interior walls and that we could select the colors. They also told us that since we were coming from college and had very little money we would not have to leave a security deposit or even the first month's rent.

Although we knew it was not permanent, it felt like we were home for the first time in nine years.

The Vitellos' had operated a florist business in Delmar for many years. The sunken yard next to the house had been used as a nursery and had only recently been seeded with grass. A few days after we moved in there was a heavy rain. The next day the boys were playing on the new lawn and it gradually turned into a sea of mud. When we finally realized what had happened they were both covered from head to toe and a crowd of neighborhood children had gathered to watch the new kids on the block turn into rolling mud pies.

Since the house abutted the busy main street, we used the sidewalk at the front of the house as a boundary to keep the boys far away from the traffic. Three and a half year-old David nodded okay. Two and a half year-old Brian wanted to know if he was allowed to have one foot on the sidewalk and one foot beyond the boundary toward the road. I told him that that would be okay as long as one foot was on the sidewalk. Then he asked if it would be okay if both feet were on the grass beyond the boundary so long as one foot was touched the edge of the sidewalk. I agreed that this too would be acceptable so long as he maintained contact with the sidewalk. He was not challenging our boundary that would come much later; he just wanted to know exactly where the boundary was.

One day when I arrived home after work, I noticed that there was a dead squirrel on the back-entry stoop and that the back door was locked. I couldn't imagine the sequence of events that would lead to that outcome. Later I learned that Brian had found the squirrel in the yard and proudly carried it inside to show Reg. She of course was still traumatized from the Central Park "squirrel encroachment episode" and screamed in horror. David nodded and took the squirrel from Brian and threw it outside. Reg insisted that he lock the door in case it was still alive. It all made perfect sense once she explained it to me.

"Mr. Ralph" was an excellent gardener and occasionally provided us with wheelbarrows filled with fresh vegetables during our two-year stay at his rented home. Mrs. Vitello was an excellent baker and would occasionally include a homemade apple pie in the wheelbarrow of edibles. My mother was an exceptional cook and baker so I rarely found anything that could compare to her work. However, Mrs. Vitellos' apple pie was better than my mothers' were.

On Memorial Day in our second year in Delmar, Brian and David set up a refreshment stand to sell lemonade as the Decoration Day parade passed our house. I still cherish the image of the two of them sitting at the card table in front of their Fisher Price cash register. It's priceless.

One day a frog jumped into the basement from an open window. There was a large drainage hole in the corner of basement, which was always filled to the brim with water. Whenever I entered the basement, the frog would dive headlong into the drain, so it was impossible to catch him. I noticed that the hole was just slightly larger in diameter than a coffee can. The frog was mine.

I attached a pulley directly over the hole and attached a coffee can to a string that lead from the pulley to the top of the staircase. I filled the can with water, hoisted it about two feet above the hole, and secured the string. On my next trip to the basement, I released the string and the can fell into the drain hole. Hearing the commotion, the frog followed and took refuse in the drain. I slowly raised the string and put the lid on the can. The frog was released to the back yard and a screen was placed over the open basement window.

Reg and I made a playroom for Dave and Brian in the basement. We painted the walls, laid down and old carpet, build easels for each of them, and created smocks from my old shirts. I built an HO gauge train layout on a 4 by 8 feet piece of plywood. They helped create papier-mache mountains and scenery. I'm sure I enjoyed the whole process at least as much as they did.

1969.4   DEPARTMENT OF MENTAL HEALTH

In May of 1969, I began my career in Mental Health Care Administration. My first job was as a budget analyst in the Management Division. My first assignment was to find a more accurate method of predicting year-end expenditures. The predictions made by the methods they were using varied so widely from month to month that the Budget Director couldn't be sure if they were going to be on budget until well into fourth quarter of the year. The quantitative analysis courses at Cornell emphasized the use of computer simulation models for predictive purposes. There were no personal computers and the Departments' computer, which took up an entire room, was very limited and was not available for ad hoc use. I found an old teletype machine in the engineering office that was connected via modem to a time-share computer in the next town. It recorded data by punching holes in a paper tape. I wrote the computer program in the "BASIC" language and sent it at 10 characters per second to the remote computer. I sat for hours with a computer handbook in one hand and a mathematical simulation manual in the other. Gradually the program became more complex as the causes of the problems with earlier predictions became apparent. Eventually it became clear that if monthly expenditure reports and accounting categories were standardized and submitted in accordance with a regular schedule the simulation model, which only I could run, would no longer be needed, as the simpler methods would become accurate enough with more reliable data. Therefore, while the computer simulation didn't last very long, the process of constructing it helped discover the solution to the budgeting problem and provided me with skills that would be useful in the future. In a few months, I was promoted within the Budget office but I really wanted to move to the Program Division, which was responsible for the operation and funding of services and supports for our patients.

1969.5 & 1942   THE CITRUS TOWER

After visiting with Mom and Tony for several days, Reg, David, Brian, and I were off for our first visit to Disney World. The day before we left, we purchased cowboy hats to provide sun protection that the boys would voluntarily wear. We drove south for about 100 miles and saw the Florida Citrus Tower. It is one of the tallest points in Central Florida, allowing us to see miles of citrus groves on a clear day. The tower is 226 feet high and the boys were anxious to run to the top after the two-hour trip in the car. I jogged behind. About halfway up, the spiraling staircase I saw what might have been a black cowboy hat or a white cowboy flowing past a window.

> (1942) A window near my room revealed one of the boys at the orphanage leaping from the top of the roof of the 30-foot high boy's dormitory. We

called him Buck Jones after a popular daredevil Western Movie star. He had constructed a makeshift parachute from an old sheet and was truly expecting to soar across the yard just as he had seen the soldiers do it in the Movie Tone Newsreels at the Saturday Matinee. He crashed with a loud thud and lay lifeless of the ground. As the staff rushed to help him, he slowly moved his head in disbelief, apparently surprised that the flight that he had envisioned so perfectly but planned so poorly did not go off as expected. He went back to St. John's Hospital in Brooklyn where I had first met him a few months earlier. He was well known there. He seemed to be totally lacking in fear.

(1969) I panicked as my terror drove me scurrying up the remaining stairs dreading what I might not find waiting for me at the observation level. I didn't know exactly what or who had fallen from the ledge. The boys never knew why I was so glad to see them or why I stayed so close to them on the way down. Next, stop . . . Disney World, where dreams come true and nightmares (no matter how recent) are not allowed.

CHAPTER 5   *THE SEVENTIES*

In the Western world, socially progressive values that began in the 1960s, such as increasing political awareness and political and economic liberty of women, continued to grow. The hippie culture, which started in the latter half of the 1960s, waned by the early 1970s and faded towards the middle part of the decade. It involved opposition to the Vietnam War, opposition to nuclear weapons, the advocacy of world peace, and hostility to the authority of government and big business. The environmentalist movement began to increase dramatically in this period.

Many industrialized countries experienced an economic recession due to an oil crisis caused by oil embargoes by the Organization of Arab Petroleum Exporting Countries. The crisis saw the first instance of a high inflation rate and slow economic growth, and began a political and economic trend that emphasized free trade, open markets, privatization of industries, deregulation, and enhancing the role of the private sector.

The partial merging of the lower social class, with the lower middle class, resulted from the economic boom of Post-War America afforded the average American a level of self-determination, individuation, and economic prosperity.

In Asia, affairs regarding the People's Republic of China (PRC) changed significantly following the recognition of the PRC by the United Nations, the death of Mao Zedong and the beginning of market liberalization. The United States withdrew its military forces from their previous involvement in the Vietnam War, which had grown enormously unpopular. In 1979, the Soviet Union invaded Afghanistan, at the request of the Afghan government to expel the multi-national insurgent group called the Mujahedeen. The insurgents received military training from the CIA in neighboring Pakistan and elsewhere, as well as weapons and billions of dollars from the United States, United Kingdom, Saudi Arabia, and other countries. The decade-long war resulted in millions of Afghans fleeing their country, mostly to Pakistan and Iran. Hundreds of thousands of Afghan civilians were killed in addition to the rebels in the war. (The weapons we supplied would later be used against us when we invaded Afghanistan in 2001.)

The 1970s saw an initial increase in violence in the Middle East as Egypt and Syria declared war on Israel, but in the late 1970s, the situation in the Middle East was fundamentally altered when Egypt signed the Egyptian–Israeli Peace Treaty. Anwar El Sadat, President of Egypt, was instrumental in the event and became extremely unpopular in the Arab World and the wider Muslim world. He was assassinated in 1981. Political tensions in Iran exploded with the Iranian Revolution that overthrew the Pahlavi dynasty and established the Islamic Republic of Iran.

The economies of much of the developing world continued to make steady progress in the early 1970s, because of the Green Revolution. They might have thrived and become stable in the way that Europe recovered after World War II through the Marshall Plan; however, their economic growth was slowed by the oil crisis but boomed immediately after.

Technological advances of the decade included microprocessors, videogames, the Liquid Crystal Display, word processors, Email, digital cameras, pocket calculators, floppy disks, food processors, and the Hachy sack.

Best-selling books of the decade were Love Story, Wheels, Jonathan Livingston Seagull, Centennial, Ragtime, Trinity, The Silmarillion, Chesapeake, and The Maturase Circle,

The average new house cost $23,450 the average salary per year was $9,400 a gallon of gas was $0.36, bread was 25 cents a loaf, and the average cost of new car was $3,450

US Population was 203,392,031 and the life expectancy for men was 67.1, and 74.7 years for women.

1970.1   LEARNING TO RIDE

The following spring, Reg and I lay in bed, the morning was warm, and the window overlooking the driveway of our newly rented home in Delmar, NY was open. It was such a relief to be working again with two years of graduate school at Cornel University behind us. David had received a new bicycle for Christmas and now that the snow had melted, he had been riding in the driveway. Brian, now only three, was beside himself that David had a two-wheeler and he was still riding a tricycle. One morning the sounds of spring from the window were interrupted by a series of grunts, a few huffs, and puffs followed by a crash and a long moan. It was Brian, up before breakfast, on David's bike  teaching himself to ride a two-wheeler by holding on to the railing of the back stoop. He repeated this until we couldn't stand it anymore. We brought him in, cleaned up his bloody knees, and bruised arms. By the time, I left for work that morning Brian had gotten the promise that when he learned to ride David's bike he would have one of his own. That afternoon when I returned from work and drove into the driveway, he was waiting. He ask me to watch him ride down the long driveway. He did great until he turned around to see if I was still looking. He veered off the driveway into a large maple tree. One last groan and a new world opened for Brain. Soon David and

Brian were riding their two wheelers side by side. Together, real brothers in a real family, this is how I often remember them.

1970.2   FIRST PROMOTION

After working for about a year and a half as a budget analyst, I was asked to take a Civil Service Exam to become a Program Analyst. Budgeting held little interest for me. Ninety-five percent of the budget was predetermined by existing commitments and the remaining five percent was divided among all manner of options, many of which reflected political boondoggles. While it was clear that any meaningful change would be implemented through changes in the budget, it was also clear that the Budget Office was not the place where those decisions were made. Since I had spent most of my time in the budget office working on special projects for various Department managers, I had learned little about the practical details of constructing a multimillion-dollar budget. This would prove to be a serious problem for me in the future when I would be responsible for producing a six hundred-million-dollar multi-agency statewide budget in Georgia.

At that time the Department of Mental Hygiene Program Analysts were traveling change agents. We worked with State hospital directors, community leaders, and local service providers to begin the process of shifting services, patients, and resources from large remote state institutions to small local community services and supports. I spent Tuesday, Wednesday, and Thursday traveling between Long Island, Brooklyn, and Staten Island. It was hard for the entire family for me to be away so much, but I felt that I was playing a key role in a process that was long overdue and sorely needed. State mental hospitals had become holding areas for incapacitated, disenfranchised, or unwanted people. Many patients, having once been admitted had little chance of being discharged. With very diverse populations and few effective treatments, hospitals across the country had grown much too large to be well managed and adequately staffed. Much of their focus had shifted from treatment to merely providing segregated protective supervision. Sadly, at this writing 45 years later, while many of the patients have been moved from the institutions to the communities, many of the needed resources have been diverted to other uses. As a result, the prisons and streets are heavily populated with people who cannot retreat to the safety of the hospitals and cannot find the services and supports they need in the community.

Life is a dream for the wise, a game for the fool, a comedy for the rich, and a tragedy for the poor.

Sholom Aleichem

1970.3 NIEDERSTEIN

In the late 1930s, Karl Niederstein, opened a German restaurant on the Sunrise Highway in Lynbrook, L.I. In the 1970's it was a great favorite among the German American population and many others in the area. Our local extended family ate several meals there on special occasions. Also, because it had a small playground with several amusement rides, it was a great favorite with the young children in the area and their grandparents. Pop Pop Straub enjoyed taking David and Brian to the park whenever we visited them in the warmer weather in Valley Stream. It was hard to tell who enjoyed the outings more. The park was closed before Gregory was old enough to join his brothers on their grandfather outings.

A grandfather is someone you can look up to
no matter how tall you grow.
Author Unknown

1971.1 GREGORY VINCENT

Reg and I had always wanted to have three children and in 1970 with our biological clocks ticking, graduate school behind us, David and Brian soon to be starting school, and a solid career begun, we decided that this was the time.

Reg's mother (Nana) who had been staying with us for the past few weeks in anticipation of Greg's arrival, watched David and Brian as I drove Reg to St. Peters hospital to deliver our third child. It was on that snowy ride that we decided that if we had another boy his name would be Gregory. Sonograms were not yet in use so we didn't know if we were having a boy or a girl. In our early years  of marriage, all of our friends with children had girls, so it was an adjustment when our first child was a boy. However, after raising two boys for five years, I was relieved when Gregory arrived and I looked forward to continuing the now familiar family life that we had created. Gregory was as lovable as he was adventurous. He would cuddle in my arms or slide down a flight of carpeted stairs from the bedrooms to the living room with equal ease. Gregory shared his middle name of Vincent with Reg's father William Vincent Straub. Now all three grandfathers were honored by being the eponym of one of my sons.

David *Arthur* Gerhard .... *Arthur* Gerhard .... my Father
Brian *Thomas* Gerhard .... Anthony *Thomas* DeSant .... my Stepfather
Gregory *Vincent* Gerhard .... William *Vincent* Straub .... Reg's father

With Reg and my three sons, my cup overflowed. I knew that the conditions of my own childhood were in the past and would not be repeated . . . my boys were secure. And, I was secure as well, for each of my three sons had so insinuated themselves into my life that they had changed who I was, how I felt, and how I lived, they had given more to me than I would ever be able to give to them

> *"The soul is healed by being with children."*
> Fyodor Dostoevsky.

1971.2   OUR FIRST HOUSE

With Gregory's arrival came the need for more space so in August, six months after his birth, we purchased our first house at 11 Herber Ave, in Delmar, NY and a new sense of stability and permanence settled over our family. It was within walking distance of David and Brian's Elementary school on Delaware Ave, and the local A & P supermarket and it was but a short drive to my work. Our new street was named after the artisan who built our four-bedroom home with its Chestnut molding and a staircase to the walk-up attic. The lot backed to a raised but rarely used train track, which The Mohawk Hudson Land Conservancy has now converted, into a nine-mile long nature trail leading from Albany to Voorheesville.

We used the workshop in the basement to create the first of what was to become a family tradition, homemade Christmas tree ornaments. The excelsior birds' nest was filled with eggs made of small red glass globes, a stuffed cloth cardinal and a wooden clothespin latch completed the decorations, which were shared with family and close friends. Through the years, the excelsior wasted away into a few barren strands and small glass shards served as reminders of the once glittering eggs; and yet it decorated our holidays for many years past its prime. It wasn't merely an ornament; it was a symbol of our family playing, creating, and loving together. Eventually only the wooden clothespin remained with a dab of glue reminding us of its former beauty. And now, even the symbol is gone, but the family remains with a variety of new decorations, new homes, new cities, and new members

.

> *Our family is a circle of love and strength, with every union and*
> *every birth the circle grows. Every joy shared adds more love.*
> *Every crisis faced together makes the circle stronger.*
> *Author Unknown*

1972.1   THE LILY PAD VISION

As I gained experience working with others to improve conditions at state hospitals and encourage the development of community-based alternatives to the large institutions, I became convinced that the institutions could never be improved sufficiently to overcome their inherent shortcomings. Adding to the problem was the fact that there was no clear plan as to what an alternative service system might look like and little interest among funders to create such a plan. However, there was money available for conducting extensive site plans of existing facilities. These plans were routinely used to help design renovation schemes that would modernize old facilities.

I was able to work with the architects who were hired to conduct a hospital site review and have them expand their role beyond remodeling the facility to remodeling the service system that provided the context in which services were provided. The report was quite controversial, but it began the process of developing the principles and planning tools that would occupy much of my professional life. The plan was initially called the lily pad model, because primitive blackboard sketches of a community rich in services resembled a pond with lily pads scattered throughout the various neighborhoods. The lily pad model was later named The Balance Service System and it was widely distributed as a series of monographs before it was finally published in book form in 1981.

I could not have known that the Republican champion, Ronald Regan, would soon undo all of the federal legislation that was needed to create community mental health centers and the work of Rosalyn Carter and the *Commission* on *Mental Health.* These laws would have provided the financial incentives necessary for the states to meet the needs of persons in distress.

We have to get the word out that mental illnesses can be diagnosed and treated, and almost everyone suffering from mental illness can live meaningful lives in their communities.
Rosalynn Carter

1972.2 & 1942   MAINE

During the summer of 1972, we vacationed at Balch Pond at Sanford, a small town in southern Maine. The water was freezing and I was content to sit by the shore and read. Gregory played in the sand near Reg, and Brian and Dave swam out about 50 feet. The water was shallow but I put my book aside to watch. Soon Brian climbed onto the dock and jumped back into the lake. Then Dave climbed up onto the dock. He waited.

> (1942) Jeff was one of the oldest boys at the orphanage and he took several of us younger boys about a mile down Foster Ave to Sayville's public beach on the Great South Bay. The beach has since been replaced by a marina. The swimming area was completely enclosed by a U-shaped dock. Wire netting below the dock prevented the ever-present jellyfish and horseshoe crabs from entering the swimming area. We all walked out to the deepest end of the dock. The markings said 12 feet. Jeff jumped in as the rest of us lined up on the dock. As the youngest, I was last in line. Each of the boys ahead of me jumped into the water where Jeff would catch them and return them to the dock. It looked like great fun. When my turn came, I jumped in but instead of seeing Jeff's arm come to lift me out of the water; I saw his feet slowly drifting upward as I sank into the dark green abyss. When I woke up, I was lying on the dock with

a crowd of people standing around. I never knew exactly what happened, needless to say, Jeff never took me to the beach again.

(1972) Then, Dave jumped into the lake. I was so proud and relieved that he had not let his fear define his relationship to the water, as I had done 30 years earlier. All three boys became great swimmers and years later Dave would become a SCUBA diver.

1972.3 ASSISTANT PROF, NY SCHOOL OF PSYCHIATRY

Many of the Doctors who were working at State Psychiatric Hospitals at that time were completing residencies in psychiatry, which typically took four years. For some the residency was extended into a fifth year due to language problems or other issues that prevented them from becoming Board Certified after four years. In days passed some doctors spent many years as "fifth year residents." They helped staff the wards of the psychiatric hospitals, which had difficulty hiring sufficient numbers certified physicians. Much of their training was concerned with the use of psychoactive medications among the chronic and severely disabled patients that populated the hospitals at that time. It was becoming apparent that in the future, many psychiatric services would be provided in community settings, and that psychiatry would become more closely linked to other medical and ancillary services. I was appointed an Assistant Professor and asked to teach a class to some of the fifth-year residents that would attempt to expose them to the latest trends in Mental Health and some of the various roles that psychiatrists might find themselves, as patients moved from remote institutions to local community mental health centers. It took a great leap of faith on their part to accept ideas that ran totally contrary to their daily experience and prior education. A leap that some could not take. I met with the group of about 12 physicians for 3 hours each week for about 6 months. I provided reams of handouts that supported the classroom presentations, but there were no exams or other assignments. It was agreed from the onset that this was to be more of a conscience raising experience than an academic course of study.

1973.1   VOORHEESVILLE

Early in 1973, I accepted a position as the Director of Research and Evaluation at a Community Mental Health Center in Buffalo, NY. We sold our first home on Herber Ave., in Delmar, NY and began packing for the move. However, at the last minute the salary for the multi-sourced funding of the position changed from the state payroll to the county payroll. The years that I had worked at Republic Aviation, the Veterans Administration and the US Army had no provision for retirement and I felt that I needed to accrue more time in the state retirement system, so I decided not to take the position. We quickly found and purchased the house on Stonington Hill Road in Voorheesville, NY where we lived from Feb 1973 to Aug 1977.

I built a grape arbor as my stepfather had done some 30 years before and a plywood Teepee for the boys to play in. A row of cedars was installed to provide privacy and a pair of weeping willow trees was planted to absorb the water in the recessed back yard.

We were very active in the renewal that was going on in the Catholic Church at the time and soon began holding prayer meetings in our living room one evening a week. I prepared a bible reading and played the guitar; the small group sang and shared their insights and part of their lives with each other. While the group has long disbanded, some of us continue to stay in touch and visit whenever possible.

We had traded in our two-tone Plymouth sedan for a red Volkswagen van to accommodate our growing family and their friends. One of the members of the prayer group owned a small auto body shop and knowing how difficult it was for us having only one car in the suburbs he fixed up an old car and gave it to Reg and me. It was quite old but usable and would allow Reg to get around town while I was at work. It was going to be a major change in our life.

The next week a friend who I knew to be very poor, arrived at the prayer meeting asking for prayer because his car had broken down and could not be fixed. He worked many miles from his home and had several children who depended upon his being able to get to work. He left that evening with the keys to the car that was given to us the week before. I entered a car pool with three men who lived nearby and worked in the same office building where I worked. This allowed Reg to have use of the van several days a week.

We met Charlie at an area wide renewal meeting. He had lost his eyesight in a tragic accident while volunteering as a firefighter. He lived about 75 miles from Delmar, was attending a training program at the Northeastern Association of the Blind in Albany, and needed a place to live, so we invited him to stay with us. He moved into our spare room a week later.

We had many interesting times with Charlie; including the time, he returned from a weekend visit with his family and brought back his ancient and visually challenged Seeing Eye dog. He was too old to work and was now Charlie's 200-pound pet; he was huge. Charlie was now riding with us in the car pool, and on a day when the car being used was a small two-door coupe he decided to bring the dog to work, he opened the car door, and the dog jumped into the back seat and sat upright on the lap of the startled passenger. If only Charlie could have seen the expression on the face of the dogs' new traveling companion. We asked Charlie to leave his dog at home except on the days when I was driving the van to work since, unlike the cars in the pool, it had enough room for the dog to have its own seat.

For a few years, like most of the fathers in the neighborhood I became a Little League umpire. On one occasion, the small crowd became particularly nasty with their negative comments and disparaging remarks. I stopped the game and told crowd that: "The analogue to what you're seeing here today isn't to be found in Yankee Stadium but in the sand box in your back yard. These are children at play; all they need is your love and support, not a reason to hate the children they are playing with."

One Halloween the boys built a "haunted house" in our basement. They put up sheets to create a path through a maze of horrors. I thought it was great work but Reg came running up the stairs screaming as the trial run turned a little too realistic for her sensitivities. The neighborhood kids loved it.

When the boys expressed a wish for a dog, Reg and I thought that a small pedigreed dog would be a good idea. We decided to get a Cairn Terrier. At first, I thought his legs were too short but I quickly noticed they reached the ground which is about all you can expect from them. Unfortunately, I may have missed a few key phrases in the description of Cairn Terriers' behavior when I was doing research about which breed to bring home. Such phrases as "barking might annoy the neighbors" or "digging and chewing can be very destructive" or "have a mind of their own and can make training difficult" and most importantly "needs a fenced yard to prevent him from running." I recall running knee deep in snow through miles of back yards passing widows of curious neighbors trying to catch McTavish, who seemed to delight in my misery. McTavish did not deserve the title that I gave him, "the world's worst dog." Actually, I was the worlds' worst master for bringing him into the wrong environment. We sold him at a great loss and replaced him with a gerbil which came with his own fenced in yard.

One Christmas we invited several children from the inner city of Albany to spend the day with us. We had a small party and gave out gifts. I was never sure if we helped them in any way, or in our attempt to help, we merely highlighted all that was missing from their lives. A "fuck you" found scratched on the bathroom door convinced me that at least one of the kids was as uncomfortable with the situation as I was. The following year we didn't make the kids sit through the humiliation of being the target of our naïve attempt to help, we just delivered some presents to a few families that had identified   themselves as wanting help at Christmas. In spite of the issues I dealt with as a child, I never felt hopeless or that I wouldn't someday be successful and happy. Without that dream, I can't imagine what my life would have become. I hope those kids were able to find a dream that they could reach for that didn't depend on charity, but on the strength that they would find within themselves.

I travelled a lot on business and often brought home a state-owned car that I used for the trips. I foolishly left the car unlocked one day and Greg and his close friend Kerry hopped in and pretended to go for a drive. When Greg released the emergency brake, the car began to roll backward down the sloping driveway. Greg jumped out and tripped beneath the car, it ran over his legs. Carrie yelled that the car had rolled away and I came out to find the car across the street and Greg lying on the driveway. I could see the tread marks on his legs and I rushed him to the emergency room. He didn't have any serious injuries but the tire marks on his thighs lasted for weeks.

From time to time I drive pass the old white house (now colored blue with its' new siding) and remember those days when the family was together and all things seemed possible.

1973.2   THE DEAD FISH

After leaving Bill and Norma Straub and their family at the roaring gorge and lush forests of Letchworth State Park, we headed east for a place to park our pop-up camper beside the St. Lawrence River. Wanting to show the boys that fishing can be fun (even though I hated it); I took Dave and Brian to the marina and rented a rowboat with a small outboard motor. We loaded our newly purchased gear and slowly made our way out of the marina toward the river. When we left the protection of the cove, I soon realized that the river was moving so rapidly that I was not sure that it would be safe to turn the boat broad side to current. Fortunately, there was a small island part way out into the river and I thought that the water might be calm on the downstream side of the island. Although the only thing on my mind was getting the boys back safely to shore, I headed out into the deepest part of the river and the island, which I believed, held the solution to my dilemma. I had never driven an outboard motor boat before, so I cautiously turned it one hundred and eighty degrees in the calm waters of leeward side of the island. I told the boys that the water was too rough today to catch any fish and that we were headed back. As we glided into the mooring place at the dock, I noticed a large dead pike floating near the boat. I scooped it up with our net and we took it to the campground shower. The underside of the fish had been eaten away, but the top was still intact. We hung the fish on a string that Dave and Brian held so that only the good side was visible to Reg when we walked back to our campsite. At first Reg looked shocked, because she knew that I had never caught a fish in my life much less a 2-foot long pike. The boys were beside themselves with glee as they fooled their mother into thinking that we had caught the fish. Becoming suspicious about never being shown the back of the fish, Reg soon caught on and we all had a good laugh. Some laughed about the fish prank; I laughed with relief that we were all safe on dry land and that the water on the leeway side of an island really is calm enough to allow a small boat filled with precious cargo to turn safely around.

1973.4   COMPUTERS

Early computers required the use of cards with punched holes to enter data and programing instructions as they had no keyboards or screens. After a few years, computers could be accessed by remote teletype machines with keyboards but still no screens. With few computers available, timesharing services began to fill the gap in the growing industry. I began using a timesharing computer as part of my first job in the budget office of the Dept. of Mental Hygiene in 1969. Later I used the service to gain an understanding of the relationships between the components of complex mental health service networks.

In 1973, I met Dr. Dolph Ebeling, who had just retired from General Electric's research and development facility, the Knolls Atomic Power Laboratory. He had started his own software development company and was interested in the computer simulation projects that I had developed. Some of his customers were in the health field and I began consulting with him and served as an intermediary between his high-tech staff and the health care professionals whom he served. He began his business in the basement of his home, but soon bought the Glen-Sanders Mansion in Scotia, NY. The two-story mansion was built as a trading port in 1658, three years before the founding of Schenectady. It was the first settlement on the north side of the Mohawk River and was a family home until 1961. It was transformed by Dolph and Silvia Ebeling into a business office and training center. It currently houses an Inn. The ancient home was restored and furnished with 17th and 18th century furniture, but equipped with the latest computers and tele-communication, audio-visual, and other electronic equipment. I worked with Dolph until 1980 on many interesting projects with several health care organizations in New York and New England.

In 1977 I bought my first home computer. It was a TRS-80 and had 4K of memory. (Not enough for a single email.) It used the B.A.S.I.C. programing language, and with so little memory, programs had to be limited in scope and very efficient. Today my cell phone has more computing power than those used in the first NASA space modules.

In the 1960's and 70's no one really knew how computers would evolve and be used, but it was assumed that computer users would have to be able to write the programs needed to control a computer. This belief was so deep-seated that some colleges were accepting a computer language to meet the second language requirement for a bachelor's degree. I took several colleges courses in computer operations and languages, so my second language wasn't French or Spanish, it was Fortran; and I never had a job in the computer field. It was just a tool that I found to be very useful. Today few computer users have any programing skills or even the remotest idea of how computers actually work. That knowledge is as unnecessary as a knowledge of mechanical engineering would be to drive a car. Well-designed programs are now controlled by user friendly interfaces consisting of menus, icons, spoken words and even eye movements.

It's hard to discuss the future of computing because by the time a new idea becomes generally understood, it's already outdated and the rate of change is exponential.

Consider virtual reality, augmented reality, wireless technology, biometric security, flexible display, and holographs. In 2015 they were all seen as tomorrows dreams. But today, just 2 years later they are either in production or design. If skyscrapers had developed at the same rate as computers since 1971, the tallest building would reach half way to the Moon. This is truly a new and exciting time.

1974.1 ADJUNCT PROFESSOR, EMPIRE STATE COLLEGE

While working full time at the N.Y.S. Dept. of Mental Hygiene as the Director of the Bureau of Planning Coordination, I accepted a part time position as Adjunct Professor of Public Administration, at the State University of New York's Empire State College. I taught "Principles of Supervision and Personnel Management" to a small number of students. Other, more challenging teaching opportunities ended my work with Empire College but, I enjoyed teaching and I believe that if I had taken a more direct route to a graduate education I might have sort a career in academia.

1975.1 FRANCES CROAKE STRAUB DIES

Nana, as her grandchildren called her, was only 66 years old when she died in 1975. She had been ill for several years but it was only in the last few months of her life that she began to appear frail. But her natural unassuming and good-natured spirit stayed with her until the end. I had seen many people who were at the last stage of their lives, but Nana remains as my role model not only of how to maintain your own sense of dignity, but also how to ease the burden for those who are seeing a loved one leave. She is buried in the Holy Rood Cemetery, Westbury, NY in a plot that she would all too soon share with her husband Bill and her youngest daughter Terry. Today when I think of her, I remember her laugh, and her thoughtfulness, but mostly I remember how much her family loved her. At her funeral 9-year-old, David paused until everyone had left the gravesite and he kneeled and kissed the grave of his beloved Nana.

It is as grandmothers that our mothers come into the fullness of their
grace.
Christopher Morley

1975.2 ASSISTANT PROFESSOR, SUNY STONY BROOK

After giving a lecture at State University of New York at Stony Brook Long Island, NY, I was asked by head of the Health Sciences Department if I would be interested in teaching a graduate level course the following semester. I told him that I would like to teach the class but it would be difficult since I was living in the Albany area at the time. He offered to pay my roundtrip airfare between Albany and MacArthur airport on Long Island each week and send a car to take me back and forth from the College to the airport. I accepted.

I was given an Assistant Professorship of Health Sciences Administration. The course was "Mental Health Systems: Administration and Planning." Six students signed up and I created a reading list and a syllabus. There were no exams and one major paper that the students had the entire semester to develop. It was quite disappointing as some of the papers appeared to be rewrites of work submitted for other classes and the others lacked the vigor I had experienced at Cornell. If I had an opportunity to do it again, I would have raised the students' expectations by giving weekly quizzes on the reading list to be sure that they were taking the material seriously. I decided that the course would require more of my time than the students' time so I decided to stick to giving visiting lectures.

1975.3 & 2015   THE PLANE WITH NO LIGHTS

After graduating from Cornell in 1969, I was frequently asked to return and present a colloquium to the graduate students of the Sloan Program in Health Administration. On one occasion, the return trip to Albany was postponed until well after dark due to bad weather. After the long delay, the pilot announced that even though the weather was getting worse he would fly the small 6-seater plane back to Albany if he could get one passenger to come with him. Everybody refused, that is, all but one, anxious to get home to my family I agreed to fly with him. There was no control tower at the small Ithaca airport so the pilot had to call the Tower at nearby Elmira Airport for clearance to take off. They told him that there was an Allegheny Airline jet in the area, which might try, to land because of the worsening visibility but that they had lost track of him. He taxied away from the terminal and waited a few feet from the only runway. After a few minutes, he said that the Allegheny plane must have gone further since it hadn't appeared yet, and he revved the engine. Just as he began to release the brakes and move onto the runway, the Jet (huge in comparison to the tiny prop plane) roared past and touched down a few yards past the point where we would have entered the runway. Everything was quiet. After a deep breath, we entered the recently vacated runway and headed for home. What an exciting story to tell Reg about my flight home. Little did I know what might lie ahead? There were only the two of us on the plane so the pilot asked me to sit in the copilot seat. It was a great view looking out over the lighted instruments of the dashboard and seeing the lights of the towns and villages that we passed as the plane's beacons flashed our presence for all to see. There was a sudden and severe jolt and the plane was engulfed in total darkness. The instrument panel, the wing lights, the beacons the interior lighting . . . all were gone. The pilot said that the jolt must have loosened a connection and that he was going to try to jerk the plane and see if the lights might come back on. He maneuvered the plane into several sharp turns and bounces. On one practically sharp jounce, the lights snapped back on. Later that night when I finally arrived home, shaken but well, I anxiously told Reg of my harrowing adventure.

(2015) It is now 43 years later and I am writing this story, which I have told countless times to all who would listen. And it is only now that I realize that the pilot was having fun at my expense. He knew that the airliner was landing, and when he heard it on his earphones, he pretended to move forward to stop just in time to make me believe that we just had a near miss. The lights are all controlled with, of all things, a light switch, which he turned off after one on the many bumps on that "dark and stormy night." I couldn't see him turn it back on because it was dark. I suppose that he is still enjoying his side of the story about the man he fooled into thinking that he almost died twice in the same night. My story however, which I really enjoyed telling, is now ruined forever. Sometime seeing the man behind the green curtain can take the fun out of life. I guess you don't have to actually face death in order to be glad to be alive.

1976.1 COMMUNITY MENTAL HEALTH CENTERS

The Joint Commission on Accreditation of Hospitals[+] was founded in 1951, to help improve the nation's health care. It created The Accreditation Council for Psychiatric Facilities in 1970 to accredit psychiatric facilities and substance abuse programs. In 1975, even though it was still in draft form, the Council began using the Balanced Service System as its conceptual model for the creation of an accreditation methodology for the nation's Community Mental Health Service Programs. My friend, Rich Dorgan served as the Division Director of the Council until 1976 when he left to complete his Ph.D. In 1976 Rich and I wrote the principles and standards for the agency's handbook, "Principles for the Accreditation of Community Mental Health Service Programs and began the National Community Mental Center Accreditation Training Program by training trainers who would then train Joint Commission accreditors. We took few vacations during that two-year period as I used most of my free time writing and traveling.

[+]*Now known as the Joint Commission on Accreditation of Healthcare Organizations*

1976.2 DIDASKO

On December 28, 1976, a group of men, including myself, who had been attending the Highland Lake Bible Camp near Port Jarvis, NY created the Didasko Christians Association, Inc. It is a New York Domestic Not-For-Profit Corporation. I suggested the name Didaskō, which is a Greek word that means, "To teach." The previous camp organizer, a Lutheran Evangelist, would no longer be able to continue in that role. The new group recruited speakers, rented space, advertised events, and financed the annual encampments. Our family attended the Bible Camp for about 7 years beginning in 1974. Its informality and charismatic style was exactly what I was looking for at the time as it was both deeply spiritual and yet not tied to any particular set of ritualistic behavior or dogmatic teaching. It was a time when I enjoyed religious activity. I look back on those days now and remember how secure and reassuring it was to have no feeling of doubt or uncertainty. It provided a confidence and self-assurance that now seem so shallow and tedious. Perhaps it is the certainty that causes so many people to adhere to fundamental ideologies, even those that defy ethical, logical, or scientific principles.

We can easily forgive a child who is afraid of the dark;
the real tragedy of life is when men are afraid of the light.
Plato

1977.1   GEORGIA ON MY MIND

When the NYS Commissioner of Mental Hygiene announced that he was leaving, most of the senior staff left for greener pastures. I waited about a year before leaving. At my last meeting with my supervisor, he called me into his office and said nothing, not one word. I waited see how long he would let it go on. After 30 minutes, I left having decided to take a position in Georgia that I had previously been offered. Later his motives became clear when it became known that he had assigned one of his staff to abstract much of the content of my book, which was widely disturbed but still in draft form, to create a watered-down version of the community service system that it described. I guess he didn't mind stealing my work he just didn't want me around to witness the process.

We sold our home in Voorheesville to friends from St Mathews Church. They rented it for a few weeks until their home sold. I flew to Atlanta and found a house on the bus line that pasted the State Capitol office complex where I worked.

Unlike the annual fiery blaze of the Adirondack Mountains in upstate New York, the foliage in Georgia never caught fire; it just smoldered its way through autumn. The scenery wasn't the only disappointment for while we painted the rooms of our new home, and I built a treehouse in the backyard for the boys to play in, and joined the local church, but it never really felt like home.

1977.2   DIRECTOR: BUDGET, PLANNING & EVALUATION

I took a position with The Georgia Department of Human Resources, which oversaw the Departments of Mental Health and Mental Retardation, Education, Social Services, Vocational Rehabilitation, and some other smaller Human Service agencies.

My position was Director, of the Office of Budget, Planning, and Evaluation, my primary responsibility was to create and manage the $600,000,000 annual budget. By the time I arrived the Director of Mental Health, who was part of the major reform planned for Georgia, had already been fired. It became apparent within a month of our arrival that the changes, which Jimmy and Roslyn Carter had begun to make to the

Georgia Human Service System, were now on hold as Carter's popular successor as governor George Busbee, would not maintain the level of tension needed to make major reforms. The by-word of the Department of Human Resources was "evolution not revolution." While no one would stand in the way of change if it should happen to occur, there was resistance to initiating any change that would upset the status quo. I was a fish out of water in this environment, as all of my prior work, teachings, and writings were about the changes that I felt were long overdue to the services and supports provided to disabled and disadvantaged people. I was able to edit the draft version of the book and begin to get it ready it for publication.

I may have been the worst budget director the agency ever had, even if I didn't hate the job I still wouldn't have been very good at it because my interests and abilities lie elsewhere. However, I was able to use my spare time to continue to conduct weeklong workshops and to give lectures at Colleges including the University of Georgia in Athens. I also continued to train surveyors around the country to use the newly created standards for accrediting Community Mental Centers, which were based on my book, "The Balance Service System." On one occasion, my friend, and co-author Rich Dorgan, another trainer, and I arrived late one night to give a presentation the following day. We stopped in the hotel coffee shop, my two colleagues ordered tea, and I ordered a decaffeinated coffee. The server soon delivered three cups of hot water, two tea bags, and an orange tinfoil packet of Sanka instant coffee. The server stood by as my friends dunked their tea bags in the hot water. Seeing an opportunity for a little humor, I began dunking my tinfoil packet in my cup, awaiting the predictable reaction. After a few moments, the server politely suggested that the waterproof packet needed to be torn open and the content poured into the cup. I obeyed, stirred and sipped. Then turning to her in astonishment, I praised her brilliant suggestion and told her that this was the best instant coffee I had ever drunk. I imagine that she enjoyed telling her friends about the world's stupidest customer as much as I enjoyed retelling the prank.

1977.3   FATHER PETER GERHARD

Father Peter gerHard O.P. was a friend and a Dominican Priest.

> *The Dominican Order began in the middle ages. Its priests traveled among the people to preach, and survive by begging and through persuasive preaching.*

Father Peter's real name was John Peter Gerhard but he never used his full name in his ministry. He was born in Rhode Island in 1923 and died in Ohio in 2005.

We met him on our first Sunday in Doraville, GA. After Mass in Holy Cross RC church, we introduced ourselves and the three of us soon became friends. Although we share the same last name, we are not related.

Father Peter and I began capitalizing the "H" in the middle our last name in our private communications: "gerHard" after reading the following passage in the bible:

> *(Genesis, 17 5-15). No longer, will you be called Abram; your name will be Abraham, God also said to Abraham, "As for Sarai your wife, you are no longer to call her Sarai; her name will be Sarah. The "H" added to their names represented the breath of God, meaning that God was with them.*

Reg and I had been active in the Charismatic Renewal in Albany and Voorheesville and we joined Fr. Peter to form a Prayer group at Holy Cross. We met one evening a week. I generally led the group with weekly teachings and music. As the group expanded, we began having weekly planning sessions at our home prior to the meetings. Peter seemed to long for the closeness of a family, which he did not find with his fellow priests at the church. The leadership team of the Prayer Group seemed to help fill that need for him, and we all welcomed his open and unpretentious style and personal warmth.

Fr. Peter had asked me to prepare a sermon to be delivered at Sunday Mass. I wrote a sermon about what it meant to be the salt of the earth i.e. salt enhances and preserves. I never delivered the sermon as changes with my job caused us to move back to New York. I was enrolled in the Atlantic Permanent Deaconate Program and Peter told me that he didn't believe that I would ever become a deacon. I was surprised by his frankness, but he knew me better than I did. I left the Deaconate program in Albany two years later.

Peter visited us in Delmar several times on his trips to New England to see his brother. In 1992, I visited him in New York City. After his retirement, he lived in the rectory of a large church in the Yorktown area of NYC with several other retired priests. He had changed and seemed fearful and suspicious. I asked him if he would ever consider living with Reg and me or with his brother in New England, but he could not abandon the community that he had committed his life to, even as it failed to provide him with the close-knit community that he always longed for.

A few years later, he moved to a Dominican supportive living community in Steubenville, Ohio. We traded holiday cards until 2005, when we received a letter from a priest informing us that Peter had died. He was buried on the grounds of the Dominican enclave in Ohio.

1977.4   INSPIRATIONS

I made several presentations in New Hampshire. One of those trips took me to Keene, NH, which is only about 100 miles from New York State but not easily reached by public transportation, so I decided to drive. Before the presentation, as I had done before every presentation I gave, I listened to a tape of Judy Collins singing, "Bring in the Clowns." I found the song mesmerizing and believed it to be one of the most beautiful songs ever written. It's a theater reference meaning "if the show isn't going well, send in the clowns (or fools) for a laugh; which is followed by, "Don't bother, they're here", meaning we are the fools. It reminded me of one of my core beliefs that I should be prepared to be the clown or to be seen as foolish when taking an unpopular stand on behalf of those who cannot advocate for their own cause. It never failed to move me and keep me humble before the presentation whether it was a one-hour seminar or a five-day workshop.

Later that afternoon, on the drive home I passed through quiet bucolic farmlands with a scattering of small roadside stands with only an occasional crossroad. At one particularly poor looking farmhouse, I noticed a garage sale sign and decided to pull into the driveway. Among the usual array of household items was a small Irish accordion. While I didn't play the accordion, I did like collecting a variety instruments and playing with them even if I never learned to play them well. The price tag read $10.00. A young boy was proudly in charge. I told him that I couldn't pay $10.00 for such an old worn accordion, but that I could pay $20.00. He was unsure, and had to check with his mother who could be found overseeing the transaction from behind the kitchen curtain. In a few moments, he returned and he told me that his mother had agreed to the revised price. I kept the accordion for several years and did learn to play it well enough to pick out a few songs that I knew well and I was able to add basic cords to some of them. An old friend saw it one day and told me that his grandfather had played such an instrument in Ireland before he immigrated to America. He left that afternoon with the accordion. I never met his grandfather but I imagine that he did not have to send in the clowns as his playing was going well.

Sometimes we listen, sometimes we play,
and sometimes we just dream.
RJG

1977.5   NEW ORLEANS

One of the sessions to train surveyors to assess Community Mental Health Centers for the Joint Commission on Accreditation of Healthcare Organizations was scheduled for New Orleans. I thought that this would be a great time for Reg to join me as I had spent so many days away from home. The three boys stayed in New Jersey with Reg's brother Gerry and his wife Susan.

We had some time to explore in the evenings after the training with the two other trainers. We had dinner at the Pontchartrain Hotel Restaurant; I had Oysters Rockefeller. I extended the trip so we would have time together when the training was over. We walked through the French Quarter on Bourbon Street and heard the Jazz band playing at Preservation Hall. We had our first beignet at the bustling Café du Monde, which has been in operation since the Civil War. Later we ate shrimp boiled in beer and red beans and rice in a white tiled restaurant where tables had holes in the middle for the shrimp shells.

On one of our strolls, I saw a white dress in the window of a shop and I wanted to buy it for Reg. She said no and we left without it, but I still regret not buying that beautiful dress for my beautiful Reg.

We took a cruise on Lake Pontchartrain and saw the same huge causeway that we had driven across 17 years earlier in 1960 when we were traveling from San Antonio, Texas to Fort Dix, New Jersey.

Before we left, we purchased a signed photo entitled "Cathedral in the Fog." It shows the early morning fog on Jackson Square partially obscuring the St. Louis Cathedral. It was taken in 1937 and the vender has made a living selling copies for many years. We had the photo matted and framed and it still hangs on our living room wall.

1978.1   RESPONSIVE SYSTEMS ASSOCIATES

Four of us who were conducting workshops and publishing materials about improving the quality of life for persons with developmental delays, psychological or significant social problems met at our home in Georgia to form a Limited Liability Corporation. I have long since stopped identifying with the small group but it continues today as Responsive Systems Associates (RSA) of Atlanta, Ga. The Balanced Service System and scores of booklets, monographs, and training materials were published under its auspices.

1978.2   TONY DIES

My stepfather Anthony Thomas DeSant died on 18 Apr 1978. Reg, Dave, Brian, Greg, and I drove from Georgia to Florida for the funeral. Mom wanted a Catholic priest because Tony had been raised Catholic. However, the local priest from Blessed Trinity Church, in Ocala, Fla. had to be bribed to attend the funeral because Tony had stopped attending church many years earlier. Like many clergy who sometimes lock themselves up in small-minded rules, instead of ministering to those in need, this priest was upset that Tony had left the church while totally ignoring the fact that the church had made him an outcast when his first wife left him. Divorce was not allowed, so remarriage was not legal, and living with someone outside of marriage was sinful. Forced celibacy was the only option acceptable to the church and totally unacceptable to most people. The church claims that an honest separation by two knowledgeable people through divorce is unholy while an annulment supported by the dishonest claim by uninvolved clerics that the marriage never truly existed is holy. The absurdity is offensive to all human sensibilities.

In 1952 when Tony's first wife Marie (nee Still) DeSant died in Florida, he married Mom, nine years after my half-brother Richard was born. The application for their marriage license indicated that Mom and my father Arthur Gerhard Sr. were never married, a fact that I had not known before reading the application.

The wake was attended by seven or eight people and I told Mom that I knew that Tony had made many sacrifices to take Artie and me into the family. I know that he would have preferred to live out his life with Mom and their son Richie.

After Tony's death, I learned that the reason that he never adopted Artie and me was because my father had provided some financial support that would have ceased if we were adopted.

Tony was buried at Forest Lawn Memory Gardens, in Ocala, FL in the plot that he would share with Mom 11 years later. It lies near the plots of my grandmother Hattie Holder Mills and my brother Artie. Whenever Reg and I visited the cemetery, we would put flowers on all of the family graves.

1978.3   THE HILL LAY IN THE RAVINE

In October 1978, we returned to New York from Georgia. Our new home on Greenwood Lane in Delmar, NY was ideally situated adjacent to an undeveloped 30-acre wooded area for the kids to play in and a 6-minute commute to my work in Albany. However, it was in terrible condition when we moved in. Every room required significant renovation. Nevertheless, within a year we had added a bedroom, expanded the ½ bath to a full bath, added a second layer of glass to the massive windows, redid the kitchen and upstairs bathroom, converted the 1½ car garage to a 2-car garage with a loft for storage, and painted and redecorated every room, hall, and closet.

The house was surrounded by massive white pine trees. Many areas of the yard were covered with 4 to 6 inches of pine needles. Over the years, this maintenance free woodland was converted into an award-winning landscape. One of the greatest challenges was the back yard, which was only about 8 feet wide. To the right was a steep hill about five feet high; to the left was a ravine about 10 feet deep. One day after work, I used a shovel and a wheelbarrow to move about a cubic yard of soil from the hill into the ravine. The boys seemed stunned when I told them that I intended to move the hill into the ravine. At first, they laughed, and then I suspect that they may have believed that the old man had finally lost his senses. However, I continued to move dirt from the hill to the ravine until a small flat new backyard area began to emerge. Their collective response was immediate and delightful, for now seeing the true potential; they all chipped in and did their share. In a few weeks, the yard was almost double its original width and the steep hill was transformed into a terraced knoll that would eventually support a cascading waterfall that fed the fishpond. This once narrow pathway became one of the major features in our landscape.

Now when I look at my back yard, or when I visit their homes, which now sport their own landscaping, I remember the three wonderful little boys who once played and worked so hard in my back yard and laid the hill to rest in the ravine.

Nostalgia is a file that removes the rough edges from the good old days.
Doug Larson

1978.4   THE BARTER SYSTEM

With the backyard now large enough to grow a lawn, I needed a place to store lawn equipment and other outdoor tools. I had met a local carpenter and asked him to build a large shed on the lower level of yard. He presented a handwritten proposal and it became apparent during our discussion that he really wanted to be able to use his computer to create more professional looking documents for his future proposals for home construction and repairs. I told him that I could create such a program for him. When completed, the program itemized all of the material required, provided three levels of quality, calculated labor costs, and tabulated the data in a professional looking proposal with his own business logo.

He was quite pleased with the results and agreed to build the shed as payment for program. Today a few dollars could purchase a product that is far superior to what I created, but in the seventies, there were few general-purpose computer applications available, and each problem was solved with its own unique computer program. The shed turned out to be much larger and better than anything I could have constructed.

1979.1   WILLIAM V. STRAUB DIES

In the last year of his life, Reg's father Bill Straub lived a Spartan life, alone in a small apartment near his oldest son Billy. Reg and I visited him a few weeks before he died. Bill spoke frankly to Reg that he knew that he was dying. The cancer was gradually reducing the once strong and vital man that I had grown to admire, to a weakened shell who was becoming more and more dependent upon his eldest son. Many will face this nature process, but it's hard to witness in a man who had been the pillar of the family for so many years. Bill died on May 3, 1979. Reg's parents, who had once been so important to her, were gone and she now was orphaned. And at the time that she needed them to help her grow into the new role of family elder, they were not here for her. The next generation may never feel quite ready to become the eldest in the family.

We acquire the role of elder, whether we desire it or not and whether we're capable of fulfilling the role or not.

1979.2   ASSOCIATE COMMISSIONER

When I joined the Department of Mental Hygiene[+] in 1969, I dreamed that one day I would become the Commissioner. Now ten years later I was close to fulfilling that dream. I was the Associate Commissioner, in charge of Program Planning and Operations. Don Miles, my friend and contributing author of the Balanced Service System was the Deputy Commissioner for the Program Division. While I was the third ranking Program Division executive in an organization with over 30,000 employees it gradually became clear that we were not getting the consistent level of support we needed from the Commissioner, and that my job, which once seemed so full of potential, was going to end in frustration and disappointment. Don and several other senior staff left the Department a year later. Some worthwhile efforts continued, as before, but the plan for systematic restructuring, which I believed was needed, ended. The hope now is that the progression of gradual changes will someday provide the breadth and depth of services and supports needed by the diverse population of people that the agency serves.

> [+] *In 1978, the Department of Mental Hygiene was reorganized into the autonomous Office of Alcoholism and Substance Abuse, Office of Mental Health, and the Office of the Mental Retarded and the Developmentally Disabled.*

1979.3   IRAN HOSTAGE CRISIS

The Iran hostage crisis had its origins nearly a half-century before it began. The tension between Iran and the U.S. stemmed from a conflict over oil. British and American corporations had controlled the bulk of Iran's petroleum reserves. In 1951, Iranian prime minister Mossadegh, planned to nationalize the country's oil industry. The C.I.A. devised a secret plan to overthrow Mossadegh and replace him "with a leader who was receptive to Western interests." Mossadegh was deposed and a new government was installed. The new leader Mohammed Reza Shah Pahlavi was secular, anti-communist, and pro-Western. In exchange for tens of millions of dollars, he returned 80 percent of Iran's oil to the Americans and the British. Many Iranians bitterly resented Americans intervention in their affairs. The Shah was a brutal dictator whose secret police tortured and murdered thousands of people.

On November 4, 1979, a group of Iranian students stormed the U.S. Embassy in Tehran, taking more than 60 American hostages. The immediate cause of this action was President Jimmy Carter's decision to allow Iran's deposed Shah who had been expelled from his country, to come to the United States for cancer treatment. However, the hostage taking was about more than the Shah's medical care: it was a dramatic way for the student revolutionaries to declare a break with Iran's past and an end to American interference in its affairs. It was also a way to raise the intra- and international profile of the revolution's leader, the anti-American cleric Ayatollah Khomeini.

In April 1980, frustrated with the slow pace of diplomacy, President Carter decided to launch a military rescue mission known as Operation Eagle Claw. The operation was supposed to send an elite Delta rescue team into the embassy compound. However, a sandstorm caused several helicopters to malfunction or crash. Eight American service members were killed in the accident, and the operation was aborted.

My friend Jerry Matthiesen who I first met at the Officers Training Course in Fort Sam Houston and later befriended as a fellow student at the School of Anesthesiology at Walter Reed Army Hospital was part of the backup medical team for Operation Eagle Claw. Who knows what role I may have played if I had remained in the Army. Jerry and Carol's daughter Michon, who was born at Walter Reed, is our God Child. Jerry died in 2011.

The students set their hostages free on January 21, 1981, 444 days after the crisis began, and just hours after President Ronald Reagan delivered his inaugural address. Many historians believe that hostage crisis cost Jimmy Carter a second term as president. With his loss, Roselyn Carter, the much-needed national champion for mental health reform was gone from her position of strength and influence. The reforms that had shaped much of my professional life were about to end.

1979.4   HOUSE GUEST

A friend and neighbor's unsuccessful suicide attempt left her with several very serious medical problems. We invited her to live with us as she recovered. Her depression grew deeper as she realized how her actions and their consequences were going to effect the rest of her life. While we offered whatever patience and understanding we could, her depression was oppressive to those around her. We joined her children in wondering if somehow we were contributing to her distress. After a few weeks, she returned home and took a fatal overdose of medication. While her death did not cause us to grieve in the same way as her family, it did trigger strong emotions, questions, and memories. I gave a eulogy in which I said that the fabric of her life was comprised of many threads and when they were taken all together, they painted a beautiful Tapestry.

CHAPTER 6 *THE EIGHTIES*

The decade saw great social, economic, and political change as wealth and production migrated to newly industrializing economies. As economic liberalization increased in the developed world, multinational manufacturing corporations relocated into Asia, Mexico, and West Germany.

Hostility to authoritarianism resulted in a wave of political reforms in many communist countries. The Solidarity movement began in Poland, and spread to Hungary, Czechoslovakia and Romania. The Soviet Union abandoned political hostility toward the western world and the Cold War ended. Mikhail Gorbachev became leader of the Soviet Union and initiated major reforms to the government through increased rights of expressing political dissent and allowing some democratic elections (though maintaining Communist dominance). Gorbachev pursued negotiation with the United States to decrease tensions and eventually end the Cold War. The fall of the Berlin Wall marked the beginning of German reunification. The European Community's enlargement continued with the accession of Greece, Spain, and Portugal. In China, the Tiananmen Square protests resulted in many deaths and arrests.

Developing countries across the world faced economic and social difficulties as they suffered from debt crises and widespread famine. Major civil discontent and violence occurred in the Middle East, including the Iran-Iraq War and the Soviet-Afghan War. The Arab–Israeli conflict resulted in the Lebanon War. This was a response to the constant terror attacks on northern Israel made by terrorist in Lebanon. The First Intifada (uprising) in the Gaza Strip and West Bank began when Palestinian Arabs mounted large-scale protests against the Israeli military presence in the Gaza Strip and West Bank. The United States launched an aerial bombardment of Libya in 1986 in retaliation for Libyan support of terrorism and attacks on US personnel in Germany and Turkey. There was continuing civil strife in Northern Ireland. Canada, Zimbabwe, Australia, and New Zealand fully separated from the United Kingdom, independence was granted to Vanuatu from the British/French control, Kiribati from joint US-British government and Palau from the United States.

After a five-year hiatus, manned American space flights resumed with the launch of the space shuttle Columbia. The shuttle program progressed smoothly until the NASA Space Shuttle Challenger disintegrated 73 seconds after launch. Other disasters included the Chernobyl nuclear meltdown in the Ukraine, and the oil tanker Exxon Valdez grounding which spilled between 260,000 to 750,000 barrels of crude oil.

As the decade progressed, cars became smaller and more efficient in design. New fuel-mileage standards spelled the end of big-block engines. National safety campaigns raised awareness of seat belt usage to save lives in car accidents. Similar efforts arose to push child safety seats and bike helmet use.

The decade also saw the beginning of the AIDS pandemic, expansion of the role of women, a greater acceptance of Gay rights, and opposition against Apartheid and international condemnation of racial segregation policies.

In the United States, MTV was launched and music videos began to have a larger effect on the record industry. Cable television became more accessible and by the middle of the decade, almost 70% of the American population had cable television.

The 1980 Summer Olympics in Moscow were disrupted by a boycott led by the United States to protest the Soviet invasion of Afghanistan. The 1980 Winter Olympics are remembered for the "Miracle on Ice"; where a young United States hockey team defeated the heavily favored Soviet team and went on to win the gold medal.

Personal computers experienced explosive growth, going from being a toy for electronics hobbyists to a full-fledged industry. The IBM PC, Commodore 64, Macintosh, Walkman, Boom box, VHS, Synthesizer, Pac-Man, Nintendo, and Rubik's Cube became household names.

The best-selling books of the decade were The Covenant, Noble House, E.T., Return of the Jedi, Storybook, The Talisman, The Mammoth Hunters, It, The Tommyknockers, The Cardinal of the Kremlin, and Clear and Present Danger.

The average new house cost $68,700.00, the average salary per year was $19,500.00, a gallon of gas was $1.19, Bread was 50 cents, and the average cost of new car was $7,200

The U.S. Population was 227,224,681 and the life expectancy for men was 70 and 77.4 for women.

1980.1   ARAPAHO

In 1980, while making presentations at several Community Mental Centers in Oklahoma I did some consultation with an Arapaho Indian Tribe.

> *(The Arapahoe Indians in Oklahoma are part of the Algonquian Tribe that lives in the area of the Upper Platte and Arkansas rivers.)*

After the workshop, one of the tribal medicine men took me aside. He told me that each person in his tribe was placed under the sign of a particular animal at the time of their birth and that their spirit was absorbed into this animal in death. Each animal represents the general characteristics of the person. He told me that if I were Arapaho I would be an Eagle. People of the Eagle are spiritual leaders in the tribe.

Some Native Americans tribes such as the Arapahoe refer to the eagle as an earthly incarnation of the "Animikii" i.e. the Thunderbird or Great Spirit. +

I was both honored and humbled that this well-respected man thought of me as having the potential to become a spiritual leader. I hope that he is not too disappointed that I have not progressed to become a real spiritual leader in my own community. There was a time when I thought that I might someday fulfill that role.

I believe that the terms Spirit, Psyche, and Soul are all describing the same motivating force that creates an individual's thoughts and feelings and actions. Some believe this motivating force to be eternal and that it will occupy many bodies over time, others believe that it will occupy only one body and spend the rest of eternity without a body. These opinions are based on the belief that the Great Spirit is a supernatural being, which creates human Spirits, Psyches, or Souls. Others, like me, believe that the Great Spirit is merely the compilation of all that society believes to be good and powerful and that humans create Great Spirits to codify and enforce that, which they judge to be righteous. My beliefs have eliminated many opportunities for spiritual leadership, which require a religious affiliation. We are all spiritual beings simply because we are all human beings, but because spirituality has historically been so closely linked to religion, it's now almost totally impossible to separate the two. One of my great disappointments in life is not having found an outlet for what I believe to be a gift that I might have shared more fully had I pursued a different path or if I had been more willing to find the opportunities that occurred in my day to day life.

1980.2   PRIVATE SECTOR

While most of my working life was spent in the Public Sector working for State government or non-profit service organizations, I did briefly venture into the private sector. After a few meetings with the CEO of a local company that manufactured and installed radiant glass heaters, I was asked to serve as the Chairman of the Board of the company. I maintained that position for about one year when I decided that I wanted to devote all of my time to the field of Mental Health where I was beginning to make a positive contribution.

(Radiant Glass panels emit long infrared rays, which are readily absorbed by objects, including the human body. These same rays warm us from the sun. Since the panel warms the people in rooms rather than heating the air, the air

temperature can be lower than with conventional heating and still achieves the same level of comfort at far lower costs.)

1980.3   CIRCULAR SLIDE RULE #2

I created a circular slide rule to help transpose songs from one key to another. With each additional iteration, more and more functions were gradually added. Most of the functions are specific to the guitar. The reverse of the last version shows the notes played on each fret of each string on the Guitar, the five primary cords in each key, the major, minor, and seventh cord associated with each note, and the fingering for each cord. The obverse transposed notes from one key to another, the position to place the capo to achieve specific cord transpositions, the 12 tones of the chromatic scale, their corresponding key signatures, and the associated major and minor keys, and the number of sharps or flats in each key signature. I have to admit that when my son Brian gave me a hammered dulcimer, after having set the guitar and the slide rule aside several years ago, it took me several minutes to figure out what the bloody thing did and how to use it.

1981.1   THE BALANCED SERVICE SYSTEM

Although we never sold all of the 10,000 copies that were printed, the book seemed to have an impact that far exceeded its sales. I was asked to speak at numerous state, local and non-profit organizations about the principles and policies that the book presented.

Although excerpts of book, "The Balance Service" (BSS) had been published in 1976 by the Joint Commission Accreditation of Hospital and was widely cited in professional journal articles it wasn't actually published until 1981.

As First Lady of Georgia, Rosalynn Carter had overhauled the state's mental health system and she continued her work on behalf mentally ill people as First Lady of the Country. Abstracts of the book were used by staff of the President's Commission on Mental Health to develop its final report. Volume two of the Commission's report draws heavily upon the ideas and structures of the BSS. The report led to the development of the Mental Health Systems Act of 1980. Unfortunately, the Act had hardly become law when newly elected Ronald Reagan immediately caused the Act to be repealed. At that point, there was little hope that the reforms outlined in the book would ever be initiated. Ten years of work were put on hold awaiting a new resurgence of concern and commitment.

At this writing in 2016, we are still waiting and I try to repress my resentment.

1981.2   SPREADING THE WORD

As the materials about the Balance Service System slowly spread through the distribution of unpublished materials, lectures and workshops I was increasingly asked to make presentations to colleges, government agencies, and non-profit organizations. During the decades surrounding the 1981 publication of the book, The Balanced Service System, I made about 150 presentation in 25 states and several visits to Canada.

The workshops varied in length from two to five days and varied in content, which included understanding the role of Values and Moral principles in the evaluation of service programs, the use of computer simulation as a tool in planning for change, empirically based system design, and assessing program effectiveness from the perspective of the patient/client, and many other topics.

I enjoyed teaching and believed that I was good at it. When we left Georgia in 1978, one of the women from the prayer group approached Reg and told her that she hoped that I would continue to teach. I did continue to teach, although no longer in church, and I know from some of the comments I received, the messages that I delivered had an important impact on some who heard me. I was never able to affect the systematic changes that I had hoped for, but perhaps simply planting the seeds for others to reap will eventually help create some of the societal changes needed by persons who lie outside the mainstream of society.

1981.3   THE LAST GOD CHILD

We met Ed & Nancy at St Thomas RC church in Delmar, and soon joined their large circle of friends. They were both very active in peace, justice and environmental causes. Nancy was battling Hodgkins Lymphoma but fortunately went through several long periods of remission. When their second daughter Elizabeth, was born on May 4, 1981 they asked us to be her godparents. Elizabeth is our 13th and last Godchild.

Elizabeth's older sister has Autism, which involves delays in the development of many basic skills, including the abilities to easily socialize or form relationships with others and to communicate effectively. Elizabeth went on to become a brilliant and successful lawyer, while her sister Sarah struggles to understand why she is unable to move ahead with the life that most of us take for granted.

Nancy knew that Ed would need help with his daughters when her body finally gave in to the leukemia and she asked Reg and me to help. In time, Ed remarried a woman who shared his religious convictions and understood from personal experience the challenges that families face when trying to balance the needs of children with widely divergent needs and goals.

However, even after Ed's marriage we stayed in touch with Elizabeth and Sarah: with Elizabeth and her husband who live in Buffalo by letter and email and with Sarah who lives in a nearby group home, with occasional outings to our home or to McDonalds.

A LIST OF OUR GODCHILDREN			
CHILD	PARENTS	BIRTH DATE	God Parent
Joseph Piazza Jr	Joseph & Norma Piazza	7/13/1954	Ron
Susan Straub	Bill & Norma Straub	11/06/1959	Reg
Scott Schleyer	Joseph & Barbara Schleyer	1960±	Reg
Kathleen Craig	John & Grace Craig	1960±	Both
Michon Matthieson	Jerry & Carol Matthieson	1962±	Both
Carolyn Straub	Bill & Norma Straub	8/15/1970	Ron
Kevin Hettenbach	Joe & Terry Hettenbach	11/22/1970	Reg
Adrienne Straub	Gerry & Susan Straub	4/22/1974	Both
Karen Stornelli	Jesse & Dotty Stornelli	1975±	Both
Kristen Dorgan	Richard & Barbara Dorgan	2/1976	Both
Kristen Donnelly	Joseph & Mary Donnelly	1976±	Both
Nathan Bush	Richard & Theresa Bush	1977±	Both
Elizabeth Fox-Soloman	Ed & Nancy Fox-Soloman	5/1981	Both

1982.1   CHERISHED VISITORS

When I think back on the lives of our three growing boys, it is possible for me to ignore the continuity that linked the numerous stages of their individual lives. Instead, I can see, in its place, a steady progression of little boys of various ages who once shared our lives but who have moved on as their older version displaced them. I remember the infant in candy-striped pajamas, a little boy in red boots, and the young lad who sang while he rode on his wooden pony. I remember Little Leaguers and teenagers; I remember them all. I recall the long procession of cherished visitors, each with their own charm, and each so unique from their predecessors, and each with a limited amount of time to share with us. It is as though we didn't raise just three children, but hundreds of children at a variety of ages and each distinct from all the others. When the children finally left home, the event divided my life. It felt like a part of me had broken.

The changes that are so clearly observable in children with their rapid development and continuous transformation and refinement, continue into adulthood. As my brother-in law Gerry says, "This very moment is pregnant with new possibilities... "But in adults, changes are less obvious because they are less frequent and less striking. This is reflected in Ericson's Eight Developmental Stages in which the first three stages of life all occur in less than one decade. The second decade witnesses only two new stages while the last three stage each take ever-increasing lengths of time to develop. I suppose we maintain our identity amidst this instability because of some sort of executive personality that provides continuity as it oversees and coordinates the comings and goings of our ever-changing selves.

1982.2	RITES OF PASSAGE

When David turned 16, we would use the weekends to drive to the large parking lot near some State office buildings. He would then take the wheel of the car that would eventually become a major source of his growing freedom from the constraints of childhood. He soon mastered all the required maneuvers and one day as we prepared to return home, instead of taking the keys and driving home, I suggested that he drive us home. It was the first time that he had driven on a public roadway. I don't know which of us was prouder. The scene would be repeated twice more as Brian and Greg aged-out of childhood. It has become a rite of passage in the twentieth century. Like other coming-of-age rites, it reinforces the skills or beliefs that are essential to the culture that employs them. Some other rites of passage are listed below.

➤ During Bar and Bat Mitzvahs Jewish youth demonstrate their commitment to their faith and their respect Jewish law.

➤ Young boys of some Amazon tribes demonstrate their readiness for manhood by enduring the pain of many ant bites.

➤ At 16 Amish youth enjoy unsupervised weekends away from family during Rumspringa to experience the outside world. Those returning are baptized as members of the church

➤ In Central and South America, some girls celebrate their Quinceanera at age 15 with a Catholic mass and the renewal of baptismal vows followed by a fiesta.

➤ Preteen Inuit boys go into the wilderness with their fathers to test their hunting skills and acclimatize to the harsh arctic weather.

➤ At 11 some Muslim girls in Malaysia, celebrate Khatam Al Koran, to demonstrate their maturity at their local mosque by reciting the final chapter of the Koran at the ceremony.

➤ In Africa, a Maasai tribe boy's circumcision marks his transition to warrior. He'll live 10 years in warrior's camp to learn needed skills. A ceremony marks the transition to senior warrior, he may then marry the woman of their choice.

➤ In Ethiopia, prospective grooms must jump naked over a castrated bull four times, to leave their childhood and become a Maza.

> In the Vanuatu island in the South Pacific, young boys jump off a 98-foot-tall tower with a bungee-like vine tied to their ankles, barely preventing them hitting the ground below.

> In Japan, Seijin-no-Hi on the 2nd Monday of January is when 20 year olds dress in traditional attire for a ceremony and receive gifts at a celebratory party.

> In parts of China, wearing traditional dress is part of the coming of age party and ceremonies Ji Li (for girls) and Guan Li (for boys) honoring their turning 20.

> Traditionally young Apache girls performed the 4-day Na'ii'ees ceremony, in the summer after their 1st menstruation where they reenact the Apache Origin Myth.

1982.3   SNAKES, TOADS AND MOTHS

As the landscaping around the property gradually matured I decided to replace the stairs that lead from the driveway up to the front door. The stairs included low voltage lighting. Of course, the lights attracted moths and other insects each evening. On one particular evening, I noticed a toad sitting in the shadows below one of the lights which lie across from a stone walled garden. It only took a few seconds for the moth to disappear and for the hungry old toad to retreat back into the shadows to await its next meal. Eventually a new moth appeared and the cycle began again. A few days later I saw a small snake slip out from between the cracks in the rock garden and capture the toad. The moths flourished until a new toad appeared and the cycle began anew. It seems that all the world is a restaurant.

The gardens progressed and wild life flourished. The gardens were featured in two local garden shows and the property was officially recognized as a wild life sanctuary.

1983.1   A REFLECTION ON FAITH AND RELIGION

My first exposure to religion came when I was six in 1941, when my foster mother, Mrs. Morgan took me into St. John's Roman Catholic Church in Central Islip. It was mid-day and the church was empty as we strolled down the aisles and Mrs. Morgan showed me the statues. It struck me as a creepy place: all that blood, nails, and thorns. Lighting the candles however, was fun for me; but I now imagine that it was not fun but fear that motivated Mrs. Morgan to light candles, for her two sons who were by then caught up in World War II. I don't believe we ever returned. She might have gone back without me or perhaps one candle was enough; surely, she needed no sensory reminder of the reason for her petition.

My first baptism took place in the Episcopal chapel at St. John's Hospital in Brooklyn, NY, in the summer of 1942. I was little more than a spectator: a wet spectator. The orphanage which was about to become my home was run by the Episcopal Church and all who entered needed to be cleansed, which included baptism and circumcision. I had no idea what was going on, for the minster's explanation was brief and totally unrelated to anything in my experience. I remember him as a kindly man. I also remember tasting apricot nectar for the very first time in the hospital; it was delicious and more vital to me then the baptism. The thick, sweet fruitiness remained a favorite of mine long after the balance of the mundane hospital menu and the religious ritual were forgotten.

My first real awareness of God occurred on a warm Sunday morning during one of the mandatory services at St Ann's Episcopal Church across South Main St. from the orphanage. While idling time during the pastor's sermon I looked up at a stained-glass window above the altar. (Many years later, I learned the church was famous because its windows were made of Tiffany stained glass.) It was a depiction of Christ as The Good Shepherd. He stood with a lamb on his shoulders; I found this concept very comforting. I needed a shepherd who I could trust and who I could rely on to be with me when the wolves come to take my family away. To be cared for and loved forever just as I am, was the balm that I needed, and the one that I would return to later in life. The Good Shepherd experience did have a significant impact on me, and so, I asked my mother to give me a Children's Bible Story book for Christmas. In the cottage, we lived five to each bedroom, organized by age group. As the youngest boy, I was in the group of second, third and fourth graders. Several women worked as housemothers at the cottage. They rotated shifts. When Mrs. Owen was working the evening shift, she would sit on my bed and read stories to us. When the Bible storybook arrived, I would request stories from the Old Testament. The others didn't object. The stories were as exciting as the tattered books in the meager library of comic books that the cottage maintained in the living room. I was also quite proud of the fact that I actually owned a book.

When we left the orphanage a year or so later, Artie and I left God behind as well. My mother had been raised a Southern Baptist but by the time I met her there were no outward signs that religion played any part in her life. My stepfather, Tony, had been raised Catholic, however, when he and his first wife, Marie, separated she refused to give him a divorce. Consequently, Mom and Tony "lived in sin" as cohabitation was called in those days. Tony was irate and frustrated that the church would not grant him an annulment, which allowed his former wife to hold his life hostage to her hatred. When he died, I had to bribe a priest to come to his funeral because he was not a member of any parish. Tony was caught up in the "Catch 22" resulting from the tangled web of rules created and enforced by a church hierarchy that doesn't personally have to live by them. *(Catch 22 is a problematic situation for which the only solution is denied by a circumstance inherent in the problem.)* He could not return to his first wife because she left him and moved a thousand miles away, but he could not end the marriage because she would not agree to it, and he could not remarry because of the existence of the first marriage, and the Church condemned his relationship with Mom because they weren't married. Reality played no role in the Church's decisions. The situation was made more painful for Tony because he knew of annulments that were allowed in similar situations, where the petitioners were powerful, wealthy, or well known. (I personally know of a case where similar rules were waved for a well-placed parishioner.)

My next experience with religion occurred in high school. Students could leave school an hour early each Thursday afternoon to attend religious instruction. The town was predominately Catholic and much of the school emptied as the students walked the half mile to St. John of God Church. Two or three of us walked a few blocks to the Episcopal Church. The minister was uninteresting and certainly uninspiring, but I continued to attend. One day the minister took me aside and told me that someone had seen me and a girl walking in the fields across from the school and although he admitted that he had no idea what we were doing there, he freely accused me and the totally innocent girl of immoral behavior. I was outraged that he could so easily jeopardize the girl's reputation on a baseless accusation. In the 1950's a girl's reputation could easily be tarnished by the words of a minister, true or not. And a stained reputation could cause a girl to be criticized, ridiculed, or even isolated. I never knew who gave him the information or whom he might have spoken to, but I never told the girl about the slander and never returned to the Church. (The girl lived a few blocks from the school and the field was a shortcut to her home.)

While in college when I was dating Reg, I would occasionally go to Sunday service at the Episcopal chapel on the hospital grounds or go with Reg and our friend Mike to Catholic services. I found the Catholic services to be inexplicable. The priest stood with his back to the congregation speaking in Latin, which few understood. The motivation to attend seemed to have little to do with what was in evidence at the service but based in beliefs about what might happen to you if you did not attend and the belief in a magical transformation performed by the priest that could never be referred to as magical. I was at a complete loss as to why anyone would ever attend. I went because Reg was there.

Two years later, as Reg and I began to get more serious with each other, I began to get more serious about attending the Catholic Church and in 1958 I was baptized for the second time. The priest insisted even though I had already been baptized. In 1960, I was confirmed at a ceremony that included Reg's youngest brother Gerry and in the church where we would soon be married.

During the 1970's Reg and I were active in several Catholic renewal movements including Marriage Encounter, Cursillo, and the Charismatic renewal. We also attended a family Bible camp that was predominately Lutheran, for several years.

I enrolled in The Albany Dioceses Deaconate Training Program and completed one year of the three-year course of study when we moved to Georgia. I then enrolled in the Atlanta Diocese program and completed one year there. On our return to Albany, I tried to reenroll in the Albany program and met with the Albany board to discover where I stood with the program. After that meeting, when it became clear that the Albany Diocese was not going to accept the 13 months of work and study I did while enrolled in the Atlanta Program I left totally disillusioned about the program and my place in it. Deciding not to continue in the program caused both guilt and relief. I had been struggling with the fact that women were not allowed to become Deacons and I was considering protesting the decision by completing the training and then accepting whatever ministry might be offered to me, but refusing to be ordained until women were also ordained. I knew that the protest would not change the policy, but I also believed that the reason that this totally unjust, unnecessary, and unscriptural policy was preserved because other men who believed that the policy was a grave mistake stood by and did nothing. And now I too was doing nothing; leaving the program was the easy way out so I would not be placed in the uncomfortable position that the protest would have provided. Perhaps one day a man with more fortitude and determination will take the stand that I avoided.

Several years later one of the deacons and his wife met with me and after a brief conversation, they realized that I was relieved to be out of the program. They were satisfied with what they had learned and the conversation ended before they might have learned about the reason for the relief was my concern about the ethics of continuing in the program knowing that I would never be ordained because of the planned protest. I think they preferred to believe that I didn't really want to be a deacon and that I was relieved to be free of the responsibility.

While I am disappointed that they and their colleagues are content to accept the policy without protest, I have no right to criticize them as I had taken the easy way out and simply walked away.

My faith journey took me from a place of few questions to a place of few answers through places populated with many questions and the answers that spawned them. The eventual loss of my personal God was like the loss of my brother to death or the loss of my sons to manhood: fully expected . . . but arriving all too soon. My faith journey was, as with much of our interior lives, was always alone, but only occasionally lonely. Religion moves the believer to individual growth which when truly obtained it's defined as failure, for the believer must never outgrow the church. For example, Faith in creation, which can be experienced, rather than in the creator, which cannot be experienced, is heresy. Trust in the gift, which can be understood, rather than in the giver, which cannot be understood is heresy. To achieve a spirit of wholeness rather than a spirit of holiness is heresy. I believe that many people, including myself, look to God for what we can only give ourselves. To paraphrase

Pogo, "We have met the solution, and he is us." We seem to foster belief instead of knowledge but I can no longer offer belief without doubt. As I age, I have less belief and more respect for other ideas as my life has distanced me from early certitudes.

I am a spiritual being trying to express my true self within the constraints of a limited physical body and a physical being trying to express my true self within the constraints of a limited spirit. Life is not about becoming spiritual any more than it's about becoming physical, they are both an inherent part of our human nature. I believe life is about using our nature in ways that are the most fruitful, the most gracious, the most merciful, and the most just. Some of what we call growth is often merely change. I believe that true growth is not Godly but pragmatic. What we understand as Godly is merely that which works best for the common good. Peace is preferred to war, mercy is preferred to revenge, love is preferred to hate, and action is preferred to indifference, not because one is inherently Godly but because the outcomes are inherently better. I do not stand in opposition to religion for I believe that it is the other side of the coin to my own beliefs. Religion and I seem to be in general agreement about humankind's quest for fruitful, gracious, merciful, and just lives. I think we merely disagree on the source of that motivation. Perhaps the Holy Spirit, which is given, and the Human Spirit, which is learned, are simply different terms for the same phenomenon. Or, perhaps they are not.

Interestingly I have changed my opinion about religion and God many times, but it has never changed my belief that I was always right. Evaluating the cogency of my own opinions seems to be more difficult than evaluating the cogency of Gods existence.

"Two things are infinite: the universe and human stupidity but, with regard
to the universe, I have not yet acquired absolute certainty."
Albert Einstein

"Tell people there's an invisible man in the sky who created the universe,
and the vast majority will believe you. Tell them the paint is wet, and they
will touch it to be sure."
George Carlin

1984.1   WOLFENSBERGER

Wolf Wolfensberger influenced public policy and practice regarding persons with disabilities and developmental delays through his writing and workshops, which included The Principle of Normalization. Normalization involves the acceptance of people with disabilities, with their disabilities, offering them the same conditions as are offered to other citizens. It involves an awareness of the normal rhythm of life – including the normal rhythm of a day, a week, a year, and the life cycle itself. It involves the normal conditions of life – housing, schooling, employment, exercise, recreation, and freedom of choice previously denied to individuals with severe, profound, or significant disabilities. His definition is based on a concept of cultural normativeness. Services should be as culturally normative as possible, to establish or maintain personal behaviors and characteristics that are as culturally normative as possible. Thus, for example, "medical procedures" such as shock treatment or restraints, are not just punitive, but also not "culturally normative" in society. Normalization also requires social and physical integration, which later became popularized and widely implemented. He authored and co-authored more than 40 books and monographs, and wrote more than 250 chapters and articles. I read much of his materials attended many of his workshops. He was one of the most influential people in my professional life. I led or participated in several workshops and program evaluations based on his ideas. I believe that his work should be required reading in any program aimed at persons who will be providing, planning, or managing human services. But like so many others whose work requires significant change, he was marginalized by much of the mental health establishment. Only the ideas that reinforced the then current public policy were generally accepted. His greatest acceptance was with persons servicing or supporting individuals with development delays. After one of his workshops, he gave me his personal prayer book. Wolf died in 2011.

1985.1   WHEN THE MUSIC STOPPED

(To John Nuttall, music director, on the discontinuation of the folk
mass at St. Thomas' RC Church, Delmar, NY)

The silence muffles joyful sounds,
and special times in friendships' bounds,
familiar voices heard no more,
lost too are times when spirits soar.

Cymbals now just dust collecting
symbols lost my soul objecting,
for the song was not just singing
but for love and gifts a-bringing.

Though the rituals continue,
word and wine designed to bring you,
still a part within me's longing, back
once more in song a-joining.

Ancient rites in dogmatic form,
cannot fulfill 'lest substance born,
the substance of our lives are we,
sharing joys and misery

Though ripples on the pond we be,
a sailing to our destiny,
making very little splashing,
when we feel our hopes a-dashing.

Eviction did not tear asunder,
even though it was a blunder,
but like the house that is not home,
we miss the place we called our own.

But, joyful sounds can't stand apart,
they meet and bind and then restart,
joined together in a blend,
life's tribulations to transcend.

With the coming and the going,
discord often is a-showing,
though priests moved on to serve anew,
this town was always served by you.

Most people go to their grave with their music still in them.
Disraeli

1985.2 & 1989   EMPTY NEST ... FULL HEART

Between the weekend visits, the daily commutes and the part time respites during graduate school, the amount of time that the boys spent at home gradually diminished over several years. I saw the changes happening moment-to-moment and day-by-day. But there was one particular moment on one particular day when the life-changing impact of that process shook me to the core. The nest was not merely physically empty ... it was in some more important way – spiritually hollow.

I stood in the window and watched the old Chevy Malibu drive away with my boys, with an assortment of beloved relationships, and with a life force and a life style that could never be recreated. I didn't recognize the sound of the moan that filled the room, as I had never heard it before, and was surprised that it arose from within me. I had never felt so lost before. I was broken hearted. We had sought to help the boys become independent. Now I thought, "If this is what success feels like, how much more painful failure must be."

> (1989) I wondered how my parents felt when I left home; I never would have known that it might have been a problem for them if it were not for a single passing comment my mother made a few years before she died that alluded to her empty nest.

(1985) This was a new and exciting time ... for them, however, for Reg and me any new and exciting times would have to be carved out together to fill the time and space that their leaving created. Fortunately, we were up to the task, and although we miss our children and wish we had more contact with them, our lives are full and rich again. Only occasionally do I recall that one particular moment in time when the bright side of the dark transition could not yet be seen.

> *Before I knew the best part of my life had come, it had gone....*
> *Ashleigh Brilliant*

1985.3   BLOSSOMS MONTESSORI LEARNING CENTER

I was first exposed to the Montessori Method in 1969 when we placed David in the local nursery school, the Montessori School of Albany.

> *Montessori education was developed by Italian physician and educator Maria Montessori. It is characterized by an emphasis on independence, freedom within limits, and respect for children's natural psychological, physical, and social development. It uses mixed age classrooms, student choice of activity from a prescribed range of options, uninterrupted blocks of work time, reliance upon students' ability to discover concepts from working with*

specialized educational materials, rather than by direct instruction, and freedom of movement within the classroom.

We were both very pleased with the school and the Montessori approach. We began volunteering at the school and I became President of the Board of Directors and the following year the Chairman of the Long-Range Planning Committee. The school was located in a former church facility that was in great need of repair. The administrator and driving force behind the school, Jim Davis, was severely injured when he fell from a ladder while making some repairs. His injury and the cost of the needed renovations eventually forced the school to move across the river to Rensselaer and we lost touch with it. Jim was also the designer of the official international medallion honoring the centenary of the birth Dr. Maria Montessori.

Gus and Noreen were former members of religious communities and opened a Montessori School in their home in 1983. I was glad to accept an offer in 1985 to become a member of the Board of Directors of their school, the Blossoms Montessori Learning Center. As their reputation spread, enrollment at the school increased. Reg, who was working in Real Estate at the time, helped them find a building to house the school. It had an apartment on the second floor and the rent from it helped keep the cost of running the school to a minimum. Gus and Noreen are two of the most impressive people I have ever met. Even though tuition at Blossoms was substantially lower than other schools they still managed to help support Montessori schools and Training programs in developing countries. My role on the board was minimal as Gus and Noreen are very capable to run both the programmatic and the administrative functions of the school. But I am proud to have been associated, if only in a peripheral way, with Gus, Noreen and the other board members and staff. In 2014, NYS started to provide full day kindergarten classes in public schools. While this was good for children in general, Blossoms suffered as it was only prepared to provide half-day classes. Since most parents preferred the tuition free full day sessions as it provides more time for other employment, enrollment at Blossoms was quickly limited to its half-day preschool programs. In 2015, Gus and Noreen Cadieux decided to close the school. At this writing, they have found another Montessori teacher to open a new school at their site. I hope they succeed.

The child is both a hope and a promise for mankind.
Maria Montessori

KEYNOTE

After delivering the keynote address at a meeting of a Canadian Mental Health Association, I settled into my seat to review the afternoon's program and select a workshop session to attend. I sat for a moment stunned by what I had read. There was to be a single workshop during the first two hours of the afternoon; and I was facilitating it. I left the plenary session and found a quiet place to think. I had nothing planned and no previously developed workshop that could be quickly restructured to meet the objectives outlined in the conference agenda.

At one o'clock, I was reintroduced to the group and looked over the large conference hall, the several hundred attendees, and the dozens of tables spread out in front of me. I asked the group to image that the meeting room was a map of Canada: St. Johns and the other eastern provinces to my right and British Columbia and the other western provinces to my left. As usual, the French translator repeated the message for the Francophones. I asked the group to rearrange themselves so they would be located on the map as close as possible to the place where they worked and at a table with people who worked as close to them as possible. There was a lot of shuffling and chatter as each person headed in the general direction of their town or city and negotiated with their neighbors until all had found their place. I then asked each person to consider quietly his or her organization, job, and career and an ongoing problem that remained unsolved. After A few minutes, I suggested that the problems be shared with the others at their table, without discussion. Next, the group was asked to consider privately what they had heard from their colleagues. While they thought about each dilemma, they were asked to consider what they might personally do to contribute to the solution of the problem. Then the point of the exercise was revealed. For those who had considered ways in which they might help another person, the opportunity was provided to offer to voluntarily help; knowing that not all offers would be accepted and that the details of those that were accepted would be negotiated at a time and place established before the meeting was adjourned. This was not a call to give advice to others, but a commitment to give of themselves to help others. As I heard myself saying these words to this group of mental health professionals and advocates I thought, "Who was I to be suggesting that these people work harder, be stronger, and share more. This was going to be a disastrous flop because these people were always over-worked, over-committed, and over-extended." But, they politely continued and I could see discussions at the tables around the room. As the time wound down, I asked the groups to finish up and asked if anyone would like to share what happened or didn't happen at their table. One by one, they came to the microphone to relate their experiences. I was greatly relieved that "my workshop" was not a flop but more importantly that "their workshop" had created some important new fibers in the fabric of service that they spread across Canada. In the concluding statements, I told the group that many, like me, had not been able to make a commitment that day, but all of us had participated in a process that will likely be of benefit to others. After the workshop the conferences leaders told me that the proceedings were videotaped and asked if they could use the exercise at future meetings. Of course, I agreed. I never heard how long they continued to use the exercise, or if it helped others form helping new relationships. However, I have heard about one relationship that begun at that first workshop. An agency had a preteen boy for whom they were unable to find a "big brother" because of his age and aggressive behavior. There was a childless psychologist at the same table. While he made his living assessing young children, he admitted that he was afraid of many of the youth he served. He offered to meet the boy and decide if he could become the needed "big brother." Later I learned the boy had taught the psychologist to fish, a skill he had learned from his deceased father. Their relationship grew and the psychologist eventually adopted the boy.

Now when I look back on my career and think about how little of what I wanted to achieve was actually accomplished, I remember the boy in Canada who I never met, but who was given the opportunity for a better life because I arrived unprepared at a conference many years ago, I could not help create a system that would help thousands but at least I helped to create a family that helped one.

Not being able to do everything
isn't a reason for doing nothing
(even if it happens by accident.)
RJG

HAIKU AND OTHER POEMS

STRENGTH

Stones that once sustained
crumble into desert sand,
single rock remains.

PREOCCUPIED

Needing to be soothed
by birds healing joyful song
not ready to listen.

FORE SHADOWED

Life is the shadow of birth
extending to the grave
but who can see it.

THE DEER [1]

Gentle deer
grazing in the field
hunter's shot
saving you from yourself.

SEASONS

Spring's fulfilled in summer's joy
but autumn's splendor
belies winter's grief.

BIRDS

Birds gently gliding
on the winds of blowing storms
in the calm, they sing.

MATURING

Fallen peaks of former joys,
filling sorrows valley spaces.
Leveled feeling come together,
merged as hill and dale embraces

FATHER AND SON

Strong pride stays the course
stiff wills do not veer away
hearts collide and break.

HELPING HAND [2]

Locked away from life's own treasures,
programs' goals my only pleasures.
Is this some demon I can't flee?
or "Helping Hand" which turns the key?

HOPE [3]

In sadness, there is hope for joy,
in turmoil hope for peace.
It is placed there by the Christmas light.

THE SERVER

See the world with tears aflowing,
in my heart the call was growing.
Stop the signs of sadness 'ever.
(to inflate my self-endeavor.)
When the hopelessness of fervor,
became apparent to this server,
then I joined the world in feeling,
and my tears joined yours for healing.

FREEDOM

Independence of thought is purchased
with loneliness of heart
and Freedom with solitude of spirit.

DEATH

The weakness spreads from my sickbed
until the sun flickers and goes out.

I AM [4]

I am because of you.

WE [5]

(but for a moment, then alone again.)

We live with private fears and public cheers,
with private dreams and public schemes.
We keep our true selves hidden well
for reasons that we cannot tell.
But in a moment fleeting,
we are quickly seeing,
we are alike.
We all are
WE
It's true
we are alike.
We are quickly sharing.
But in a moment of despairing,
for reasons that we cannot tell.
We keep our true selves hidden well
with private dreams and public schemes.
We live with private tears and public jeers.

~

[1] *Winner of the 1986 Silver Poet Award of World of Poetry magazine.*

[2] *Written in response to the growing trend to professionalize all aspects of life.*

[3] *Evoked by terrorist attacks in 2015*

[4] *Short love poem written for Reg*

[5] *Pattern Poem shows our brief coming together and the inevitable drifting apart.*

1988.1 COMPUTER SIMULATION IN NEW HAMPSHIRE

On one of my many trips to New Hampshire to consult with staff attempting to develop community alternative to the State Institutions for persons with developmental delays I found myself stranded in Boston's Logan Airport in a snowstorm. Direct flights from Albany were generally limited to larger cities and I had to fly into Boston to get the small plane to New Hampshire.

While I waited for the snow to stop, I began rethinking the Computer Model that I had created to help evaluate alternative strategies. As I waited for the snow to stop, I modified the model to include the costs and savings associated with deinstitutionalization and the costs of alternative community programs and the timing of the transfer of funds. When I finally met with the NH staff, they told me that this was exactly what they needed to help with the planned transfers.

Had it not been for the snow delay this tool may never have been created; this was not the first time that serendipity helped me with my work. I showed the model to staff in New York State where I worked for twenty years and they were not interested. I made the model available to persons attending the many planning workshops that I was still conducting around the country.

Fact is, inventing an innovative business model is often mostly a matter of serendipity.
Gary Hamel

1989.1 & 2009   MOM

As Mom lay dying in the hospital bed, I could see my face reflected in her eyes, but I was alone, she was no longer there... she had suffered a cerebral stoke, from which there was no retreat. I would have liked to have a few minutes more to be alone with her, but someone entered and hung on watching my every move. I had the uneasy feeling that her curiosity about my emotional condition was more important to her than Moms physical condition.

Soon, Mom was transferred to a nursing home. She died a few days later. My brother Richie picked up her belongings; everything fit in a small shopping bag. Her other things, which had been the anchors to her identity and to part of her past, had long since been dispersed or trashed; sadly, the provenance of her artifacts and of her life were trashed as well.

At Mom's funeral, I performed grief and losing her was like burying some of my 0wn past: Artie was the only one for whom I was ever truly bereaved. While alive Mom had never gone to a beauty parlor or used makeup or hair styling. The stylist at the funeral parlor had done an excellent job and for the first time I saw just how beautiful Mom could be. There must be something to learn here, about not putting things off until it too late to enjoy them.

Mom died in New Port Richey but she was buried in Ocala, in the plot she and Tony had purchased years before. It's situated between the plots of her mother Hattie (Holder) Mills and her first-born son, my brother, Arthur Gerhard. Reg and I had to fly back to New York and could not visit the gravesite, which was an hour away from New Port Richey.

> (2009) In March, Reg and I visited Moms' grave on our return from a visit with my brother Richie and our friends Jerry and Carol from Punta Gorda, FL. Richie had never visited the grave and didn't want to come with us. He was never encouraged to be communicative so I didn't know if his decision not to join us was motivated by too much emotion or too little.

> With Mom's death, part of my past and part of my life's history had slipped away as well. Mom alone had the answers to the many questions about our past that I had not yet learned to ask. When she left, much of my childhood went with her. There was so much more that I would have liked to know, but now there's no one left to ask. I felt like an orphan again, but this time there was no one coming to rebuild the family, that role had fallen to me.

> *Death is the end of a lifetime, but not the end of a relationship.*
> *M. Albom*

1989.2 & 1953   LIKE FATHER LIKE SONS

Each of my three sons David, Brian, and Gregory have some of the traits that I recognize in myself. And fortunately, they each have many admirable traits that I lack. Some of these traits they may have inherited from their mother Reg, but I believe that they developed others by their own nurturing of the behaviors that seemed personally important and proper.

The photo of Greg (on left,) giving the High School graduation speech in 1989 and  me, giving a similar speech in 1953 documents one of the traits that I share with my sons. Greg's' speech being much warmer and personal than mine exemplifies how each of my sons has exceeded my capabilities in their own special ways.

David is ever responsive and checking to be sure that Reg and I are okay and freely shares his time and many gifts with all who seek his help.

Brian keeps us informed about Emily's progress as he continues to prove himself to be a stellar father to her. His warmth and talent have served him well. He once wrote "Like a search party for the meaning of life, you and a friend can cover more ground than you alone."

I am equally proud of each of them and amazed at how different they are from each other while maintaining a core family attribute.

CHAPTER 7 *THE NINETIES*

During this decade, living standards and democratic governance generally improved in many areas of the world, notably East Asia, much of Eastern Europe, Latin America, and South Africa.

In Rwanda, hundreds of thousands of Rwandans were massacred. The Taliban seized control of Afghanistan. The Pakistan Army overthrew the democratically elected government of Pakistan.

The Los Angeles civil rights riots occurred, with 53 deaths and 5,500 property fires in 100-square-miles. The first bombings of the World Trade Center and the Oklahoma City bombing lead to awareness in the U.S. of domestic and international terrorism as a potential threat. At the Columbine, High School massacre, in Littleton, Colorado, two student gunmen killed 12 students and a teacher before committing suicide.

After the bombings of U.S. embassies in Kenya and Tanzania by Al-Qaeda militants, U.S. naval military forces launched missiles against Al-Qaeda bases in Afghanistan.

United Kingdom handed sovereignty of Hong Kong to the People's Republic of China. Portugal handed sovereignty of Macau to the People's Republic of China. Eritrea gained independence from Ethiopia. East Timor broke away from Indonesian. The republics of Croatia, Slovenia, Bosnia and Herzegovina, and Macedonia declared independence from Yugoslavia. Czechoslovakia was split into the Czech Republic and Slovakia. The former countries of the Warsaw Pact moved from totalitarian regimes to democratically elected governments. The same happened in other, non-communist countries, such as Taiwan, Chile, South Africa, and Indonesia. Capitalism made great changes to the economies of communist countries like China and Vietnam.

The African National Congress leader Nelson Mandela was released from jail after thirty years of imprisonment for opposing apartheid and white-minority rule in South Africa. This would resolve with the end of Apartheid in South Africa.

Social liberalization continued in most countries, though coupled with an increase in the influence of capitalism. The World Health Organization removed homosexuality from its list of diseases. California voters legalized cannabis for medicinal purposes.

Israeli and Palestine agreed to the Oslo Accords. The Palestine Liberation Organization recognized Israel's right to exist, while Israel permitted the creation of an autonomous Palestinian National Authority consisting of the Gaza Strip and West Bank. The Israeli withdrawal from the Palestinian territories marked the end of the period of violence between Palestinian Arab militants and Israeli armed forces. A peace treaty was also signed between Israel and Jordan. With the end of the Soviet Union, Israel faced a mass influx of Russian Jews, many of whom had high expectations the country was unable to meet.

German reunification integrating the economic structure and provincial governments focused on modernization of the former communist East.

The Irish Republican Army (IRA) (In Irish: Óglaigh Na hÉireann) agreed to a truce marking the end of 25 years of violence between the IRA and the United Kingdom.

The European Union formed and there was freedom of movement between member states, and the Euro currency was adopted. The improvement in relations between the countries of NATO and the former members of the Warsaw Pact ended the Cold War both in Europe and in other parts of the world.

The U.S. experienced its longest period of economic expansion during the decade. The North American Free Trade Agreement, which phased out trade barriers between the United States, Mexico, and Canada, was signed into law.

The government of the People's Republic of China announced major privatization of state-owned industries in September 1997.

The first mammal was cloned, Dolly the sheep. The Human Genome Project began. DNA identification of individuals found application in criminal law. Biodegradable products began replacing products made from Styrofoam; advances were made in the recycling of waste products. Genetically engineered crops were developed for commercial use. Dark matter, dark energy, and brown dwarfs, were discovered and the presence of black holes was confirmed. The Galileo probe orbited Jupiter, studying the planet and its moons extensively. The Global Positioning System became operational. The Channel Tunnel across the English Channel opened connecting France and England.

Construction started on the International Space Station, the spacecraft Pathfinder landed on Mars, and the Hubble Telescope revolutionized astronomy. Extra solar planets were discovered orbiting stars other than the sun.

Sustainable development and environmental protection became serious issues for the international community. The prevention of the destruction of rainforests and climate change became major concerns, and the United Nations Framework Convention on Climate Change helped coordinate efforts to reduce carbon emissions in the atmosphere.

The Tibetan Freedom Concert brought 120,000 people together in the interest of increased human rights and autonomy for Tibet from China.

Violence against women took center stage internationally. More nations than ever before were led by elected women Presidents, and Prime Ministers, and women reached great heights in the U.S. government. Hillary Rodham Clinton was elected a Senator, Madeleine Albright became United States Secretary of State, and Janet Reno was appointed Attorney General. Sheila Widnall became Secretary of the Air Force and Ruth Bader Ginsburg joined Sandra Day O'Connor on the Supreme Court. Record numbers of women become top CEOs worldwide.

TV shows, mostly sitcoms, were popular with the American audience.

Technological advances included modems, cable service, and DSL led to faster connection to the Internet. E-mail became popular; E-commerce companies such as Amazon.com, eBay, AOL, and Yahoo! grew. The MP3 player, digital cameras become available. Apple introduces the iMac, the CD-ROM drive became standard, and the DVD media format and Flash memory cards were developed. Hand-held satellite phones were introduced. Portable CD players became available. Mobile phones gained massive popularity worldwide. Microsoft Windows operating systems became standard on Personal Computers. The development of Web browsers made surfing the World Wide Web easier and more user friendly.

Top selling books included The 7 Habits of Highly Effective People, Cold Mountain, Into Thin Air, and Memoirs of a Geisha, Divine Secrets of the Ya Ya Sisterhood, Chicken Soup for the Soul, The Plains of Passage, Dolores Claiborne, The Bridges of Madison County, The Chamber, The Rainmaker, The Runaway Jury, The Partner, and The Street Lawyer.

Academy Award Winning Movies: 1990 Dances with Wolves, 1991 Silence of the Lambs, 1992 Unforgiven, 1993 Schindler's List, 1994 Forrest Gump, 1995 Braveheart, 1996 The English Patient, 1997 Titanic, 1998 Shakespeare in Love, 1999 American Beauty

The average new house cost $123,000, the average salary per year was $28,960, a gallon of gas was 1.34, a loaf of bread cost $0.70 and the average cost of new car was $16,950.00.

The U.S. Population was 249,438,712 and life expectancy for Men was 71.8, and for women it was 78.8 years.

1990.1   LEAVING ACADEMIA

For the past 20 years, I had been working part time as an adjunct professor or visiting lecturer at the State University of New York and Russell Sage College, in Albany, NY and at many other colleges around the country. As my publications became dated and my contacts retired, I had fewer and fewer requested to speak, so in 1990 I retired my overhead slides, my corny jokes, my bibliography. and the human-interest stories I had used to make my points.

I was asked become a reviewer for the professional peer reviewed journal, Hospital and Community Psychiatry Journal

> *(Peer reviewed journals assess the quality of articles submitted for publication by having experts in the field evaluate their accuracy and the validity of their research methodology and conclusions. Peer-reviewed articles that meet established standards are accepted for publication and exemplify the best research practices in a field.)*

The Journal changed its name in to Psychiatric Services and was the highest-ranked mental health journal in the country. I continued reviewing the occasional article for the Journal until I began working at Parsons in 1994.

1990.2   COMMUNITY RESIDENCE

A group home for persons with developmental delays opened on Kenwood Ave. in Delmar. I was glad to accept a position on the community advisory board. It wasn't that the staff ever requested or that I ever offered any advice, it was because the history of services for disenfranchised persons makes it very evident that contact and communication with outsiders is essential to help maintain the quality of life for people living under the total control of others. When powerless people and the staff who control their lives are isolated from the community, there is a dangerous tendency for staff to become overly controlling, unkind and in some situations brutal in their treatment of their powerless wards. I believe this to be equally true for all types of institutions whether they be large prisons or small group homes.

Some board members also served as personal advocates for one of the residents. Raymond and I planted tulip bulbs in the front yard. It was fun to watch a young man use tools to create a garden for the first time. In the spring when the tulips grew, he watered them with a watering can. It was one of the highlights of the year. I remained on the board until Raymond moved to another group home. He then lived far away and I never saw him again, but I continue in 2017 to serve as his personal advocate and receive regular updates about his life and sign off on his treatment plans.

1991.1   PERSIA AND HAWAII

We were awakened at dawn by the sound of the surf. Since we had arrived by taxi late the night before, we had no idea that the "Lannan, Kihi Kai" was situated on a ledge overlooking beautiful Hilo Bay. It was a Bed and Breakfast run by former mainlander Amy Gamble. We found it in a tourist guidebook to Hawaii and made the reservation by mail. We had homemade bread, huge delicious ripe mangos, and Kona coffee for breakfast.

David was studying for one year at the University of Hawaii at Hilo. Reg and I thought that this would be a great time to visit Hawaii. Dave had a friend who had been a travel guide and he arranged several breath-taking trips to remote sections that are rarely seen by tourists. We saw green sea turtles, and the remnant of a primitive village that may have been the original landing site of the early migrants to Hawaii. After exploring lava tubes, we visited beaches of black sand, of green sand and of red sand. Dave explained that the red sand is rich in iron ore, that black sand consists of tiny fragments of lava, and that green sand is rich in the mineral olivine that forms when the magma cools.

One evening we drove 9,200 feet to the visitors' center below the Mauna Kea Observatory. The Observatory is 14,000 feet above sea level. Going all the way up requires some preparation, as there is 40% less oxygen there than at sea level. Amateur stargazing only occurs at the visitors' center, which is equipped with telescopes and the temperatures are much warmer than at the summit.

We watched the eruption of Kilauea, a 3,646-foot deep crater on the southeastern slope of Mauna Loa in Hawaii Volcanoes National Park. Kilauea is one of the largest active craters in the world with a circumference of 8 miles. It has often erupted explosively in the past 2,500 years. The most recent major eruption at Kilauea began on January 3, 1983. The vent produced vigorous lava fountains that quickly built up sending lava flows down the volcano's slope. The lava flows extending 11 to 12 km to the sea. Large areas of coastline and the coastal road were enshrouded.

Reg and Dave swam in tidal pools on hardened lava fields far from the active flow. The area looked like dozens of acres of black and gray stone, but life under the water teemed with plant life and multicolored fish, unaware that they were living in a desert. Reg and Dave snorkeled while I enjoyed the solitude.

Dave took us to a botanical garden in which we saw huge waterfalls and Azealia plants that were ten feet tall. On the highway, we passed red hedgerows made of Poinsettias. We left Dave on the big Island of Hawaii and spent the last two days of our vacation on Oahu where we visited Pearl Harbor, a Dole pineapple farm, Diamond Head, the beach at Waikiki, and the Bishop museum. The museum has the world's largest collection of Polynesian cultural artifacts and natural history specimens. To me the most impressive holding is a circular stick chart in which the patterns made by woven sticks represented ocean currents and swells. The charts were studied and memorized prior to a voyage and were not consulted during a trip across thousands of miles of ocean. Navigators used their senses and memory to guide them on voyages by crouching down or lying prone in the canoe to feel how the canoe was being pitched and rolled by underlying swells. They focused on the effects of islands in blocking and bending of swells and the interaction of swells coming from opposite directions. Seashells scattered throughout the map indicate the location of the islands.

Later, Reg and I watched in horror as the aerial bombardment of Iraqi lit up the night sky on the TV in the lobby of our Hawaiian Hotel. The invasion of Kuwait by Iraqi troops on 2 August 1990 was met with international condemnation. When negotiations failed to end the conflict and expel Iraqi, U.S. troops from Kuwait began with an aerial bombardment on 17 January 1991, this was followed by a ground assault on 23 February, which was a decisive victory for the coalition forces, who liberated Kuwait and advanced into Iraqi territory. The coalition ceased their advance, and declared a cease-fire 100 hours after the ground campaign started.

Many questioned why President Bush didn't proceed to Bagdad and remove Saddam Hussein from power. Thirteen years later his son showed the folly of creating a political vacuum by removing the leadership of a country without the possibility replacing it with a viable alternative.

1991.2   FIRST RETIREMENT

After 22 years at the Office of Mental Health and 26 years of total state service I decided to retire. My career in Mental Health had peaked years before and there was little hope that I would ever find myself in a position to play a major role in the organization again. I planned to find another job and continue working for another ten years. With my retirement income from the State, I could then afford to take jobs that paid less than I had been making and continue to build up some funds for an actual retirement.

I left the building where I had once been the Associate Commissioner without fanfare, I asked my colleagues who were planning a retirement party to send the money they might have spent on the party to a local service agency where a friend was a lifelong client. The disappointment of my failure to make any significant changes in the Mental Health Service had partially subsided and my leaving was merely the beginning of the next phase of my life.

Major changes to any large established system can only happen when a combination of major circumstances converge to create the motivation and capacity for the magnitude of change that is required. No amount work in one area can singlehandedly create change across an entire system. There were moments when I thought we had most of what was needed, but as a weak link can cause an otherwise strong chain to break, without the simultaneous and sufficient coalescence of programmatic, financial, structural, political, and community support, systematic change is not possible. Change may still occur, but it will be reactive rather than proactive and the pattern of change may not be recognizable must less desirable. This perfect storm of events happened in the field of Developmental Disabilities in the 1970's. Mental Health reform still waits for new reformers, leaders, and supporters.

> *We must let go of the life we have planned,*
> *to accept the one that is waiting for us.*
> *Joseph Campbell*

1991.3   GENEALOGY: PEOPLE OF THE PAST

After retiring, I began exploring the genealogy of our family. At first finding names and dates, was very exciting. I remember the first document I found, a 1910 Federal Census containing my mother's name. At this writing, there are over 15,000 people in the family tree. This is quite a change from the handful of names and the few fragments of other people's memories that I knew as a child.

My list of family members reads like tombstones "Name, Date Born – Date Died." As the roots of the family tree gradually began to grow in my computer, I found that it was the stories, uncovered in old documents, like wills and newspapers, which gave life to the tree and meaning to the lives. The hyphen between the dates, representing their life stories, turned out to be far more interesting than the dates.

> *For that dash represents all the time*
> *that they spent alive on earth.*
> *And now only those who loved them*
> *know what that little line is worth.*
> *Linda Ellis*

In addition to the hyphens found between the dates on tomb stones, many people also use hyphens to designate their group identity. Migration and intermarriages have produced a nation in which we all have hyphenated identities. Some people retain their hyphenated group identity names to reflect their history, perhaps out of fear of losing the culture heritage that has been forging their identity for centuries. Some examples are Asian-American, African-American and Native-American. They are telling us that they are not homogeneous Americans but that they are also unique individuals from unique cultures. Alternatively, some seem to be emphasizing the "American" portion of the hyphen to tell us that while their heritage may be unique they are in important ways similar to other Americans and want to be recognized as such. For others, the hyphen may simultaneously represent both the desire to retain a tie with their history and a need to be seen as truly American. I suppose I'm European-American, but I've never used my hyphen. I've let it go to waste because while my European background is of interest to me, it is too far removed from my current identity to require constant recognition.

I have ancestors from the Netherlands, France, Germany, Ireland, Scotland, England, Wales, and North America.

Below is a summary of a few of our earliest immigrant ancestors and the countries they left behind and the cultures they tried to bring with them. These people are part of the long line of anonymous dead who produced us and have vanished with barely a trace. Our Genealogy records contain much more information about these immigrants, their ancestors, and their descendants than I could fit in this memoir and I invite you to read it.

Every man is a quotation from all his ancestors
Ralph Waldo Emerson

DUTCH IMMIGRANT ANCESTORS

<u>Garharth Von Sweringen</u> (Ron's 6th Great Grand Father) aka Gerrit van Schweringen, was born on February 04, 1635/36 in the outskirts of Amsterdam, Holland in a town called Beemsterdam. He died in 1698 in St. Mary's, Colony of Maryland. He was the youngest son of a family belonging to the nobility, and received a liberal education.

 When he was about twenty years old, the Dutch West India Company appointed Garharth officer in charge of the sale and purchase of the ship's cargo on the Prince Maurice. It was to go to Nieuwer Amstel (now New Castle, DE) in support of the Dutch colonists on the Delaware River.

The ship sailed from Amsterdam on December 21, 1656. It was to have stopped at New Amsterdam (New York City); but on March 8, 1657, it was stranded off Fire Island, and burst to pieces. In freezing weather, the passengers and crew made their way to the barren shore where they remained for several days without fire. On the third day, they sent word to Peter Stuyvesant via some local Native Americans. Governor Stuyvesant sent a sloop, which carried them to New Amsterdam. On April 16, they sailed for Fort Casimir (a Dutch fort located on a no-longer existing barrier island off New Castle, DE.)

After the wreck Gerrit asked to be relieved from the company's service, as he intended to make his living here, his request was granted. In 1664, all of the Dutch settlements (called New Netherlands) passed to the British. After a few years in America, he began spelling his name "Garrett."

He became the Sheriff of New Castle, DE but he was forced to leave town because of an unfortunate incident in which he accidently shot a noisy drunk.

He moved to St Mary's, MD, then the capital of Maryland and opened a Public house that served as a meeting place for many Revolutionary War planning meetings, which is now an archeological site.

Garharth Von Sweringen married Barbarah De Barrette, from France on March 01, 1658/59 in New Castle, Del. After her death, he married Mary Smith on October 05, 1676. There are many more details of this adventure and additional stories about Garnet and his decedents in the Gerhard Genealogy records.

FRENCH IMMIGRANT ANCESTORS

Barbarah De Barrette (Ron's 6th Great Grand Mother) was of a Norman-French family. She was born in Valenciennes, which was a part of the county of Hainaut. The region surrounding the city was involved in a long series of wars between the French, and Spanish Kings. Perhaps the war and the related demands for religious conformity influenced her decision to emigrate to America. Garharth had 13 children, some born to Barbarah, and some to his second wife Mary Smith. In 1980, a book was published that listed over 17,000 descendants of those 13-original offspring.

GERMAN IMMIGRANT ANCESTORS

Henrich Gerhards (Ron's Great Grand Father)

The basic rights achieved during the German revolutionaries of 1848 were reversed in Germany by 1851. After the failed Revolution, immigration to America increased rapidly, and in time, New York was referred to as the fourth largest German city in the world. Many disappointed German patriots came to the United States. They became known as the Forty-Eighters; among them was Heinrich Gerhards of Siegburg, Germany.

Henrich established a framing and gilding store in the lower east side of New York City. He eventually moved his family to the Bronx, which would become the family home for three generations.

In 1861 at the age of 38, Henrich enlisted in the Union Army. He served in Company `E' of the 66th Infantry Regiment from New York. During the period of Henry's service, his company fought in 29 Civil War battles. These included the 3-day battle at Gettysburg. During which, 14,530 Union soldiers were wounded. Henrich Gerhards was one of them. His wounds lead to his discharge and both he and his wife Lena received pensions for life because his injuries. Some of his children eventually dropped the "s" at the end of the name.

Lena Eichwald (Ron's Great Grand Mother)

German immigrants first began arriving in the New World in the late 17th century, with a major settlement established in Pennsylvania. Large-scale immigration began a quarter century later, following a major war, which devastated the German Rhineland. Thousands of German refugees immigrated to England and then to New York and Pennsylvania. From this time until after the Second World War, repeated cycles of political unrest and conflict caused large numbers of Germans to flee their homelands for the United States

. Since 1820, more Germans have immigrated to the U.S. than any other national group (as of 2010.)

Lena left her home in Erdmannrode, Germany and arrived in New York City on Sep. 17, 1852 aboard the S.S. Espendola at the age of 28. "We made the voyage in about six weeks, half the time of the former voyage. It was a modern vessel and quite fast and as large as the largest of those days," noted from another passenger aboard the same ship.

Although Henrich was raised Catholic, Lena was Lutheran and he and Lena were married at the Evangelical Lutheran St Mathew's Church, in lower Manhattan on Nov. 1, 1863.

She and Henrich had six children and she died on 07 Dec 1927.

GERMAN JEWISH IMMIGRANT ANCESTORS

Although of the same nationality as other Germans, Jewish immigrants maintained a distinct culture and so they are listed separately here.

Julius Tobias (Ron's Great Grand Father) immigrated in 1851 after being wounded in the Austrian service. Perhaps he was wounded in the 1848 rebellion in Vienna.

He enlisted as a 2nd Lieutenant on Oct 26, 1861 and served in Company H, 13th Infantry Battalion Connecticut: "The Welsh Riffles." His unit fought in 35 battles during the Civil War. He also helped an escaped slave join the US Army and hid him from the slave owners' posse.

Julia Borchardt (Ron's Great Grand Mother) married Julius Tobias on Feb 15, 1849. She served as a nurse in a New Haven Hospital that had been converted into a Military Rehabilitation Center.

Aside from Julius, Julia, and their daughter Estelle, I knew very little about my Jewish family or *Mishpocheh*, [1] until I received, an email from my second cousin twice removed Amy Feigenbaum who had found my name on a genealogy web site. She been searching for my Grandmother Estelle and supplied me with hundreds of names, facts, and sources of information about the Tobias family, including Great Grand Mother Estelle's ten siblings.

[1] *Mishpocheh, from the Hebrew word* משפחה *(mišpāḥā) means distant family.*

SCOTCH IRISH IMMIGRANT ANCESTORS

Their roots go back to the lowlands of Scotland. They spoke English and were Presbyterian. They were different from their Highland cousins. They didn't wear kilts, didn't belong to clans, or speak Gaelic. But they weren't English either. They didn't support the Anglican Church. They held onto the memory of bloody massacres that their ancestors suffered at the hands of English conquerors centuries earlier especially the 1745 massacre at Culloden.

Their history in Scotland was not pleasant as they were caught, both geographically and politically, between the English to the south and the Highlanders to the north.

In the seventeenth century, when Scottish and English land-grant owners sought tenants to populate the northern region of Ireland and drive out the Catholics, the Lowland Scots fit the bill. To the English monarchy, the Lowland Scots were preferable to the Irish Catholics.

But as the decades passed, the transplanted Scots did not vow allegiance to the Church of England, detesting tithing to a church they didn't support, and were governed by laws that prevented them from voting, bearing arms, or serving in the military. They could not be married, baptized, or buried with the assistance of any minister who was not ordained by the church of the state.

The Scots-Irish of the eighteenth century considered themselves Irish. Many came from families who had lived in Ireland for 150 years. It wasn't until the Irish immigrants of the 1845-49 potato famine arrived in America that this group began distinguishing themselves as Scots-Irish. The Scots-Irish migration was largely complete when the American Revolution began in 1776. Conversely, nearly all of the Irish-Catholic immigrants arrived in America in the middle of the nineteenth century or later.

The early Scots-Irish pioneers to America settled in Pennsylvania, where they found the Quakers more to their liking than the Catholics in Maryland or the Anglicans in Virginia.

By 1730, the Scots-Irish had made their way into the Shenandoah Valley of Virginia and to the Piedmont country of the Carolinas in the mid-eighteenth century.

After the war with England ended in 1783, the restless Scots-Irish led the way behind such trailblazers as Daniel Boone. They intermarried -- the reason that so many Americans can trace their roots to this group. Today's Appalachian dialects are forms of Scottish and Irish brogues.

Many of the founding fathers, including John Hancock and Charles Thomson, were of Scots-Irish heritage. Fourteen U.S. presidents ranging from Andrew Jackson to George W. Bush boast Scots-Irish bloodlines.

John MILLS (Ron's 6th Great Grand Father) and many other Scots-Irish immigrated in 1682 into the Port of Philadelphia.

ENGLISH IMMIGRANT ANCESTORS

Christopher HOLDER (Ron's 8th Great Grand Father) Immigrated from England on 27 Jul 1656. Christopher's Maternal Grand Father (Ron's 10th Great Grandfather was Christopher Wren the famous English Architect.) The Holders were in Costal

Massachusetts at the same time and place as the original Mayflower Pilgrims. However, it took 400 hundred years for the Holders and the Pilgrims to merge when in 1997 the ninth Great Grand Son of Christopher Holder (Brian Gerhard) married the 10th Great Grand Daughter of Mayflower passenger William White (LeAnn Maxwell.)

Thomas IVEY (Ron's 7th Great Grand Father) immigrated in 1625 to Virginia and died on 25 Jan 1655. His many descendants established many businesses throughout the south. I have a copy of Joseph B. Ivey's memoirs that lists many of our ancestors.

WALES ANCESTORS

The history of Wales begins with the arrival of Neanderthals at least 230,000 years ago, Homo Sapiens arrived by about 31,000 BC.

The presence of Neanderthal genes among modern Homo Sapiens contributed to Europeans being able to resist the diseases that killed off millions of Natives from North and South America beginning in the 15th century. 2.5 % of the genome of an average person living outside Africa today is made up of the lifesaving Neanderthal DNA.

A number of kingdoms formed in Wales after the Romans departed from Britain in the 5th century, The Norman conquerors of England, led to the Welsh kingdoms coming gradually under the sway of the English crown. Under England's authority, Wales became part of the United Kingdom. Yet, the Welsh retained their language and culture in spite of heavy English dominance. In the 18th century, Wales was greatly affected by the Methodist revival and the Industrial Revolution. Industry. In the 20th century nationalist sentiment and interest in self-determination rose. In a 1997 referendum, Welsh voters approved the devolution of the National Assembly for Wales.

Hopkins WILLIAMS (Ron's 3rd Great Grand Father) immigrated to America in the early part of the 19th century. His decedents settled largely in North Carolina.

IRISH ANCESTORS

William DOYNE, (Ron's 7th Great Grandfather immigrated from Carrichfergus, Ireland in about 1647. He lived in Maryland, which was a Dutch colony at the time.

Robert SHANKLAND, (Ron's 8th Great Grand Father,) immigrated from Fermanagh, Ireland between 1720 and 1740. Our Shankle relatives settled in the Carolinas.

NATIVE AMERICAN ANCESTORS

People who have ancestry going back 10 generations or more in North America have a 40% chance of being part Native American.

Ann AYN, (Ron's 4th Great Grandmother lived with a Native American tribe and may have been a member of the Catawba Tribe of North Carolina. She got her name because when she first started attending the missionary school "Ann" was the only English word she knew, so the teacher called her Ann Ann on his records. To be considered a member of the tribe, a person must be at least one-eighth or 12.5 % Native American. If Ann was Native American, which only DNA tests can now prove, I would be only one-thirty-second or 3.125% Native American.

I hope you will go out and let stories,
which is life, happen to you,
and that you will work with these stories,
water them with your blood and tears and your laughter till they bloom, till you
yourself burst into bloom.
Clarissa Pinkola Estés

Ancestors of Ronald J. GERHARD

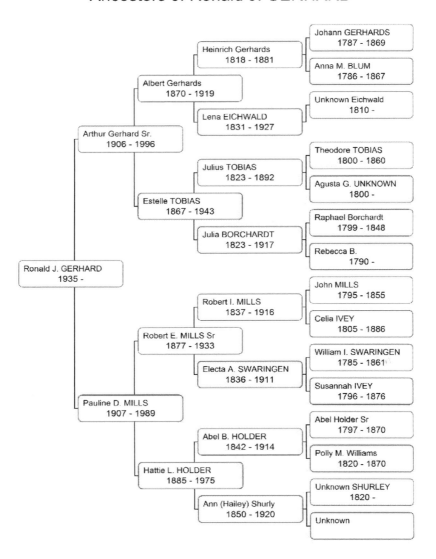

In the Tree of Life our roots are forever intertwined.

Anonymous

1991.5   SMALL WORLD

I know of 63 of my relatives who fought in the Civil War, 25 fought for the north and 38 for the south.

One of the many battles that my Paternal Great Grandfather Sgt. Henrich Gerhards fought in with Co. E, 66th NY Infantry Regiment was the battle at Gettysburg. Regiments from North Carolina were also engaged in that deadly combat. Two of the soldiers from NC were my Maternal Great Grandfather Sgt. Robert Ivey Mills from Co. C, 28th NC Infantry Regiment, and my Maternal Great Grandfather Pvt. Abel Barney Holder from Co A fifth NC Infantry Regiment. Our northern and southern ancestors likely fought against each other on July 2, 1863, the day that a ball tore into Heinrich's thigh as the NC units attacked the NY position on Cemetery Ridge. It is possible that one of my Maternal Great Grandfathers shot my Paternal Great Grandfather at Gettysburg. But the story doesn't end there.

My Paternal Great Grandmother Julia Tobias was a nurse working at Knight General Army Hospital in New Haven, CN. Heinrich spent three months at that hospital where 25,340 soldiers were treated from 1862 to 1865.

Therefore, it is possible that after one of my Great Grandfathers from NC shot my Great Grandfather from NY, my Great Grandmother from CN nursed him back to health.

My first cousin 3 times removed, Henry Clay Swaringen was in Co. K, NC 28th Infantry Regiment. He died at Gettysburg at the age of 19. I hope my grandfather Heinrich didn't shoot him.

Twenty-five percent of all Confederate casualties at Gettysburg were from North Carolina.

1991.6   ROCKEFELLER COLLEGE

After retiring from the NYS Office of Mental Health in September of 1991, I began working as a Senior Research Scientist at The Center for Human Services Research at the State University of New York at Albany. The majority of our work involved evaluating Social Welfare programs operated in New York City by the State Department of Social Services.

I had a small staff, which included PhDs, statisticians, clerks, and stenos. I was able to bring in over 1 million dollars in state and federal grant money during the four years I worked at the research center.

My office was at the SUNY Albany's downtown campus. I spent my summer lunch breaks in Washington Park among the flowers and birds and winters freezing in the aging building. I spent a great deal of my time in New York City and Washington D.C.

I was the Principal Investigator or project manager of eight-multiyear research projects. The subject of the evaluative research included Drug Addiction Treatment, Medicaid Managed Care, Day Care Centers, Infant Abandonment, High-risk Mothers, Foster Care, and Child Sexual Abuse. I also served on the National Evaluation Committee, for the National Addiction Training Center. US Dept. of Health and Human Services, Wash. DC

The research was generally interesting spoiled only by the palace politics that frequently caused studies to be watered down to mere activity counts. Bureaucrats often prevented the projects, which were advertised as Evaluative Studies, to delete any enquiry dealing with the efficacy or efficiency of the target program. Often the goal of the study was not to determine whether or not the projects were meeting their goals or actually helping people, but merely to ensure that any program for which funding was available would continue. Conducting research was generally required by funders but they rarely provided any requirement that the research be conducted in a rigorous manner.

1992.1 & 1941   NYC RAILROAD STATIONS

After one particularly frustrating day trying to interview some New York City employees, who saw my presence as an opportunity to bargain for higher salaries, I left the building with my assistant as the staff closed the building due to approaching inclement weather. The door locked behind us and as we stood on the Grand Concourse in the Bronx, scanning the three lanes of traffic for a taxi, it soon became apparent that this was not an ordinary storm. The wind was so strong that the rain was not falling but sailing horizontally. There were no taxis and the bus service that we were depending on had already been halted. We learned later that the major bridges and all tunnels in and out of Manhattan were closed due to flooding and high winds. There are no hotels in the area; our situation was looking desperate. Traffic stopped as the light turned red. I noticed a car about 50 feet and 3 lanes away that had a wooden picket fence behind the driver's seat. Suspecting this was a Gypsy cab that used the fence as a form of protection for the driver; I walked out into the center of the street in front of the stopped cars and signaled for the cab to pull over to the curb. I never believed that the driver would respond and didn't believe that he could cut off three lanes of traffic and make it to the curb even if he wanted to respond. Fortunately, I was wrong on both counts. The cab cut across three lanes of horn blaring traffic and stopped in front of us. We had only been standing there for five minutes but we were both soaked to the skin, in spite of our heavy winter coats.

I asked the driver how much it cost to go to Penn Station; he asked how much I paid last time. This was another stroke of luck. The cabbie was a recent immigrant and didn't know how to get to Penn Station much less how much to charge. I would have paid him all the cash I had just to get to a safe neighborhood or a hotel. I told him $20 dollars, but gave him $40 when we arrived a half hour later. "The Storm from Hell," as the December 11, 1992 northeaster was called created tides that swamped seawalls and knocked out electrical service to New York City's 25 subway lines, closed Airports, and submerged highways in Manhattan under four feet of water. PATH trains to New Jersey and Amtrak trains to parts of upstate New York were shut down for days. Some Manhattan streets were showered with falling glass as hurricane-force winds ripped windowpanes from the sides of skyscrapers. Coastal flooding damaged 20,000 homes and forced thousands into emergency shelters. Coastlines were rapidly and severely eroded and some sandy beaches were replaced with 6 foot vertical drops.

We waited in Penn Station while Amtrak officials determined if the tracks between Manhattan and Albany were safe to use. We finally left for home several hours later, but only got as far as Poughkeepsie and had another hour wait as the tracks that ran close to the Hudson River were tested. I arrived at the Albany-Rensselaer station 4 hours late.

(1941) Mom settled Artie and me on the Pullman train that would take us to Cheraw, South Carolina for a years' stay with our grandmother, Hattie Mills. We had been living with Mom and our Aunt Velma for the summer in Central Islip. Not having a close attachment to Mom was a blessing at times like this, as the pain of separation that most children might experience simply didn't exist. In order to be homesick, you must first have a home. Artie and I were like trees in winter, we let the ill winds of life flow through us without being rustled.

Aunt Velma, who later in life preferred to be called Aunt Ann, and her daughter Joan Brown, had spent the summer with us in the little bungalow in Central Islip where Mom lived. They had returned to Grandma's house in Cheraw, SC a few weeks earlier. Now Artie and I were to make the trip alone. Mom helped us find seats in the Pullman car and tried to take my coat, which wouldn't be needed in the warm weather of South Carolina. I would not let it go, for I had filled the pockets with my favorite treats.

In those days, many people canned their own homegrown vegetables and fruits. While vegetables were "put-up" in Mason jars with screw on lids, jars of homemade jellies were generally sealed by pouring melted wax onto the top of the freshly made and still warm jelly. When first removed from the jar with a table knife, the bottom of the wax lid was covered with sweet grape jelly and the wax could be chewed like chewing gum. This was the closest thing to chewing gum that many poor children from that generation ever experienced.

At 5 years old, I never noticed that Mom must have been living in this house long enough to harvest the grapes and make the jelly. It was just 2 miles from the foster home were Artie and I had lived the year before; but we rarely saw her and never visited her home.

Before we left the house for the train station, I went to the basement, removed the wax seals from all the jelly jars, and hid them in my coat pockets. Mom yelled, I cried and Artie watched. The battle ended when a stranger on the train offered to trade his pocket watch for the jelly-covered wax. I accepted, Mom left with the wax and Artie and I set off for our next adventure. We watched the houses and telephone poles speed by the train window until it got dark. By some creative genius, the porter magically converted our single bench seat into two beds. Artie took the lower berth and I lay in the upper berth watching through the rain-streaked window as the lights of many towns with many roads leading to many homes sped by. I tried to peer into the widows of the speeding trackside homes to see the families living inside. But, like the other families I had known, they changed all too quickly. Soon the houses and towns faded into dreams of jellied wax and pocket watches. This was a new and exciting time.

(1992) There was only one taxi at the train station, and it was fully occupied. As I stood near the cab, I overheard the passengers giving the driver the address where they wished to be taken. They only knew the name of the apartment complex, no town, and no street address. The cabbie didn't know where it was; I knew that the apartments were a few blocks from my home. I told them that I would direct them to the apartments if they would make room for me in the already crowded cab.

It was a great ride home, the family was visiting their grandparents for the holidays and we were all in good spirits.

The next day was Saturday; Donna Straub, Reg's niece, was celebrating her 25th Birthday. Her father had rented a hall and invited dozens of family members and many of Donna's friends for this coming of age birthday bash. It was still snowing, but I didn't want to disappoint Donna, so I told Reg that we would drive to Long Island even though I had just returned the night before. I was very fortunate that Reg came from a large and close family. In her family, I witnessed and then experienced family attachments. Later, as we built a home for our own family I tried to put what I learned to practice, and Reg acted as the mortar that held our family together.

1993.1   WALKING ALONE TOGETHER

On one of my travels to Jamaica, Queens I was struck by the saddnesb of what I saw. A young mother was walking with her four or five-year-old son trailing some 20 feet behind. He was struggling to catch-up but she never waited, slowed down, or even seemed to notice him or his problem. She crossed streets without ever looking for him much less holding his hand. I wondered how she could be so careless and inattentive and I wondered if I were misjudging her. This was not the suburbs with hovering parents making play dates for their kids. I'll never know if what I saw was just a simple difference in parenting styles or the beginning of a tragic ending for the little boy. I'll never know exactly what I was looking at ... but I'll never forget what I saw. Or, perhaps it merely reminded me of a boy separated from his mother in a subway car because she did not provide the attention that he needed to keep him safe.

1994.1   RETIRED AGAIN

After just three and one half years in my new career the State's fiscal crisis caused the Research Center to cut back. It took several months to find another job. Looking back, I now believe that the move from research to health care administration was a very good move for me. This would be my forth-major career move from Anesthetist to Mental Health Administrator to Researcher and now to Health Care administrator at a Child Care Agency.

1994.2 & 1942   FIRST DAYS

It was late fall and the brown leaves that so vibrantly painted the landscape with brilliant yellows, reds, and oranges just weeks before danced beneath the naked branches of the dormant shrubs, as they circled in on their icy fate. The gray shadow of a solitary young boy swaying aimlessly on the playground swing was visible from the window of my new office. It was reminiscent of another boy who had sat on another swing in another orphanage some two hundred miles away. The scenes were remarkably similar although more than five decades separated them in time. Moment and memory seemed to merge as the years dissolved and the boys became as one.

(1942) He sat waiting for the housemother to finish sending the other children off to school, and come out and take him to his first day of second grade at his new school in Sayville, Long Island, NY. He was already a week late for school as the orphanage required that all of its boys be baptized and circumcised, so he had spent the previous week at St. John's Episcopal Hospital in Brooklyn, NY with wire stitches in what was left of his private parts. As he waited for the housemother, he busied himself with the details of the steel gray swing set and the boundaries of the playground. The playground was small, with an unusually high cyclone fence, which in spite of its un-scalable height, could neither imprison nor protect, for it only ran along the Southern border of the yard. The remaining perimeter was enclosed by trees to the East with a path leading to Browns River that was little more than a creek, where one day he would catch frogs and turtles. A driveway to the North lead to the church where he would first encounter his God, and a road to the West that led to the places where his memories still resided.

The two-large white multi-story stucco buildings were filled with strange people and strange things. Even his own things were strange, purchased new for the occasion of this, his fifth home in the past four years. He would have liked to see his old plaster friend, Ferdinand the Bull, but Mr. Morgan had thrown it out when its left leg had fallen off a few weeks earlier . . . it wound up in the garbage pail together with that night's empty quart bottle of Ballantine Ale. The memories of his last home drifted through his mind, but he avoided direct contact with them. It was like seeing someone in a crowd who you'd rather not speak to, their presence lingers in the back of your mind until time saves you, they pass-by, and pretend they didn't see you either.

The absence of his most recent foster mom, Mrs. Morgan, could not be so easily avoided. He was still living in the memory of a life that was never really his, but his recollection of her was too dear to be ignored, but too distant to be enjoyed. It hung in the air around him like the smell of the soup she often cooked on chilly and damp Long Island mornings. She was the only person he ever remembered having gently touched him on purpose; a fact that he never shared with anyone, not because it was a secret, but because in his life there were no occasions for speaking of feelings.

(1994) The swing swayed as the boy walked away. I returned to busying myself with the details of organizing my first day at my new job. Strangers walked past the door, some peered in, some had words of welcome, and some perhaps had unspoken feelings about the stranger in Room 139. I thought about how much I had in common with the boy on the swing outside my office window. This new job seemed perfectly matched with my training and experience, both professional and personal. It didn't take long however, for me to realize that I was mistaken. The events that brought children to the Parsons Child and Family Center of Albany, NY where I was beginning my forth career, as Director of Health Services, were quite different from those that brought me, my brother Artie, and the other forty or so kids to the Children's Cottages of Sayville, fifty-three years earlier. In the 1940's, many families were still recovering from the great depression and Day Care centers did not yet exist. Children where often placed in the care of others because their parents could not afford to keep them home. Single working mothers, like mine, had few options, especially if they were separated from their extended families. On the other hand, most of the children at Parsons were placed there by the Department of Social

Services because of parental abuse or neglect. Their childhoods were taken captive by circumstances over which they had no control, circumstances not alleviated by those who were entrusted to protect them but actually created by them.

Many of the Sayville kids were tempered by hard lives. Most of the Parsons kids were trodden by harsh lives.

A tile contributed by the Gerhard family to the Contributors Wall of the gym at Parsons Child and Family Center, Albany, NY. shows a solitary boy sitting on a swing

1994.3   THERAPY DOGS

It was 9 a.m. and the examination room door was closed, so I knew that Linda was about to receive her daily treatment for her extensive skin disorder. It was difficult to understand just what Linda was experiencing as she screamed each morning as a nurse gently applied a salve to the dry areas of her skin. Was it anger or annoyance or perhaps it was pain or fear, Linda's disabilities prevented her from telling the nurse why she screamed, just as she could never clearly tell her other helpers what she really felt, needed or wanted. But this morning it was quiet and I knew what was happening behind that beige door.

Each morning Linda would sit at the edge of the examination table with her arms crossed and her legs dangling over the edge. But today she sat on the floor in the middle of the room with her legs crossed and her arms cuddling the big black Labrador Retriever. The nurse applies the salve as usual, but there was no screaming this morning as Linda petted the dog who was the first of many therapy dogs that would be provided by the staff of the health services unit. As the program grew social workers would occasionally borrow a dog and take a child, who had difficulty talking in the professional setting of an office, out for a walk. From time to time I would see a child holding the leash of one of the canine therapist strolling down Academy Road, chatting away with their human therapist.

The use of canines to help mankind is known throughout the world. They have been used for guarding flocks, tracking, hunting, search and rescue, leading the blind, and in assisting the deaf and physically challenged. The bond between dogs and people dates back to early history, but it wasn't until recently that a correlation was acknowledged between this bond and the emotional health of humans. Studies have shown that a person holding or petting an animal will cause a lowering of blood pressure, the release of strain and tension, and can draw out a person from loneliness and depression. Therapy dogs are used settings such as schools, hospitals, and nursing homes.

Therapy dogs are not service dogs who are trained to perform specific tasks to help people with disabilities such as guide dogs for the blind.

I was very proud of the fact that I had helped to establish this program and I was greatly discouraged when it was discontinued a few years after I retired. I suppose there was a good reason to end it, but I wonder if whoever made that decision really understood the good reasons to start it and what criteria they might have used weigh the merits and liabilities of a program that now has worldwide recognition with well documented studies proving its value.

1994.4   ALTERNATIVE TO VIOLENCE

The Alternative to Violence Program was created in the 1970's though a joint effort of some prisoners in Sing Sing Correctional Institution at Ossining, NY and members of a nearby Quaker Community. It attempts to provide participating prison inmates with some ways of dealing with stress that do not involve violent or impulsive behavior. It's based on the belief that each of us has within us the power to transform situations in positive ways. It also tries to establish a community of like-minded men or women within the prison who can support each other as they learn and practice their new coping skills. After taking a few training sessions with the Quaker Community in Albany, NY, I began volunteering at Green Correctional Institution in Coxsackie, NY. Most of the men in the dozen or so weekend groups I met with were under 25 years old and from New York City. Some of the groups referred to me as OT (prison jargon for Old Timer) and some as Real Ron (my adjective name during the sessions) and some as Real Ron from the Hood (a reference to the fact that I was born in the Bronx.)

The format is very affirming and the process, which excludes lectures, is comprised totally of experiential teachings and discussions. For example, to teach a session on "Cooperation" the class is divided into small groups of five or six and each group is seated at a separate table. Each participant is given an envelope containing several pieces of colored cardboard cut into irregular shapes. The goal is for each person to arrange his/her pieces into a 6-inch square. However, the pieces are arranged in such a way that no individual has the necessary pieces to form a square. Each person places his/her pieces in front of them on the table visible for all to see. The rules include no talking or communication of any kind, and no one is allowed to take a piece that they need to form their square from another person's pile. This can be quite frustrating as people are helpless to complete their own task. Eventually someone realizes that the rules do not prohibit passing pieces to others when you notice that you have a piece that they need. Soon all the squares are completed as the other-centered nature of the problem is mastered. Discussion follows and insights abound. There are dozens of other sessions that use a wide variety of means to teach without lecture, affirm one another at every opportunity, and begin the process of creating a supporting community.

I never teach my pupils.
I only attempt to provide the conditions
in which they can learn.
Albert Einstein

My weekends generally started on Friday afternoon with the same question: "What am I doing here?" As the two dozen or so men walked into the room, I felt that I had so little in common with them that the weekend was bound to be a flop. However, they always ended on Sunday afternoon in the same way: with hugs and words of hope that was not apparent at the onset. I also learned that biases based on stereotypes could not be willed away. Getting to know the men as individuals and not just as members of an unappreciated group was the only cure for the undeserved prejudice that I felt toward many of the men at the beginning of the weekends. For me the biases that I acquired throughout my life are a part of me, just like a physical aliment. I know it's there but I don't let it define who I am or let it control my life. I can't control how I feel, even feelings I don't want, but I can control how I respond to those feelings, including how I think about them and the credence I give them when they arise within me. Some neurologists are exploring the possibility that fear of others with notable differences from use may be encoded in our DNA. A remnant from a time when every new experience was fraught with danger. But whether the bias is learned or inherited we are still free to decide how to respond to it in the same way that we choose to respond to other impulses or emotions.

I have among my keepsakes the notes that many of the men wrote to me during closing hours of the weekends. Some had learned as much as I did from the experience.

In the long run. we find what we expect.
We shall be fortunate then if we expect great things.
Thoreau

I remember many of the men and hope that they are safe and living with loved ones, and that they are living in a way that will be of value to others. I know that this work could not change lives that faced many challenges, but if it helped to support or encourages one man at a time when he was trying to overcome his own challenges, it was well worth the effort.

I volunteered at the prison until 2001 and continued providing the occasional workshop for local schools until 2003.

1995.1   GREGORY GRADUATES FROM COLLEGE

This letter was written to Gregory Gerhard upon his graduation from college in June 1995.

Dear Greg

At times like this, I always feel that, as the father, I am supposed to say something very important. However, I do not have any earth-shattering comments for you today. Instead, some simple feelings seem in order.

I do not want to tell you how much I love you, because I want you to be free to be angry with me. I do not want to tell how proud I am of you, because I do not want you to feel the burden of having to live up to my expectations. I do not want to tell you how much I admire you, because I do not want you to feel unwarranted guilt about anything you may have done wrong.

But Greg, I do hope that every good thing finds its way into your life, and that you will recognize them, nurture them, and share them with many friends.

I really like you, and hope that someday, when you no longer need a father to support or guide you, that I may be one of those friends who share some of the blessing life has to offer.

With much LOVE, PRIDE and ADMIRATION,

Love, Dad

1995.2   CANCUN CANCELADO, COZUMEL BUENO

Reg and I decided to take a brief vacation, which included a four-day cruise followed by four days lying on the beach on Sand Key, Florida at a Sheraton Hotel.

After leaving our first stop, Key West, the cruse was next scheduled to stop at Cancun, Mexico. However, the sea was too rough for the small boats that were to ferry passengers from the ship to the mainland at Cancun. The pier at Cancun was too shallow for the large cruise ship so we were diverted to the Island of Cozumel whose port could accommodate deep draft vessels. There was little to see or do on the island as the tourist trade was just beginning to expand with the recent expansion of the deep-water piers. We joined a bus tour of the Island, which included visits to several of its Mayan ruins. Reuben, the driver of the bus and tour guide had the short stocky build that hinted of his Mayan ancestry. There were few other travelers and Reg and I were able to spend most of the day speaking to Reuben. He was very concerned that the children growing up on the Island had little knowledge or interest in their Mayan heritage and he wanted to start a library that would provide them with information about the history of the Island and the culture of their ancestors. I was reading a book about the Mayans at the time and I took Rueben's address so I could mail it to him when I finished reading it during our stay in Florida. During the next few years, I found many books and magazine stories about Cozumel and mailed them to Reuben.

Today there are 10 museums on the Island. The brochure for one of them, the Museo de la Isla de Cozumel, reads: "You will learn about how the Island of Cozumel was formed and inhabited, and how it became an important center for trade within the Mayan civilization." I never heard from Reuben so I don't if he ever received the materials I sent or if he ever managed to open his library, and I will never know if he played a role in establishing this or any of the other nine museums. It is enough to know that it exists and that future generations of Mexican children living on the Island will know that their history includes so much more than the tourist trade that currently dominates the Island's economy.

A Mayan calendar has hung over our fireplace since 1995. It reminds me of Reuben and of the children whom I never met, but who meant so much to him.

1995.3　　　　　　　　　　　　　　　CARRYING TEDDY

Teddy, whose official name was "Theodog," was a walking hug and our family pet when the boys were growing up in Delmar. The five of us each had a special bond with him; similar to the attachment we have with those exceptional people who by virtue of their warmth make everyone who knows them feel like their best friend. I often think of Teddy running through the snow as the boys' cross-country skied and played in the woods behind our house.

On one late winter evening, Teddy stood at the back door, saying nothing, just patiently waiting and knowing that I would understand and respond to his needs as had happened so often in the past. I opened the door and he strolled out on his nightly rounds of the neighborhood. A few minutes later, I had the strange feeling that something was wrong and that Teddy was in trouble and had a need that patience alone could not resolve. I dressed against the cold night and walked toward the road. There I saw Teddy, spread-eagle on a thin patch of ice, and weakened by age, unable to call for help or free himself from his frigid snare. I lifted him up in my arms, carried him home, and placed him on the family room couch, his favorite, but forbidden sanctuary. I wondered if he shared my thoughts about the implications of his infirmity as I remembered his gradual decline over the preceding year.

In a few months, I would be carrying him again, this time in the cardboard coffin provided by the veterinarian. I placed him in his final resting place, a grave I had dug for him near the pond where we had so often strolled, by the path to the woods where he had run with boys, under the large natural headstone that Gregory had found in a nearby field. The collar that I placed in a notch in the stone would be joined many years later by the one belonging to his successor Keppie, whose ashes were sprinkled on the site where Teddy was buried.

1996.1   HEALTH IS A COMMUNITY AFFAIR

Respect for Self and Others - Written for Parsons Newsletter "The Communiqué."

In 1966, the National Commission on Community Health Services wrote a report entitled "Health Is a Community Affair." In 1996, the Communiqué begins a new feature with the same title.

One difference between the two texts with the same title is the definition of "community." The community of the sixties was the government, the agencies, and the health professions. The community of the nineties is us, not just us alone, as individuals, but also us together as 'community. '

This feature will periodically explore some ways that our community can create healthier life styles for the people of Parsons: client people and staff people.

This first article addresses the most fundamental element of working together to build a healthy lifestyle, self-respect; and its common side effect respect for others.

The frailties that contribute to our need for growth are as much a part of us as are the strengths that help us to grow. The oak does not curse the acorn, but lives within it until it is able to grow beyond its shell. Similarly, we do not have to reject what we are today in order to become what we will be tomorrow.

If we respect ourselves though we may be too fat, too thin, too weak, too fearful, or otherwise imperfect, then we can respect others with their imperfections. If we can respect others, warts and all, then as a community we can serve each other without criticism, we can care for each other without condemnation and we can help each other grow without the need for keeping up or keeping score. We can work together to create a sustainable healthy life style: a life style that builds up without putting down, a life style in which affirmation abounds and every attempt regardless of how modest is supported, a life-style in which all persons are respected for who they are, not for what they have achieved. Whether our personal striving is for low fat or high esteem, our collective goal is the promotion of the striver.

Queries for the month:

How do I show respect for others and myself?
How do I strive to improve my health; how can the community help?
How are those around me striving; how can I help?

1996.2   THE QUALITY OF DAY-TO DAY LIFE

"The Quality of Day-to-Day Life," was written for the Parsons Newsletter "The Communiqué."

Last month's article addressed the issue of self-respect and its common side effect, respect for others. This month the focus is on the life-style that we create and share with others at Parsons.

Client life-styles generally fall outside the area of concern of human service providers. Usually, clients leave their homes and go to the providers' place of business. There, they receive a specific and time-limited service. This system of service works well for people whose problems are appendages to their lives. But what of those people who have life-defining problems, or life defining services? People whose service networks are so complex or extensive that they not only provide the needed aid but also actually define the life-style in which the service and all else will occur.

The transition from life-enriching service to life-defining program occurs almost daily at childcare agencies such as Parsons. It occurs whenever we shift from adding a service to the life of a client, to adding a client to the life of a service. Every time a child is admitted to one of our life-defining programs, we assume a responsibility that is far more fundamental than providing good service. We have also assumed the duty of providing for a healthy life-style. The magnitude of this responsibility is revealed by this partial list of the synonyms for the word healthy: vigorous, restorative, hygienic, fit, competent, worthy, prepared, equipped, stable, whole, abundant, etc.

Life at Parsons is defined by the structures we provide such as home, school, and neighborhood, and, by our efforts to infuse these structures with the necessities of childhood: safety, nurturing, love, and development. To these common elements, which are found in most communities, we add our professional services.

Through performance improvement and staff development activities, the quality of professional services is constantly being reviewed and improved. In an effort to establish a similar performance improvement process aimed at the quality of day-to-day life, a Task Force on Healthy Life-Styles has been established. The Task Force will provide each of us with the opportunity to help make Parsons not just a great place to receive service, but more importantly, an excellent village in which to live. As Hilary Rodham Clinton asserts, it does take a village to raise a child. For many of our clients that village is the Parsons campus.

"The enemy of the excellent is the good; the enemy of the good is the poor." S. Corey

Queries for the month:
Do I really know what it is like to live within a Parsons' program?
How does this life compare to what I desire for my own family?
What can I do to help create a healthier life style?

1997.1   BRIAN AND LEANN

We were delighted when Brian and LeAnn asked us to host their wedding in our back-yard garden. The garden was both beautiful and symbolically important as our entire family had heavily invested in its creation and maintenance.

The following was written by and read by Reg and Ron to LeAnn & Brian Gerhard at their wedding.

COMMON GROUND: Life is like a garden. Life partners are like gardeners. Building a marriage is like tending a garden.
Concept:
THE GARDEN: comes from the labor of the gardener.
THE MARRIAGE: comes from the labor of the partners.
Vision:
The Plot Plan is the gardener's dream of the beauty and purpose to come.
Your converging dreams are not a map that guides your every step, but a compass that guides your general direction and sometimes needs adjusting.
Preparation:
The soil is what the garden brings to the gardener a place for roots to grow and the capacity to nourish.
The marriage can become your soil, where you plant your roots and find the source of your nourishment.
Tilling
Tilling makes the soil ready for the seed.
Your preparation has molded you into able individuals, capable of being alone but worthy of being together. Your individual strength will be become secondary to your collective strength. This surrender of personal preeminence will not make you weaker but will create a union that is stronger than either of you could be alone
Planting
Not every flower planted will grow, but the ones that are not planted will never grow. Choosing what to include in your lives is an ongoing process of compromise, achieved through negotiation and enabled by empathy.
Watering

Water does not provide nutrients to the plants but equips them to use the nutrients provided elsewhere

Just as water prepares a plant to grow, so respect, and encouragement prepare each person to grow from what they're afraid they might be, to what they hope they can be.

Fertilizing

The gardener has to nurture, in order for nature to take its course.

Like fertilizer, a material wealth is necessary. But too much fertilizer can act like poison. Many a garden has been ruined by too much food. A shared dream should not be sold to the highest bidder

Weeding

Sometime the weeds require a hoe . . . sometimes a ho ho ho. Humor is like the drop of oil that keeps our engines from burning out.

Choosing what to remove is just as important as choosing what to keep. after all, sculpting a beautiful statue is merely a matter of removing what is unwanted to discover the beauty which was always been present within the stone.

Mulching

Mulch protects the seeds, preserves the moisture, and beautifies the soil.

Protect each other, preserve your dignity and your beauty will grow

Growth

We can't pull up the plant to see how the roots are doing. Too much inspection will kill the plant, be patient, and let it grow.

Don't be critical about how it's going, but make a commitment to keep it going. Believe in the process and be patient, if you plant your field of dreams, it will grow. Your acceptance of each other will allow you to participate in each other's beauty and their beauty will become a part of you and make you more than you could ever be alone. You are no longer together just because of whom your partner is, but also because of whom you become when you're with them.

Harvest

Edible foods to sustain the body, beautiful flowers to sustain the senses and peaceful gardens to sustain the mind are achieved by work that sustains the spirit. You are not the laborer in your garden, but its author, and participating in the natural process with a supernatural partner.

Your dreams of the harvest will sustain you when you have only faith in each other to support your hopes for the future.

The fruits of the harvest will sustain you during times of plenty.

Your memories of past harvests will sustain you in times of hardship.

Recycle

We're not separate from the earth, but a part of it, just like the soil and the water.

In the same way, we're not separate from each other, but united to each other by physical, psychological, social, and spiritual bonds.

CONCLUSION: Life is about taking care of the earth, including taking care of each other. We can do this by our work, by the example we show in how we do our work, or by leaving behind something of value for those who follow. This value may come from our efforts or the efforts of our children who accomplish the things we never got to. The thing is to try . . . to persevere . . . and to enjoy the experience.

1997.2   BREAD AND HONEY

After Brian and LeAnn's wedding, Reg and I decided to take a mini vacation trip to Canada. We drove to Montreal, stayed in an upscale hotel, visited the Notre-Dame Basilica and other beautiful sites, and ate in fine restaurants. We then drove east to Quebec City with its fortified colonial core, narrow cobblestone streets, stone buildings, and European feel. We stayed in a small hotel just outside the old city, visited several historic sights, and learned of its role in the early wars with England and ate in intimate French bistros.

Both cities were beautiful and interesting places to visit but on the way home we decided to avoid the cities and travel through the rural countryside that borders the St. Lawrence River. We bypassed the highways and took secondary roads through farmlands and small villages.

During one particularly bucolic pass, we came across a famer and his wife baking bread in their front yard in a five-foot high, wood burning, homemade oven shaped like an igloo. We stopped and purchased a loaf of bread as it came out of the oven hot and delicious. Although they only spoke French we were able to get instructions from them to stop at the next farmhouse, about two miles down the road, where that farmer and his wife would sell us honey to put on the bread.

We visited what may be two of the most beautiful cities in the North America, saw magnificent architecture, and ate in multi-star restaurants. And yet the most memorable building I saw was an outdoor oven, and my most enjoyable meal, a loaf of bread with <u>my</u> honey.

1997.3   EMERGENCY SERVICE

The following was written for Parsons Communiqué and adapted from an anonymous fable.

A small town, built at the edge of a deep ravine, invested thousands of dollars in state-of-the-art ambulance services and emergency facilities. It seems that children playing at the edge of the cliff would occasionally tumble into the ravine. The ambulance drivers kept careful notes detailing how long it took to get to the scene, to find the broken bodies, and to deliver them to the well-equipped and richly staffed trauma center. The ambulance service became a favored community activity, with many volunteers, a large support group, and an ever-increasing budget. One day a newcomer suggested that a fence be built to protect the children from the danger of falling into the ravine. After much discussion the town leaders, who had purchased the equipment, the hospital directors, who had staffed the trauma center, and the ambulance corps that had provided the volunteers, decided that a fence was not needed. In fact, a fence would divert limited resources from the established emergency services, and was therefore a danger to the children.

Queries for the month:

Are there any "ravines" at Parsons, which tempt our clients into unhealthy activities or life-styles (e.g. Violence, fast food, helplessness?)

Do we distinguish between what we need to do and what clients need to master?

Are there any favored activities at Parsons that are above review?

Are there services that our clients might need but that we do not provide (e.g., anti-violence training, healthy life-styles, vocational training?)

Are there any new ideas out there that have been avoided because the 'stranger' hasn't presented them yet?

Are there any new ideas out there that have been avoided because they would disrupt current activities?

1997.4   A PARABLE OF TWO FROGS

The following was written for The Communiqué and adapted from an anonymous fable.

A group of frogs was hopping through the woods when two of them fell into a pit. The others looked in to see if they could help. When they saw its depth, they told the two in the pit to prepare to die because it was hopeless.

Unwilling to accept their fate they began to jump with all their might. Some shouted into the pit that they wouldn't be in this situation if they had been more careful; others shouted that they should have been more obedient to Froggy rules. The remaining frogs sobbed and shouted that they should save their energy since they were already as good as dead. The two frogs continued jumping as hard as they could.

Finally, one frog took heed of the calls and lay down, spent and disheartened. The other, although exhausted and wracked with pain, continued to jump.

The group continued yelling, "Stop, save your strength." The weary frog just jumped harder until finally it sprang out of the pit. Amazed, the other frogs gathered around and asked, "Why did you continue jumping when we told you it was impossible?" Reading their lips, the astonished frog explained that he was deaf, and when he saw their gestures and shouting, he thought they were cheering him on, and so he tried harder.

Whom shall we cheer on today?

1997.5   SEAN'S ACCOMPLISHMENT

The following was written for The Parsons Communiqué and adapted from an anonymous fable.

Sean and his father were walking in a park where some boys they knew were playing baseball. Sean asked his father if he thought they would let him play. His father knew that most boys wouldn't want him on their team but he approached one of the boys and asked if Sean could play. The boy looked for guidance from his teammates. Getting none, he took matters into his own hands and said, "We're in the eighth inning and losing by six runs. He can be on our team and he'll bat in the ninth. In the bottom of the eighth, Sean's team scored but was still behind by three.

In the top of the ninth, Sean played right field. Although no hits came his way, he was thrilled to be on the field. In the bottom of the ninth, Sean's team scored again. With two outs and the bases loaded, the winning run was on first. Sean was up. Would they let him bat and lose their chance to win the game? Surprisingly, they gave Sean the bat. Everyone knew that a hit was all but impossible. Sean stepped up to the plate and the pitcher moved in a few steps to lob the ball softly. Sean swung and missed. The pitcher took a few more steps forward. Sean swung and hit a slow ground ball to the pitcher who picked up the ball and threw it over the first baseman's head into right field. Everyone yelled, 'Run Sean run.' Sean had never before made it to first base. He scampered wide-eyed down the baseline. They yelled, 'Run to second!' By the time he rounded first, the right fielder had the ball and threw it over the third baseman's head. Sean ran towards second as the runners ahead of him deliriously circled the bases towards home. As Sean reached second, the shortstop shouted, 'Run to third!' As Sean rounded third, the boys from both teams were screaming, 'Sean! Run home!' As Sean stepped on home plate he was cheered as the hero for hitting a grand slam and winning the game for his team."

The action of one boy initiated a chain of events that allowed each person to recognize and respond to the opportunity that Sean presented. As a result, the players and fans from both teams learned the joy of valuing the achiever over the achievement by making accommodations for a person with a visible challenge. Perhaps each of them will become the "one" who helps others recognize their opportunities to make accommodations for other challenged people; whether the challenge is publicly visible as Sean's or privately held like mine.

The following was written for *The Communiqué* when I returned to work in April 1998 after being discharged from the hospital where I had an operation on my back.

"Recently I spent a week in a local hospital. My years of hospital experience as an anesthetist and later as an administrator did not prepare me for the role of patient. And of course, much has changed. There seemed to be fewer staff each with much more to do than I remembered and so many gadgets . . . so much technology. Every bodily function is monitored, measured, and signaled for all to hear in coded beeps, buzzes, and bleeps.

I was struck by the efficiency of the staff. One nurse actually ran from room to room trying desperately to meet everyone's needs, but in the end, finding only enough time to tend to beeping's of the most serious kind. One apparently new nurse's aide was so preoccupied with my blood pressure that she seemed shocked to find an actual person in my bed, as she jumped when I thanked her for her efforts. She checked her watch and went to the next bed without saying a word. Nights were very hard for the seriously ill. They get so little sleep as the treatments that keep them alive and healing are just as important at two in the morning as they are at two in the afternoon. Most of them have long since given up the structures and rhythms of typical daily life and have succumbed to the cycle of the hospital where it's always time to work, where recreation is non-existent and sleep is rarely more than a series of brief naps. Each time I would awake either by pain or by the staff, I could hear the nurses scampering up and down the halls. I watched and listened to the cycles of the eternal day. I watched the sunrise each morning and the staff change with each shift. Soon the patterns revealed themselves, the peaks and valleys of activity; the peculiarities of each nurse; the recurring sounds from the other unseen but now familiar persons who resided on the other side of my door.

It all became quite predictable, except for one brief moment. That moment came when a nurse, scurrying by from my roommate to her next task, stopped at my bedside. She looked into my eyes, as though I was really there, I mean me, not just my parts, my treatment or my diagnosis, but me. She must have noticed my surprise at her attention. She placed her hand on my arm for no apparent reason, she had no injection, no blood pressure cuff, in fact no medical "ammunition" of any kind, and yet there she was, touching me as though I was a real person. In the midst of all the efficiency, all the technology, activity, pains and miracles, she touched me.

Perhaps one day I will forget what I experienced in the hospital. I may even forget that simple and un-prescribed act of kindness. But before I forget how important that human touch was to me even in my brief, transitory role of patient, I wonder about the kids at Parsons whose patient (or client) role is not transitory, but is often extended and for some it is a lifestyle. After all the technology, all the activity, all the pain and all the miracles of Parsons are done, will they, like me, be able to look back and remember a time when someone stopped, for no apparent reason and touched them?"

1998.2 DAVID AND MICHELLE

On August 27, 1998 Dave and Michelle held their rehearsal dinner and party in our gardens at 5 Greenwood Lane, Delmar, NY. The weather was perfect for a garden party and I was so glad that they had chosen to celebrate among the trees, shrubs and flowers that Dave had provided so much help to get established. The next day the wedding took place at the church that Michele and her family had attended for many years, St John/St Ann R.C. Church, Albany, NY.

Michele's son Ryan looked so handsome in his suit. The reception was held in the garden of Michele's parents, another wonderful evening. They seemed so well suited for each other, with similar temperaments and a shared love of gardening.

The in-laws that we acquired on that day have become a significant part of our life.

1999.1 IRELAND, SCOTLAND, ENGLAND

Our trip began in Ireland and our tour guide, a retired History Professor provided us with a rich and interesting account of present-day Ireland and the history that created it. We first visited the Cliffs of Moher while the Irish folk song "The Cliffs of Dooneen," played in the background. It was spellbindingly beautiful.

The Cliffs of Moher are situated on the West coast of Ireland in County Clare. They stretch for 8km and rise to 214m above sea level at their highest point. The stunning rock formations of the Cliffs of Moher are 300 million years old and are made of layers of sedimentary rock. Layers of sandstone, siltstone, mudstone and shale which are rich in fossils are the geological content of the Cliffs of Moher.

As we toured I read Angela's Ashes, a memoir by the Irish author Frank McCourt, which tells of his childhood struggles with poverty before the economic recovery that transformed Ireland.

One of the most interesting parts of the trip was a reenactment of a wake that was held for emigrants to America. Although the performance was conducted in the Irish language, the events and emotions of the drama were painfully clear.

Many Irish families immigrated to America in the late 1840's, during The Great Famine (Irish: an Gorta Mór) or Irish Potato Famine as it is referred to outside of Ireland (1845-1852). The fungus Phytophthora infestans caused the destruction of the potato plants' leaves and edible tubers. However, huge quantities of food were exported from Ireland to England throughout the period when the people of Ireland were dying of starvation and the British government refused to stop the practice. During the famine, approximately one million people died and a million more emigrated from Ireland, causing the island's population to fall by between 20 and 25%.

During this period of slow ships, poor sanitation, and rapid food spoilage, many died and most were ill during the week's long journey to America. It was particularly difficult for the very poor, like most of our ancestors, who traveled in steerage. There were no provisions for changing clothes or doing laundry. In steerage, the clothes you boarded in were the clothes you wore when you disembarked weeks later.

It was the Irish custom at this time for the friends and family of emigrants to hold a wake just prior to the departure. They knew that once the ship departed, their loved ones would never be seen again in Ireland. We can picture the drama: the small band and their neighbors singing the folk songs of spring, and songs of the harvest. Since most departed Ireland after the spring planting, that year's potential harvest was known to them when they departed. They knew that the harvest would not be sufficient to support their family if they stayed in Ireland, and sadly not sufficient for many who did remain behind. They danced around the fire and told stories of the good old days. Mothers cried and fathers felt a part of their life about to drift away with the outgoing tide. Since patriotic songs were prohibited by the English rulers of that time, poets created songs that addressed their country as a beautiful woman, and they sang of their love for her. One of the most beautiful Irish folk songs is "Dónal Óg," the story of a boy who leaves his sweetheart, never to return and the forlorn lass morns the loss of her lover i.e. her country taken by the English.

As they sang, danced, and wiped away the tears, they reviewed the details of their plans to take the short journey to either England or County Cork, where they would board their ships; Destination: the new world, Expectation: a new and better life.

In New York, the ships docked aside the Castle Clinton (later renamed Castle Garden, the predecessor to Ellis Island, which opened in 1892.) It was a large circular building on the tip of lower Manhattan; the remnant still stands as a monument to those immigrants. From there they had a clear view of New York, as there were few tall buildings and a clear view of the seascape as the Statue of Liberty would not be erected for another three decades.

We don't know if their dreams came true, or if the families would have to wait for future generations to reap the benefits of their courage and vision.

We left Belfast in Northern Ireland on the ferry to Scotland and headed up the west coast through its largest city, Glasgow (famed for its vibrant cultural scene) for the beautiful mountain wildernesses, the Cairngorms and Western Highlands, which are interspersed with glacial glens (valleys), and lochs (lakes). Then we traveled down the east coast past the battlefield at Culloden, where the Scots last hope of separating themselves from the English died. After the lost, efforts were taken to integrate the comparatively wild Highlands into the Kingdom of Great Britain; civil penalties were introduced to weaken Gaelic culture and attack the Scottish clan system. Then it was on to Aberdeen, Dundee and Edinburgh the capital of Scotland, which is loomed over by an iconic castle.

On our last evening in Scotland Reg and I went to the hotel bar for a nightcap. Reg sipped her Black and Tan and as I lifted my Chablis, I heard "Hey Ronnie" from the rear of the bar. It was Miles, a classmate from high school, he was on his way to Belfast to meet with friends. What a small world.

In the morning, we left for London with stops at Hadrian's Wall and the City of York. It's Cathedral, York Minster, one of the largest of its kind in Northern Europe.

The title "minster" is attributed to churches established in the Anglo-Saxon period as missionary teaching churches, and serves now as an honorific title. It is stunningly beautiful and unlike many churches of that era, The York Minster is brilliantly lit with hundreds of beams of light that streams in through its many beautiful lightly stained glass windows.

On our last morning in London, after seeing an Agatha Christie play the evening before, we visited a local flea market. We found several treasures and showed them to our travel guide who just happened to be passing by. She helped us identify them and told us that we did well at the market. We returned home with our treasures, a Welsh Army bugle and a silver box that was given to a British World War I soldier in 1914 as a Christmas gift from Princess Mary.

CHAPTER 8 *NEW MILLENNIUM*

A millennium is a period of one thousand years. The New Millennium (also known as 'Y2K') was a term used in the 1990s to describe the coming of the 21st century and third millennium, popularly beginning in 2000 but actually beginning in 2001. The term was also used in the 2000s, especially in the early 2000s, to describe the then present times.

Islamic fundamentalist terrorists hijacked four U.S. airliners and crashed them into the Pentagon and the World Trade Center in New York City September 11, 2001. The attack of two planes leveled the World Trade Center and the crash of one plane inflicted serious damage to the Pentagon in Arlington, Virginia, causing nearly 3,000 deaths. The fourth plane was heroically crashed by passengers into a Shanksville, Pennsylvania cornfield when they learn of the plot, preventing destruction of another structure in Washington, D.C.

NATO invited seven members of the former Soviet bloc to join its membership.

The War in Iraq began and Barack Obama, Democratic Senator from Illinois, became the 44th President of the USA making him the first African-American president in the history of the country. The economic recession deepened as jobless claims climb above 10.0%,

Technological advances included the development of Social Media, Smart Phones, and Wi-Fi.

Best-selling books of the decade included: The Harry Potter Series, The Kite Runner, The Hunger Games Series, The Time Traveler's Wife, A Thousand Splendid Suns, The Book Thief, The Help, and The Lovely Bones. Also, Life of Pi, The Girl with the Dragon Tattoo, The Da Vinci Code, The Road, The Secret Life of Bees, The Curious Incident of the Dog in the Night-Time, Twilight Series, My Sister's Keeper and Angels & Demons.

US Population was 281,421,906a and life expectancy was 74 for Males, and 79 for Females.

The average new house cost $207,000, the average salary per year was $42,148, a gallon of gas was $1.51 a loaf of bread cost $1.72 and the average cost of new car was $24,750.

> *We are all immigrants into the new millennium;*
> *some have come from the past and some from the womb.*
> *RJG*

2000.1   ANCESTRAL HOME

In May, Reg and I decided to extend our annual vacation in Georgia by stopping in South Carolina to visit with old friends Dick and Therese Bush who had moved from Voorheesville about the time that we moved to Georgia in 1978. On our way to their home, our brand-new Buick Regal had major mechanical problems and we used a loaner car to travel from their home Rock Hill SC to visit the cemeteries, villages, and home sites of my many ancestors from North and South Carolina. We also spent time with my Uncle Robert and his wife Mary in Darlington, SC.

We first drove to Albemarle, N.C. home to many Swearengin's aka Swaringen, Ivy's and Mills in the 18th and 19th century. We took many photos containing the names of dozens of early kin and spent several hours in the local library and found several valuable resources. We then drove to Darlington and spent the night with Robert and Mary. He made his famous shrimp dinner for us. The next day we drove with Robert to Rockingham, NC, which my mother always considered her hometown, and passed through Cheraw, SC. and stopped at the house where I lived with my grandmother in 1941. I recorded Robert as he told stories during the daylong trip. The sound of the motor ruined much of the tape, as it is often louder than Robert's voice. We went on to Ansonville, NC where my grandparents moved when their general store burned down in Rockingham and where almost every tombstone in three different cemeteries contained the names of relatives. My Great Grandfather John Mills built one of the churches we saw. We also saw a church built on land donated by my Great-great grandfather Robert Ivey Mills.

We went on to spent several weeks with Brian, Greg and their family and friends.

On our way home to New York we took side trips to Dahlonega, GA, Chattanooga, and Dollywood, TN and a long beautiful ride through Smoky Mountains.

2000.2   SIR RYAN

After Dave formally adopted Ryan, we held a party during our vacation at Schroon Lake to welcome him officially into the Gerhard family. We gave him a crown and dubbed him Prince Ryan. Not having a sword at hand for the knighting ceremony, we tapped him on both shoulders with a kitchen spatula. He was now a knight in good standing in the Gerhard clan and entitled to all the honors and benefits occurring there to. Honors and benefits already at the age of 12 wow.

I gave him a 5-inch thick book containing the genealogy of his new extended family with over 14,000 names.

He is our first grandson.

2001.1 & 1958   HOSPITALS AND PATIENTS

After completing the questionnaire that assured the medical imaging technician that I did not have any metallic inserts in my body or suffer from claustrophobia, she slid me into the 18-inch diameter hole at the center of the six-foot long metallic donut. It was a deep cavern, deep enough to engulf my entire body, even though the M.R.I. was only of my brain. Although I do not suffer from claustrophobia, at that moment I did get a brief glimpse of what the feeling of panic might be like for those who do.

I had spent many years working in and around hospitals, so I generally felt quite comfortable with the sights, sounds, and smells of the hospital. Even the professionally detached demeanor of the staff seemed comfortably familiar to me. As I lay there, with earplugs inserted to deaden the noise and an overhead mirror pointed toward the opening at the foot of the machine to provide the welcomed illusion of space and freedom; I imagined how terrifying this might appear to the uninitiated. And my mind drifted back to a former life when I was staff instead of patient.

(1958) Peter was a beautiful five-year boy with a quick grin, blonde hair, and kidney disease. The doctors at Mount Sinai Hospital in New York City where I was working had exhausted the few treatments that were available for him at that time. If the boy were to live, we would know today. I was alone in the pediatric surgery ward when his mother returned from a brief respite at the hospital cafeteria, where she had gone each night for the past two weeks for her evening meal.

It was time. We both knew what was at stake; if the boy could pee, he would live. We could try again later if he was unsuccessful, but the waiting was unbearable, so when his mother asked me if it was time, I said, "Yes." I got a specimen jar as his mother stood Peter up in the large crib-like hospital bed. I held the jar, Mom held Peter, and Peter aimed and pushed. The jar was like an empty tomb waiting to take either Peter or his urine. After a few minutes, the tears welled up in his mother's eyes. A force that I could neither see nor understand was crushing my chest; I could hardly breathe. If God were there, I could have crucified Him myself; this was so unfair. We were consoling ourselves, and planning to try again later when a single golden drop of urine fell into the jar. I would never be repulsed by urine again; in that moment, my image of urine was transformed from trash to treasure. Soon there was a teaspoon full; enough to prove that Peters' kidneys were working. The surgery was successful. Peters' mother wept loudly, Peter joined in; he seemed frightened by his mothers' wailing. I felt like hugging and kissing them both, but displays of emotions are reserved for patients and family. Staff must maintain their professional detachment. Staff use different mechanisms to remain professionally detached. Some insulate themselves from the pain that the patient is experiencing; others detach themselves from their emotional response to the pain. Either way, staff must remember that this is not their grief or their joy; it is the patients and their loved ones and it should not be co-opted. I generally fail detachment.

Later that evening when Peter was asleep and his mother was home celebrating with the rest of the family, I began to feed Carlos. Carlos was about 15 months old. He had never been home; his parents were unknown. He lived in a cast from his chest to his toes and his legs were spread about a foot apart by a metal rod embedded into the cast. His malformed hips were surgically repaired, but there was no surgery for his cerebral palsy. He twisted in my arms trying to suck on the nipple of the bottle that I held for him. When his head lurched, he failed to get a sip, and he cried perhaps from frustration, perhaps from hunger. When he succeeded, his head lurched, he gagged and threw up most of what he had worked so hard to get, and he cried. I could not hold Carlos in my arms as I had held so many other babies from the nursery and the pediatric wards. He could not sit on my lap; his cast kept him rigid. He could not lie on my shoulder; his spasmodic movements kept him at a distance, and he could not laugh, or smile or coo or do any of the things that generally make babies so adorable. Finally, the bottle was empty, half in him, and half on the towel in my lap where he regurgitated. His urine smelled of the medications he took and his flailing prevented hurrying through the diaper changing process. I did not like caring for Carlos. More than that, I did not like Carlos. Although I believed he was condemned to a life of frustration and loneliness, of pain and sorrow, I felt no empathy, not even sympathy; all I could feel was repulsion. Me, who could no longer be repulsed by urine, was repulsed by the innocent little boy who produced it.

That night in bed in my dormitory room, I tried to think about the joy of Peter, but all I could remember was Carlos, and I was ashamed. I realized that I was as frail in my way as Carlos was in his. (Sometimes I have feelings about myself but, sometimes, my feelings have me

(2001) In about half-an-hour the M.R.I. was over and I left feeling reasonably assured that the test was just a precaution, needed more to satisfy the compulsive needs of my neurologist than to guide his treatment of what would likely turn out to be nothing more serious than a viral infection of my facial nerve and not a brain tumor. After all, I was still quite healthy and life was good. But, from time to time, I remember Carlos and I wonder if his life is good and if he ever found someone to hold him who would not be repulsed.

2001.2 ARIZONA AND NEW MEXICO

Our old friend Sue Murry had moved to Scottsdale. AZ several years before and we decided to see her and tour the southwest. We rented a Lincoln Town Car, spent a few days with Sue, and saw a Hope Indian Hoop dance at a local museum and Taliesin West, Frank Lloyd Wright's winter home and school. We then proceeded west to Sedona, and Prescott, and then north to the Grand Canyon. Since words can't adequately describe the Grand Canyon I'll simply say, "Go see it."

As we drove east past Tucson we were hit by a major snowstorm which prevented us from going north to Utah to see our old friends Jerry and Carol Matthieson. We spent two days in Albuquerque and Santa Fe and visited the Georgia O'Keefe museum. In Santa Fe, I bought a wedding ring and had it blessed by the local priest. I had lost mine for the second time. When we stopped in the southern New Mexico City of Las Cruces, a TV reporter interviewed Reg and wanted to know what thought about the recent vandalism at the picturesque church. She suggested that we pray for the vandals. We saw Tombstone and the Wild West reenactment and drove back to Sue's through the Sequoia National Forest.

2001.3   VIRGINIA FAMILY VACATION

In August of 2001, the family all chipped in and rented a large home near the beach on Sandbridge Island, just south of Virginia Beach, VA. The photo shows the eight of us all wearing matching white shirts. I later added inserts of Emily and LeAnn parents and grandmother. I made a wooden jigsaw puzzle from a family photo from that vacation so Emily wouldn't forget what we looked like. It was a wonderful get away. It was the first time that we were all together on vacation. The boys and their families took a side trip to an amusement park, while Reg and I visited a local nature preserve.

On the way home, Reg and I visited Williamsburg and Jamestown VA. We then drove to St. Mary's City, MD and toured the archeological sites including the former public house owned by Garret Van Swearingen. Members of the local historical society gave us a tour of the museum and shared many documents with us. They were glad to meet a sixth great grandson of Garret, who is one of the key profiles at the museum. I later sent them some information that I had accumulated.

2001.4   SEPTEMBER 11

Airliners against a clear blue sky, now remind me of the images from
the World Trade Center. It wasn't the beginning of war;
it was the end of peace.
We must be the survivors of the peace.
RJG

I was entering the Parsons parking lot to attend the Tuesday senior staff meeting when the NPR radio show was interrupted with a special bulletin. A commercial airplane had just crashed into the World Trade Center in New York City. I thought that it must be a mistake; surely, it must have been a private plane. A commercial pilot would never make such a mistake. But it wasn't a mistake; the terrorist who had commandeered the plane had deliberately crashed the plane into the building. A second plane soon followed.

The September 11, 2001 attacks were a series of four coordinated terrorist attacks by the Islamic terrorist group al-Qaeda on the United States. The attacks killed 2,996 people, injured over 6,000 others, and caused at least $10 billion in property and infrastructure damage and $3 trillion in total costs.

Four passenger airliners were hijacked by 19 al-Qaeda terrorists. Two of the planes, American Airlines Flight 11 and United Airlines Flight 175, were crashed into the North and South towers, respectively, of the World Trade Center complex in New York City. Within an hour and 42 minutes, both 110-story towers collapsed, with debris and the resulting fires causing partial or complete collapse of all other buildings in the World Trade Center complex, including the 47-story 7 World Trade Center tower, as well as significant damage to ten other large surrounding structures. A third plane, American Airlines Flight 77, was crashed into the Pentagon. The fourth plane, United Airlines Flight 93, initially was steered toward Washington, D.C., but crashed into a field in Stonycreek Township near Shanksville, Pennsylvania, after its passengers tried to overcome the hijackers. It was the deadliest incident for firefighters and law enforcement officers in the history of the United States, with 343 firefighters and 72 law enforcement officers killed.

Reg's Cousin Jim Goodwin worked at the World Trade Center but was on jury duty on the day of the attack. The phone lines were completely overloaded and his sons, who lived out of state, were frantic trying to determine if he had been among those who had escaped. There are many stories of those who by chance happened to be out of the building that day and some about those who by chance happened to be in the building on that day.

Work for Peace by pursuing the virtues of Truth and Justice.
RJG

2001.5   HARD-WIRED FOR UNITY

The following article was written as part of a Parson Child and Family Center effort to develop the capacity to provide spiritual support to its clients.

Neuro-Theology

Scientists from the University of Pennsylvania[1] the University of California at San Diego[2] and others in Japan have been studying an area of the brain called the limbic system for many years. This is the area of the brain generally concerned with self-preservation, preservation of the species, and expression of strong emotions.

Researchers have found that the reduction of sensory stimulation that occurs during meditation causes changes in the brain. These changes reduce its capacity to identify where the self ends and where the rest of the world begins. The meditator perceives these changes as a feeling of being one with the universe.

On a more modest scale, ordinary praying, or the participation in ritual behaviors such as genuflecting, chanting, incantation and singing often bring on feelings ranging from inner harmony and a sense of community membership to spiritual unity.

We are apparently "'hard-wired" with the capacity to experience unity with our environment and our fellow travelers. We do not have to answer the meta-physical question: "Is God the master electrician who built the system, or merely the by-product of electrochemical activity?" However, in my opinion, we do have to provide our clients with the opportunity to fulfill their capacity to experience the sense of community membership as a means of counteracting the feelings of anonymity and isolation that many of them feel.

As we search for ways to reduce violence and increase cooperation, I do not believe that we should avoid the very activities that our minds are hard-wired to respond to with the very outcomes that we seek.

Concerning costs, I think we need to compare the cost providing these opportunities with the cost of not providing them. It may be a bargain when we examine both sides of the ledger.

Concerning the proposal to hire a staff member to champion this cause, I think we need to consider alternative means of meeting the goal if this proposal is not currently feasible. If this is a priority, we will not abandon it because one approach will not work. We will simply find another approach.

1. Dr. Andrew Newburg and Dr. Eugene d'Aquili

2. V. S. Ramachandran

2001.6 A CELEBRATION

The following monologue was presented to help celebrate the 40th anniversary of Parsons Pediatrician Dr. John Abbuhl.

In 1961, many in this room were not yet born, I was a young army officer and worried about the impact of the Berlin wall and the Cuban missile crisis on our country and my family, and .... <u>Dr. Abbuhl began treating children at Parsons.</u>

In 1966, Mao's Cultural Revolution began in China, the U. S. stepped up military assistance in Viet Nam, and ....<u>Dr Abbuhl was treating children at Parsons.</u>

In 1971, some here were still not born, the Martin Luther King memorial in Atlanta was under development, and ....<u>Dr Abbuhl was treating children at Parsons.</u>

In 1976, Dr. Braga, who has since retired, began working at Parsons, the effects of Watergate were beginning to fade, and <u>Dr Abbuhl was treating children at Parsons.</u>

In1981, a few in this room were still not born, Ray Schimmer was 17 months away from beginning his career at Parsons, the AIDS virus was first identified, and ....<u>Dr Abbuhl was treating children at Parsons.</u>

In 1986, the Chernobyl nuclear accident rocked the world, the U.S. invaded Panama, and ....<u>Dr Abbuhl was treating children at Parsons.</u>

In 1991, Nelson Mandela was freed after being imprisoned for 27 years. The Soviet Union and the Berlin wall were dismantled and ....<u>Dr Abbuhl was treating children at Parsons.</u>

In 1996, I arrived and I found ....<u>Dr Abbuhl treating children at Parsons.</u>

Today, in 2001, I am semi-retired. The world is changing at a faster rate than ever before.

But ....<u>Dr Abbuhl is still treating children at Parsons.</u>

During these past 40 years, the country has had 10 presidents and 4 wars, but Parsons has had only one Dr. Abbuhl.

Dr. Abbuhl, the program says that you are being honored for those 40 years. But we all know better, we know that you are really being honored on behalf of the 17,000 children that you have cared for during those 40 years. So, on their behalf; we say congratulation for the years, but thank you for the caring.

2002.1 EMILY {FDG}

Before Emily was born on 29 Nov 2002, Reg and I thought that it was very possible that we would never have any natural born grandchildren. So, when she arrived it was more than the usual jubilation. The fact that our first natural grandchild was a girl was also important, as our three children were all boys.

In December, we drove to Georgia to meet her in person. Brian and LeAnn had her dressed in red and lying on the floor in front of the fireplace in the living room. She was a beautiful sight. You could read a book by the light from her smile.

It now has been thirteen years since her birth, and every meeting, every letter, every photo, and every phone call has been a joy.

During that first holiday visit, Reg found an ad for a cabin for rent on nearby Lake Lanier. We rented the cabin each March for the next several years, until Brian and LeAnn purchased a cabin in Clayton, which they let us use each March for many years. We had many wonderful family weekends together, and many moments of pure delight with our favorite granddaughter (fgd), Emily.

2002.2   FEBRUARY IN FLORIDA

Reg and I decided to participate in one of those marathon real estate marketing efforts in order to get a free week in a Fairfield condominium in Florida. While in Florida we stopped at Ocala cemetery where my brother, mother, grandmother and stepfather are buried. Then it was on to the Epcot Center and Disney World in Orlando. We spent a few days with our friends Jerry and Carol in their "spare" condominium in Ponta Gouda. It was on to Lakeland for a visit with my aging aunt Esma and her husband WD Overcash. WD was a skilled carpenter and he had built a hammered dulcimer, which no one in his immediate family could play. I was delighted when he offered it to me. I later discovered that it is impossible to tune properly but I like having something that he built. Our last visit was with my brother Richard, in New Port Richie. He and his wife Lois had moved into an apartment and sold their home to Lois' daughter Donna and her husband. Richards's health was beginning to fail but we enjoyed out brief time together.

2002.3   TERRY

After being successfully treated for breast cancer, Reg's younger sister, Teresa, developed leukemia. With her strength depleted from her battle with cancer, it soon became apparent that she would not survive this final insult to her frail body.

On one visit, she joked that as the youngest sibling there were few pictures of her in the family albums. Reg began making frequent trips to visit Terry during her prolonged treatment, and I began sending Terry "authentic" photos of her childhood for Reg to bring to the hospital. There was a photo showing only the backs of a distant man and a young girl strolling on the beach that I labeled, "Terry and her father enjoying a morning walk on her 8th birthday." There was a photo taken from dirigible 4,000 feet over a baseball stadium with an arrow pointing to tiny figures in the bleachers claiming to be Terry on her first date. A girl diving into the pool just as a seagull swooped down to obscure her face from the camera, became Terry's spring day at the park. With many  downloaded photos from the internet and the help of Photoshop, a small album took shape, showing what Terry's youth might have looked like in the hands of an inept photographer.

Reg and I were delayed in traffic and arrived just after Terry died. Terry's Uncle Robert Straub, a Redemptorist Priest, arrived from Mexico to preside over the funeral mass. Terry's husband Joe wrote the eulogy and asked me to read it at the mass. It was long, emotional, and difficult to read as Terry's family and friends looked up from the pews of the church trying to come to grips with the reality of the tragedy that had unfolding around them.

Terry is buried at Holy Rood Cemetery, near her parents and the site where her eldest brother would join her three and a half years later.

2002.4   MY FATHER'S GRAVE

While doing research for our family tree I discovered the location of my father's death certificate. I ordered a copy and was surprised to find that he had lived the last few years of his life near Birmingham in Bessemer, Alabama. The certificate listed the informant as Tressie (nee Bowles) Parker, and gave her address. I wrote to her and asked if she had known my father. She had, in fact during her teen years she and her sister Nanette had lived with him and his wife, who was their Aunt Ethel. We spoke on the phone and she sent me several photos of my father, his brother my Uncle Julius and his sister my Aunt Mildred and information about his brother my Uncle Harold.

Tressie's sister Nanette (nee Bowles) Jenkins lived near Atlanta and we arranged to meet in September when Reg and I would visit with Brian and LeAnn in their new house in Suwanee, GA. She drove with Reg, Brian and me to Lanett, AL; the town where my fathers' wife was born just across the GA boarder. Nanette spoke about my father for the entire trip and I recoded her stories with a small tape recorder. We visited the gravesite were my father lay besides his wife Ethel.

2002.5   BOSTON REUNION

In March, our God-daughter, Michon Matthiesen invited Reg and me to join her and her parents in Boston where she was completing a PhD in Theology at Boston College. We stayed in a Hotel with a view of the harbor. Michon gave us a tour of the city and we reminisced with her parents about our brief time together 40 years before, filled each other in about our lives, and ate seafood with our old friends from Walter Reed, Jerry, and Carol Matthiesen. Jerry had remained in the Army working as an anesthetist and retired as a Lt. Colonel and they lived in a retirement community in Arizona. We would meet with them again before Michon moved to Rhode Island to begin her career as a professor. Jerry died soon afterward and we would see Michon for what hopefully will not be the last time as she prepared to move west to take a tenured teaching position at the University of Mary in Bismarck, ND.

2002.6   SAN DAMIANO FOUNDATION

Reg's younger brother Gerry had worked with various television channels and became disillusioned with both the content of the work and with his limited role in their production. He had the temperament of an artist and could never be satisfied making material that was not his own art, created by him, and produced by him. He first tried using his creative skills in the making of motion pictures as a free-lance artist working for non-profit organizations. While it gave him the opportunity to produce material with some social value and to hone his skills and develop his confidence, he could never be satisfied producing work controlled by others who did not share his vision.

Thus, the San Damiano Foundation (SDF) came into being. The 501.3c not-for-profit organization produced films depicting the good works done by other people and organizations who would then use the films to raise money to support their efforts. The motto of SDF was "Putting the Power of Film at the Service of the Poor"

Gerry asked me to be a member of the Board of Directors of SDF in 2002, a position I held until the demise of the organization in 2010. It gradually became clear that the personal characteristics that drove Gerry to create SDF would continue to plague his work in SDF. The Board thought that the films were too long and too preachy. Gerry could not edit down his own works because he saw them as the works of beautiful art that they are. One might just as well ask Michelangelo to cut down his statute of David so it would fit in your living room. The members of the board however, were concerned that the length of the films would greatly reduce their audience and thus the amount of money that could be raised and be put in Service to the Poor. Gradually the purpose of the organization expanded from simply focusing on the work of those who directly serve the poor to spending more and more time on theology and prayer. It seemed apparent to the board that the only films that provided a major source of income for the service organizations were those that emphasized how specific people in dire circumstances were helped. Gerry was unyielding, and the tension with the board remained until 2010 when other issues arose that provided the catalyst for the board to vote to fire Gerry.

I felt confident that the organization would be better off if Gerry made some changes, but I also knew that he was unwilling or perhaps unable to make those changes. So, while I agreed that the board had every right to fire him and sufficient reason to do so, I also felt that the conflict could also be resolved if the board resigned. They, including me, could be replaced, but Gerry was the organization, only he created the films and raised the money needed to produce them. If he left, the organization would cease to exist, but Gerry would continue to make his long running films with their preachy content, the only difference would be that he would no longer be attached to an organization with tax-exempt status that was needed to attract funds. He would need a new organization. Having the board resign seemed to me to be the most efficient and least hurtful way of freeing the board from Gerry's trying ways and allowing the work to continue. I was the only member to resign. All of the others voted to fire Gerry. As predicted, with Gerry gone, the organization no longer served any useful purpose and it was gradually dissolved. Gerry created a new organization and continued making very beautiful but very long films. I miss him

. Aside: Gerry asked me to help edit one of his books entitled "Dear Kate." The book contains a series of letters that a father wrote to his daughter. After repeated unsuccessful attempts to have Gerry reduce both the volume and the redundancy in the work, he sent me a mockup copy, which he thought I would not need to edit. It had only one page that said,

> *"Dear Kate,*
> *Oh, never mine.*
> *Love Dad"*

Gerry has a great sense of humor especially involving word play. The finished volume has 479 pages which one reviewer described as long and rambling. We all know that, but we don't care, we love him anyway.

At this writing, his new organization, Pax et Bonum Communications has gradually morphed from making films about others, which he now refers to as infomercials, to running his own Santa Chiara Child Care Center with his 3rd wife Ecarlatte, in Haiti. He continues to write books, and raise funds for his work by giving lectures and presentations to schools, colleges, and Catholic service organizations. His daily logs about his work in Haiti is so compelling that they have become a major source of income for the center and a source of spiritual enrichment for many of its readers.

2003.1   BABY SITTING

When Emily was about eight months old, Brian and LeAnn asked Reg and me to babysit her as they took a long-deserved vacation to the coast of Mexico. Baby sitters received about $10 an hour in those days, but we would have paid many times that amount just to be able to spend time with Emily.

Of course, Reg and I were thinking that Granddaughter number two might be on the way. But as it turned out Emily proved to be quite sufficient for both her parents and for us. She provides everything that we might ask of a granddaughter.

2003.2   EMILY'S SONG

Emily's Song: A "Lover-bye" by Ron Gerhard (September 2003)

Melody	G A B A B C B A B B A G A F# G A A B C A G F# G G A B A B C B A B B A G A F# G A A B C A G F# G
Verse 1	Oh there once was a man who lived down by the sand, and he dreamed of the things that could not be. So he worked and he toiled to build a better world, in the hope you'd soon join our fam i ly.
Chorus	G B A A A A A A D B Little girl, growing bigger, Emily G B A A A A A A D B Little girl, growing wiser, Emily. B D E E E G F# D D E E E E D B Growing bigger, growing wiser, we stand here firm beside her. A B C C B A G A G She's our love and our joy our Emily.
Verse 2	The man was blessed with a son who was loved by everyone and he followed in the footsteps of that man. And as time passed that boy came to spread peace, love and joy and when he grew, his love became our Emily.
Chorus	
Verse 3	Oh there once was a ship and it took a lengthy trip to this land so its Pilgrims could be free. From that band, your mother came so that you could do the same and be pilgrim in this land of liberty.
Chorus	
Verse 4	Your foundation has been laid and the dues they have been paid, so your free to build your dreams Emily So spread your wings and fly away, but come back another day 'cause our love binds us closely Emily.
Chorus	

2003.3   REFUGEES FROM HOPE

The following monologue was written as part of an agency-wide effort to reduce violence at Parsons Child and Family Center, Albany, NY.

REFUGEES FROM HOPE: SOCIALIZATION, OUR PRIMARY SERVICE?

At a time when culturally supported opportunities for social development are decreasing, other profound changes in our culture are increasing the need for cooperation and collaboration among our citizens. Therefore, the socialization of long-term residential clients may provide their best opportunity for becoming productive citizens.

In simpler times, individuals had little trouble finding their place in the world. Their culture prescribed their place in society. Beliefs and customs provided the lens through which they viewed the world, and the needs of the group-defined individuals' responsibilities. Family, clan, and neighbor members ensured that children knew and obeyed the rules. Rites and rituals celebrated group milestones and reinforced group membership. Group loyalty was the most valued personal virtue.

A generation ago, anthropologist Margaret Mead identified an historic turning point in the course of human history. For the first time, people generally shared the belief that the elders of society would no longer be the transmitters of the culture. The prevailing assumption was that it was 'natural' for the behavior of each new generation to differ from that of the preceding generation. Members of a generation were modelling their behavior not on that of their elders, but on that of their peers. At a time when economic and social changes are opening new avenues of opportunity, our culture is losing the road signs that had helped prior generations find their way.

Examples of vanishing road signs:

  Nationality is losing significance as a definer of individual identity. We are becoming one world, however the political and social structures that may one day guide our journey in "the New World order" have yet to be developed. The answer to the question, "Who am I?" is in part a description of my heritage. However, when my family history tells me that I am from everywhere, it feels a great deal like being from nowhere.

- Marriages have crossed ethnic, racial, regional, economic, and religious lines and are producing generations who do not closely identify with the groups that were the centerpiece of their grandparents' identity. As the lines that divided us dissolve, we become one people. The answer to the question, "Who am I?" is in part a description of my group affiliations. However, as the traditional groups merge or fade, with whom shall I affiliate and who shall I be?

- Extended families that once provided ties to the past and to other family members are now frequently unknown or unavailable. The answer to the question "Who am I?" is in part a description of my ancestry and my family connections. As the links to current and past relatives weaken, does my sense of self weaken as well?

- Many neighborhoods that historically provided residents with opportunities for social and personal support are being replaced with subdivisions where homeowners disappear into the caverns of attached garages or with city streets where residents are constrained by time or fear. The answer to the question "Who am I?" is in part a description of my commitment to a local community. As the supports die away, my opportunities to give support die with them. When they are gone, to whom can I be committed?

- Scientific revolutions have created the potential for technological changes that are so profound that we can't always be sure if a particular change is a good or bad thing. The answer to the question, "Who am I?" is in part a description of my role in society. If I cannot understand my rapidly changing and increasingly technological society, how do I define my place in it?

- Increased food production, medical and social advancements have released women from the age-old necessity of devoting themselves almost completely to reproduction and nurturance. This dramatically altered, for both men and women, gender defined roles. The answer to the question "Who am I?" is in part a description of my gender identity. If that identity has lost much of its historic meaning, have I lost much of my meaning as well?

Implications for Child Care Agencies:

The loss of culturally embedded support groups has cast many of our youth into the role of immigrant: immigrants, not into a new place, but immigrants into a new time. These immigrants, like our ancestors, band together in clubs and gangs for mutual support and individual identity. And like our ancestors, the short-term security provided by their membership in the "commune of immigrants" destines them to a marginal role in the broader society. But unlike our ancestors many of today's youth cannot even hope to make the transition from gang to citizen.

For children from dysfunctional homes the situation is even more precarious. When immigrants arrived at Ellis Island, they were examined. Those found to be wanting were exiled and returned to their native land where they might find hope for the future. When society rejects modern day immigrants, there is no homeland to which they may return. They are in a sense refugees. Many clients of child caring agencies are among the exiled immigrants of our society, the refugees from hope.

The only culture known to many clients is the transient pop-culture of youth and the only society they know is the one that rejected them. Therefore, the preeminent role of child caring agencies is to help clients define their place in society and the motivation that comes from finding something of value to which they can commit. It is not sufficient for child caring agencies to commit clients into the lives of its programs. Agencies must also place a sense of commitment into the lives of its clients.

Like their culturally normative counterparts (i.e. our homes, our schools, our neighborhoods, etc.) the activities, routines, and rhythms of program life are derived from an underlying ideology. If we were to examine these elements at child caring agencies, what Ideology would we be able to discern as the definer of daily life? Would we find that the campus is the staffs' workplace or the children's habitat? Does the staff own the residence, and allow children admittance, or is the residence the children's home and the staff but guests and servants? The question is not which perspective is present, for it is likely that they are all present; the question is which perspective dominates and defines the quality and nature of daily life. Would we identify through observation the cultural values and principles that children are being socialized to internalize? Or, would we merely find the program values and principles that instruct staff how to work but ignore the instruction of children in how to live. Caring for children is primarily about socialization. Socialization is the means of helping children to learn to use the freedom of adulthood to collaborate with others for constructive ends. Human Resource professionals advise us in our hiring practice, to hire for attitude and to train for skill. This axiom reflects the relative value of attitude vs. skill in our society. Applied to children this principle would have us see the training of children in job and social skills as secondary to helping them develop a healthy positive attitude about their life.

Each generation is becoming the first native-born immigrant into a new time. Our clients are to be socialized into a culture that adults have not experienced. How can we help children become part of a culture that we don't totally share or understand and which is constantly shifting? We can provide the same level and direction of effort that we provide or witness in good parents, in good neighbors and in good role models.

Every relatively permanent group, like a family or a neighborhood gang, creates norms and customary ways of behaving. Our primary goal then, is to create a group identity whose norms and customs will serve our clients even when our service to them ends. A few examples of how we might reach this goal follow:

- Our children learn positive values at our dinner table, and at our sides. Therefore, time spent with staff should be primarily about modelling and secondary about treatment, training, or control.

- Our children learn positive values in our houses of worship and community organizations. Therefore, we should provide the same variety of opportunities for our clients.

- Our children learn positive values by seeing what we cherish and what we abhor. We teach them by what we watch and what we ignore, by what we cultivate and what we neglect. Therefore, we should be as concerned with what is playing on the agency TV as we are with what's on the treatment plan.

- Our children learn that blood is thicker than water. Therefore, we should create a counterpart that will provide a primary group for the children who share their lives with unrelated persons to which they can be committed.

It is possible for our need for proficiency in the technical aspects of our respective professions to obscure our responsibility for socialization. Many professional schools prepare students best to provide transient services in professional workshops such as hospitals, clinics, and courtrooms. In these and most other service sites, the service is an adjunct to the life of the client. However, in child caring agencies the primary service is day-to-day life. In this setting and in other life defining venues, our companionship and our character may be as, or possibly, more important than our professional proficiency.

In Greek mythology, the guardian of Thebes, asked travelers, "What walks on four feet in the morning, on two at noon, and on three in the evening?" Oedipus solved the riddle by saying, "Man crawls on all fours as a baby, walks upright in the prime of life, and uses a staff in old age." Old age or the Third Season of our lives is when, having learned as much as we can during our First Season and earned or contributed as much as we can during our Second Season, we endeavor to enjoy the fruits of our labors, a time when for the first time in our lives we are truly free. Unchained from the restrictions of our parents and educators, and free of the constraints of bringing up the next generation and earning a living.

Before retiring and entering my own Third Season, I conducted a final workshop for some of the staff at Parsons Child and Family Center. It was based on the Alternatives to Violence Workshop that I had facilitated for many students of public schools and inmates at correction facilities. During a brief rest period, I was asked where I go to relax. I replied, "I go home because my wife thinks I'm adorable and my dog thinks I'm God." As unlikely as these ideas may seem, they do provide an insight as to how the affirmation I received at home gave me the confidence I needed to conduct these workshops. It is possible that most of the seeds of change planted during my many workshops were eroded by staff changes, competing programs, time constraints, or lack of support long before they could take root and help make significant institutional change. This is one reason why cultural change is so difficult. A culture whether that of an organization like a school or a prison or of a nation like the U.S. is a broad web of complex embedded systems; however, the programs that might be used to change them, like the Alternatives to Violence Program, are generally limited in both scope and longevity. Even those seeds that do gain a foothold are not likely to survive to effect the unborn seventh generation, which would be an indication of their lasting success. But, I did not participate in the Alternatives to Violence Program because I believed that I was helping to bring about a great cultural change, but because I believed that it is possible for each individual to change and improve their lives in ways that would take generations for a culture to accomplish. So not being able to do everything did not provide me with a reason to do nothing. The following story makes the point. *While walking along the beach during a low tide a man saw that the sand was littered with starfish that the high tide had carried in and then abandoned. When the man came upon a child tossing starfish back into the sea he said, "You're wasting your time, there are so many you can't possible save enough to make a difference so what does it matter?" The child picked up another starfish and tossed it back into the water. "It matters to that one," the child explained.*

2003.5   AUSTRIA AND GERMANY

In the fall of 2003, Reg and I took a two-week vacation to Austria and Germany. The first week was an 8-day cruise on the Danube River from Vienna, Austria to Nuremberg, Germany. It started in Vienna and we toured medieval towns in Austria's Wachau Valley. Savored the tastes of authentic dishes, learned about local legends, and understood why Strauss immortalized the "Blue Danube" in his waltz. At Passau, which lies at the confluence of the Inn, Ilz and Danube Rivers we had a guided walk along the town's narrow streets through Old Town and past traditional patrician houses and visited the baroque St. Stephen's Cathedral, heard a concert played on the 17,000-pipe organ, Europe's largest church organ. At Regensburg, one of Europe's best-preserved medieval cities we saw the largest groupings of 13th- and 14th-century church spires, towers and patrician houses north of the Alps and the 12th-century Old Stone Bridge. It was getting dark as we strolled past St. Peter's Cathedral. Later back on the ship Reg noticed that one of her earrings was missing. I remembered hearing a dull clink as we passed the church, but paid no attention to it, as there were other people strolling and distracting background noises. I went back to the courtyard with a flashlight and much to our surprise I found the earring just where I heard it fall an hour earlier. We visited Mozart's home in Saltsburg and the chilling stadium in Nuremberg where Adolf Hitler held many mass rallies. I remember seeing movies where thousands of people in that stadium were enthusiastically saluting and supporting Hitler and his policies. The country was in economic recessions because of the strict sanctions imposed on it after World War 1. The country rallied behind Hitler because of the problems they faced, apparently unaware that the solutions that he proposed would lead to one of the biggest tragedies in human history. I wonder if I had been a member of that crowd, out of work and fearful for my children's future, would I have joined the mob. The question terrifies me as I'm afraid of the answer. We all have the capacity for evil especially when mislead by fear.

Watching some of today's politicians play on peoples fear by exaggerating our problems bears an uneasy resemblance to the Nuremburg rallies.

During the second week, we visited the German cities and towns, which were the former homes of our German ancestors. We drove our Hertz Opal station wagon from Nuremberg where the cruise ended to Wurzburg where family records were archived. The following day we found documents for Reg's grandmother among the aging records. I had studied German enough to identify the column heading on the forms I would find in the archives, so I could tell if the document recorded a person's birth or their death. Next, we visited Eltmann the home of Reg's grandfather, Florian Straub who immigrated to America in 1888. Eltmann is a town of 5,500 inhabitants in the Hassberge district of Bavaria, Germany. It lies on the south bank of the Main River. The Bed and Breakfast ("Übernachtung mit Frühstück") that we had booked had closed but we were able to find another close-by. We never saw who provided the breakfast, when we left our bedroom we found the table set with piping hot coffee and bacon, eggs, cereal and rolls.

The following day we drove to Oberaurach, Bayern, Germany. We walked into the church where Reg's grandmother Maria Josepha Kaspar was baptized, 135 years earlier. Even though Oberaurach was a small town, it served as the social and economic center for the rural area. Neuschleichach is a tiny village within walking distance of Oberaurach. Reg's ancestors lived there but it was too small to have its own church.

I had written to the Blenks and arranged for us to meet Hubert Blenk, (Reg's third cousin,) his wife Lieselotte, their son Christian, and their daughter Carina at their home for lunch. Lieselotte had prepared sauerbraten made of wild boar and "Kartoffelknödel" (potato dumplings) the size of tennis balls. Christian spoke enough English to facilitate our conversation. We invited Hubert to visit us in America but he said, "Hubert, nicht fliegen. " (Hubert, doesn't fly.) Christian, on the other hand said he would love to come to America. He made two trips one with his girl friend and one with his mother. We enjoyed the visits as much as Chistian did.

2003.6 THE KIRCHENVERWALTER

Erdmannrode, Hessen, Germany was the home of my Great grandmother Lena Eichwald from 1831 until 1852 when, at the age of 21, she immigrated to America aboard the ship "Espindola." The town is a small, remote rural village in southern Hessen, with a population of a few hundred. As with many small towns in Germany, the center of town is comprised of a village square and a church. At the center of the square was an ancient tree with low draping limbs supported by huge wooden piles.

At the edge of the square was the church. A young girl played in among the tombstones in the churchyard. I could not help but to imagine young Lena Eichwald over a century before, playing among these same landmark tombstones or climbing the tree that was now too old to provide any benefit to the towns' children, but only shade to the towns' adults and nostalgic for days and people of the past. I felt somehow divided in this place. It was a part of my ancient history, my roots; and me but also separated from me by time, from the life I have experienced, and from the more recent history that I could only imagine.

We spoke to the girl in English; she replied in German and withdrew around the corner of the church. In a moment, her Grandfather appeared and greeted us in German and then in poor English as he realized that our German was less than marginal. I asked him if he was the Bürgermeister (major of the town), he laughed and told us that he was the Kirchenverwalter (church caretaker.) The photo show the Kirchenverwalter, with his granddaughter and me standing in front of the church which my great-grandmother attended over 100 years earlier.

Like the other small-town churches, we had seen in Germany, this church didn't have a sign indicating its denomination. Since the building was stark in comparison to what we had seen in largely Roman Catholic "Katholisch" Bavaria, we asked "Heir Kirchenverwalter" if the church was Lutheran. He didn't understand. I remembered that this denomination is Evangelical or "Evangelisch" in Germany. He understood Evangelical and then saw the connection to Martin Luther and nodded "Ja Luther."

He introduced the girl we had already briefly met as his granddaughter and she warmed to our presence. Then he became very solemn, asked if I was English, I told him that I was an American, but that some of my ancestors were English. Apparently, that was close enough for him to relay the following story: He had been a tank driver during the Second World War. He fought in North Africa in the German "Afrika Korps" under Field Marshall Erwin Rommel (The Desert Fox). While the Germans were not defeated in Africa until May of 1943, British forces in Egypt captured Heir Kirchenverwalter in 1942. Since he had witnessed the cruelty with which the German tankers had treated English prisoners, he had expected to be robbed, tortured, and then killed. Instead, he had a shower, a hot meal, a cigarette, and a safe place to wait out the rest of the war. He had been waiting 61 years in this tiny remote village to find an Englishman to thank for the kindness shown to him. His eyes filled with tears as we shook hands and I told him that his hospitality would serve to settle the score and he opened the doors to the ancient church where my great grandmother had worshiped as a child.

We examined the church, the courtyard, and the small village. It was all so quiet, peaceful, and beautiful that I asked myself, "Why would anyone ever leave?" On the other hand, it was so remote (a gas station attendant just 50 kilometers to the south had never heard of the place) so isolated and lifeless that I asked, "Why would anyone stay?" Of course, the "leavers" and the "stayers" all had their reasons, reasons that no doubt had more to do with who they shared their lives with than where they chose to live them. We may never know whom Lena left behind or why a future in an unknown place seemed to her to be a better life than a future with known family and neighbors.

As we drove out of town, we stopped on a hillside and looked back at the bucolic countryside that spread out before us. We took pictures that couldn't possibility fully capture the beauty, and talked about Lena and how she might have had this very scene imbedded in her memory as she left the town for the last time to build her new life in America, in New York City with my Great- grandfather Heinrich Gerhards from Siegburg, Germany. *(Although born in Sieglahr, District of Koln, Prussia, Germany, on his marriage license he listed his hometown as Siegburg. Sieglahr was a small town near the city of Siegburg.)*

2003.7   SIEGBURG

After leaving Erdmannrode, we drove west to Siegburg, in the district of Rhein-Sieg-Kreis, in North Rhine-Westphalia, Germany. I had made reservations at the Hotel zum Stern. The address was Markt 14-15, 53721 Siegburg. We drove around the small city of about 35,000 people for half an hour along cobblestone streets and could not find a road that connected with Markt. I stopped the car to recheck the map and noticed that there was a narrow alley in front of us with small sign saying "Hotel zum Stern." Another example of how good luck often surpasses good planning. We parked and checked in; our second story room had a balcony that overlooked the marketplace

in the huge main square in the heart of the city (in photo.) There were many street vendors, shops, bars, and restaurants within a few yards.

Across the market square from our hotel was St. Servatius Roman Catholic Church, completed in 1220 AD. We were going to meet Wolfgang Baum there the next morning and we decided to tour it and its second story museum. There were dozens of artifacts housed there; many were hundreds of years old. I had contacted the Catholic Diocese serving the area months before trying to determine if there were records there that might contain information about the Gerhards family. They referred me to Wolfgang, a well-known retired dentist whose hobby was genealogy. I spoke to him by phone while he was vacationing in Italy, and made plans to meet him at the church. In the evening, we strolled through the square and down side streets and boulevards. We bought a German doll for Emily. Later we ate in a quaint little restaurant the Sieburger Brauhaus, and bought a beer stein with its name and motto "zum rotten lowen" which means the Red Lion, painted on it. It was such a pleasant place; we wished we could have stayed longer.

Wolfgang Baum arrived the next morning and our hearts sank as he told us that there were no records at the church. He then explained that the church records were transferred to the civil archives "bürgerlich archivieren"across the river in Bonn during the Second World War, because it had a more secure repository. We drove at 150 k/h (93mph) for 10 kilometers on Audubon #565 across the Rhine River on the bridge to Bonn as Reg and I held on for dear life in the speeding Audi.

The archive had strict rules about the use of the card catalog, the number of persons allowed to work together in addition to meeting the approval of a matronly supervisor who seemed very skeptical about my presence. Wolfgang was able to convince her that we needed to go together but that only he would handle and documents. Reg was not allowed in as a party of two might be approved a party of three was strictly forbidden, and she used the time to stroll the beautiful grounds.

Wolf was literate in English, German, ancient German, and Latin. He would use all of these skills by the time he finished this project. We (meaning he) used the card catalogue, which was written in German, to locate an index book, which listed the events that took place at St. Servatius Church during the period when my great grandfather Henrich Gerhards lived in the area. The index book, written in Latin by the parish priests, was a chronological listing of every baptism, first communion, wedding, and death at which a priest officiated. I had obtained the year of Henrich's birth from his marriage license, so Wolf began his search at 1818. He ran his gloved finger down the page of the ancient document as he read each entry. Then he stopped. "This can't be correct," he said. In April of 1818, a woman whose first name was Anna, the same as Henrich's mother, and whose last name was "Gierards" which is similar to Gerhards had a baby. Five months later the same woman had another baby; a boy named Henrich. Not only was he convinced about the error, but he also had a very logical explanation about how it might have happened. The parish priest allowed the documents from each event to accumulate on his desk. When the pile grew high enough he would arrange them chronologically and begin entering them into the index book. Perhaps he had a glass of wine or two as he wrote late into the night. By the time he reached the end of the pile, his handwriting was beginning to devolve and his attentiveness began to fade. So, when Henrich was born in September the priest began to make the entry and instead of entering Henrich's mother's name, he entered the name that was already in mind from the April birth, which was only a few lines above Henrich's entry. He asked the supervisor to see a copy of the original documents. After several minutes, a large dusty bound volume of documents written in ancient German script arrived from the elevator from the basement. Wolf turned to the page where he expected to find what we were looking for. Henrich Gerhards was born to Johann Gerhards and his wife Anna Margaretha Blum. The document also proved that the priest did not make the mistake. The mayor of Sieglahr made a spelling error on the original document and only Johann's signature at the bottom of the page provides the correct spelling of the name. The information on this page led to several other documents going back several more generations.

Wolf asked the archive to make copies of all of the documents and mail them to him. He later found additional documents from the church records.

A few months later, he sent the documents to us together with an English translation of each.

Henrich's wife Lena (or Caroline as one U.S. document claims) was Lutheran and at the Lutheran record center, the day before traveling to Erdmannrode we discovered that the records were all written in the ancient German script and no one there could read them. The one Lutheran minister who could interpret the ancient script only worked a few days each week. We were so fortunate to have made contact with Wolf. I was able to add two additional generations to Henrich's father's branch of the family tree and four generations to his mother's branch because of his work.

2004.1   YATMA

In 2004, the Youth Advancement Through Music and Art (YATMA), program received a $25,000 grant from the Bill & Melinda Gates Foundation and brought its program to Parsons Child and Family Center in Albany, NY. It provided private and small class instruction in a variety of musical instruments, voice, dance, creative writing, and visual arts. YATMA students learned how it feels to be successful, to commit themselves, to work with others, and to learn about themselves. I was asked to join its' Board of Directors and I served as a member from 2004 until 2006 and as Board president from 2006 until 2009. The organization was later renamed "Educational Mentoring Through the Arts and Humanities" (EMTAH) and then renamed MERGE as it moved from Albany to Massachusetts and then to Pennsylvania.

In addition to serving on the board, I also developed a computerized Student Evaluation and Tracking System (SETS), which I donated to the organization. "SETS" is a comprehensive assessment program that assists organizations in tracking both qualitative and quantitative data that reflect student and teacher performance. MERGE now sells the software package to organizations associated with its mentoring program and to other service organizations seeking an effective evaluation system.

2004.2   LAKE LANIER CABIN

While we were baby-sitting, Emily a year and a half earlier, Reg found an ad in the local paper for a cabin for rent. It was on Lake Lanier, which lies just north of Suwanee, GA. The lake was created by the construction of Buford Dam on the Chattahoochee River in 1956.

The cabin was located in Flowery Branch, GA, but it was originally constructed in Macon, GA, hundreds of miles to the south during the civil war. The owner had the cabin moved and reassembled on a lakeside lot. It had a very small beach area but it was too steep for Emily to manage and a two-story boat dock, which we used for sun bathing. We spent the month of March at the cabin for several years until Brian and LeAnn bought a second home in Clayton, GA. It was close enough to Suwanee to allow many family visits during the month.

There was a public beach nearby, and we took Emily there so she could play in the sand. She occasionally spent the night with us at the cabin. Even our dog Keppie was allowed to come on our trips south during those years, as both the house and the yard were quite rustic and pet friendly.

2004.3   FLYING AT LAST

Knowing that I had once wanted to be a pilot, my three sons, David, Brian and Gregory chipped in and purchased for my 69th birthday, a 20-minute flight in the World War II P-51D Mustang fighter plane.

> *The P-51D is a single-seat fighter powered by a supercharged engine, and armed with six .50 caliber machine guns. The trainer, which I flew in, was modified into a two seater with two complete sets of controls.*

> *Because it had a long range and could fly above 15,000 feet, it provided safe escort to bombers in raids over Germany in 1944. Mustang pilots claimed 4,950 enemy aircraft shot down. Prior to its introduction bombers heading for Germany from England had no fighter plane escorts for the last and more dangerous leg of the trip as the older fighters ran low on fuel.*

> *Until 1950, the Mustang was the main fighter of the U.N. when jet fighters such as the F-86 took over that role. Many remain in service today for air racing, and at airshows.*

I was able to take the controls for part of the flight and the instructor performed some acrobatics before landing at the Schenectady airport. A video of the flight and a certificate of completion provided a record of the adventure.

As I look back on my early dream to become a fighter pilot, I now believe that I was never aggressive enough to have become a very good fighter pilot. If I had successfully completed flight training, I probably would have been designated a bomber pilot or navigator. Fortunately, I never had to find out.

2005.1   BIRTHDAY IN GEORGIA

Dear Dave and Michele,   March 2005

Since you cannot be with us today in Flowery Branch, GA, I thought I would join you, via this e-mail, in Voorheesville, NY. Today, at dinner, I hope to say three things to those gathered around our table.

First, since today is not really my birthday, and since it is not really any of our birthdays, we can celebrate each of our individual births today and collectively the birth of our extended family, including those who sit elsewhere but who reside here with us in our hearts.

Second, there once was a man who died. St. Peter gave him a tour of heaven and hell so the man could choose where he wanted to spend the rest of his days. In hell, the man saw a great table set with a huge and delicious feast. It had food and drink of every kind, prepared in a way that would make your chef friend Joey O'Brien's mouth water. In spite of all this food, the people at the table were hungry, because they had splints on their elbows and could not bend their arms to eat or drink. In heaven, the man saw a very similar scene, a similar table with the same glorious spread of delicacies, and the same splints on the guests' elbows. However, they were all filled with joy and good food, for they used their spoons to feed each other. Our family had made a heaven on earth for me, because we nourish and support one another. Thank you all for providing this wonder for me to witness and share.

Third, in the twenty-third psalm the psalmist tells us that his cup runneth over with God's blessings. My wish for all of you is for bigger cups, so that you all might find, capture, and savor all of the treasures that life has to offer, and that you will continue to share them with one another.

Please wish Ryan a Happy Easter from all of us.

Dad

BILL STRAUBS DEATH

Love One Another: A Eulogy for William Arthur Straub

(March 14, 1935 – November 7, 2005)

May God, give you peace.

I'd like to begin by thanking Donna for giving me her notebook so I could scribble down the words to this eulogy. And I would also like to say how proud we all are of Donna for being so brave during this hard and sad week.

I suppose Christ had a dilemma. He knew we would be better off if we could be like him. But he also knew that because he was perfect, we couldn't truly be like him.

Some people never try to help others because they think they can't do everything.

Some people don't even try to be good because they know they can't be perfect.

This is where people like Bill come in…good enough to learn from but not so perfect that we are intimidated by them. Bill was a regular person just like us. Yet, he was different. Bill performed many roles in life, but no matter what role he performed, the people around him could learn from him.

Bill was a fireman. He was willing, on a daily basis, to give his life for others.

As a fireman, I'm sure he wasn't perfect; but I know other firemen learned from him the value of sacrifice, the value of always doing your best.

Bill was a carpenter. Whether he was working on a commercial building or making a bookcase, you could be sure that the work was as good as he could do it because Bill never cut corners –except when he was driving to the job.

Maybe we could get the funeral director to drive fast to the cemetery.

Bill was a fisherman…a legendary fisherman, like his father.

Bill taught many of us how to fish. His son Billy –Captain Billy –may think he is a better fisherman than his father was, but I'd like to remind him that he needs sonar.

Firefighter, carpenter, and fisherman: those were the roles Bill performed. But they were not the roles that were closest to his heart. If Bill were to define himself, it would be by the roles he performed in his family: husband, father, grandfather, brother, uncle, nephew, and cousin.

Those are the roles we will most remember him for, because they are the roles that touched us most personally. When it came to love, Bill was a man of few words; but he was a man of many actions.

There are few of us in this church who have not felt some act of love from Bill Straub.

As he was dying and we were gathered around his bed at home, each of his children told me countless stories of his selfless love in action.

Christ gave his life away all at once in one dramatic moment.

Bill gave his life away in many small, everyday moments of putting the interests of others ahead of his own interests.

He would drive Donna anywhere, anytime, for any reason.

But not just Donna, he drove our elderly Aunt Jean anywhere she needed to go also.

Bill freely gave his time, his talent, and his treasure. For years, Bill supported his cousin Father Bob who is a missionary priest in Mexico.

When his sister Terry was dying, Bill was at her side day after day for years –while still driving people around, putting windows in people's houses, watching his grandchildren, and helping Billy with his boat.

If this eulogy were to include individual testimonies from each of you…we would be here for a week – at least.

But I would bet that the common thread running through all our personal stories about Bill would be this: he would want each of us to show our love for each other by our actions. This is the same message we hear in our churches, our synagogues, and our mosques: "Love one another." Bill was not a theologian. He was a man of faith. He was here in this church early every Sunday morning for first Mass.

As his brother, I think this is what Bill's life is telling us: Draw the circle of your loved ones closer. And then draw the circle larger to include more people.

Bill knew the relative unimportance of material things and the supreme importance of relationships. Bill was a great friend to many…I see his great friend John seated out there. Bill loved his wife, his children, and his grandchildren more than his own life.

In death, Bill will always live in our memories.

May you rest in peace, Bill.

Delivered by Gerard Straub

Written by Ronald Gerhard with help from Gerard Straub

St. Raymond of Penafort R.C. Church, East Rockaway, New York

Thursday, November 10, 2005

2005.3   LINCOLN CENTER

One of our old friends from Voorheesville, Dick Hagan invited Reg and me to join him and his wife, Susan, to see a play at Lincoln Center. When lit, the large plaza at the Center that contains the Opera House, several theaters, and a sparkling fountain is a spectacular sight.

We saw "The Light in the Piazza," a play with music and lyrics by Adam Guettel. Based on a novella by Elizabeth Spencer, the story is set in the 1950s and revolves around Margaret Johnson, a wealthy Southern woman and her emotionally stalled daughter, Clara, who spent a summer together in Italy. When Clara falls in love with a young Italian man, Margaret must reconsider not only Clara's future, but also her own deep-seated hopes and regrets as well. The play was enjoyable but the companionship was joy.

After the show, we ate in a small Italian Restaurant before returning to their home in Westport, Connecticut for the evening.

It takes a long time to grow an old friend.
John Leonard

2005.4   THANKSGIVING IN GEORGIA

We spent a few weeks in November in Georgia and enjoyed Thanksgiving Day at Brian and LeAnn's home. The table was set with the beautiful china, glassware, and silver that LeAnn inherited from her grandmother Clara Hennessey, who had died two years earlier. Since LeAnn worked full time and was attending Graduate School to become a teacher, she had few occasions to use her beautiful dining room.

We played with Emily who enjoyed taking her ring of plastic keys into a kitchen cabinet that LeAnn had emptied for her. She would bid us all farewell as she tucked herself into the cabinet and left on her vacation, only to return a few minutes later with twinkling eyes and a smile that could melt a glacier as easily as she melted my heart.

2005.5   AILING BUT NOT SICK

After spending the holidays in Georgia, it was time to return north. LeAnn drove us past the DeKalb Peachtree Airport to the Chamblee MARTA station in her Honda CRV. Reg and I would take the 38-minute ride the subway on MARTA's northeast/gold line to the Hartsfield-Jackson International Airport and then take the flight home that would leave two-thirds of our family a thousand miles behind.

As we approached the station, we all where sorry to be parting but said little as we put on smiles to hide our sadness. Then three-year-old Emily who had sat quietly in her car seat behind LeAnn said, "I don't feel well, but I'm not sick." We knew exactly what she meant, as we all shared her feeling but could not have expressed it as eloquently. Since that day, I too have been "not sick" each time I think of her and her wonderful parents a thousand miles away.

2006.1   BURBANK CALIFORNIA

Many of The San Damiano Foundation board meetings were conducted via conference call, with only those who lived near Burbank, California actually in attendance. However, in 2006 with many important items on the agenda it was decided that we should all gather in a face-to-face meeting. Gerry had assembled a remarkable array of people for his board. His easygoing yet charismatic style and compelling work seems to attract talented people of good will. I felt honored to be among them, my only real achievement was to marry his sister.

Reg joined me on the trip and we extended our stay so we could spend time with Gerry, Kathy his wife, and his daughter Adrienne and her husband Bill McBride. Adrienne and Bill were expecting their first child in a few weeks.

We spent one day with Kathy visiting Santa Barbara on the California coast, with the Santa Ynez Mountains as a dramatic backdrop. White stucco buildings with red-tile roofs reflected the city's Spanish colonial heritage. Upscale boutiques and restaurants offered local wines and seasonal fare. We visited Mission Santa Barbara, founded in 1786, which houses Franciscan friars and a small museum. The photo was taken on Stearns Wharf where we enjoyed a leisurely lunch with Kathy.

2006.2   FRANK DOHERTY DIES

Frank was the grandfather to my son David's wife Michele. He was a gentle man and was present at all of the many family gatherings and was loved and admired by all. As he lay dying in St. Peters Hospice, in Albany, NY, Michele asked me to write and deliver the eulogy at Frank's funeral mass at St. Ann/St. John R.C. Church in Albany, NY. It is included below.

A Eulogy for Francis C. Doherty

(October 16, 1920 – February 27, 2006)

Many of you have known Frank all of your lives. Some of you have known Frank for most of your lives. While some - like me – have only known Frank for a few years. But to Frank, the length of our relationships didn't matter to Frank, because he didn't ration friendship in small doses - friendship was how he chose to live.

Almost a century ago, in 1907, Frank's parents Patrick and Celia Doherty came to this country from Ireland. I imagine that they, like other immigrants of the time, had a dream, a dream that their future son Frank would someday live to see his own child grow and prosper here in America. We can assure Celia and Patrick that their dream has been fulfilled. Frank lived to see - not just one child- but four children - Barbara, Kathleen, Michael, and Thomas and 15 grandchildren and 11 great-grandchildren grow and prosper - here in America. And from time to time - they each remember - they remember your courage to do what was right for your family - and they remember that Frank continued that tradition by doing what was right for his family.

Whether he was taking the kids to the park, on train rides, or to the museum, Frank was always there for his family. Whether they needed a leader, a colleague or just a helping hand, they could always turn to Frank. I asked his grandchildren what they remembered about their gramps, they told me that he was shy enough to blush, sensitive enough to care, ordinary enough to chat with over a cold beer, and special enough stay connected to all their lives.

Today, we pay tribute to Frank. Frank worked for 40 years as a conductor for the New York Central Railroad, and who helped restore historic airplanes with the Empire State Aeronautical Museum. And who earned his membership in the American Legion Fort Orange Post by serving as a member of that "band of brothers and sisters" which Tom Brokaw called "The Greatest Generation," those who fought for our country in the Second World War. Most importantly, Frank maintained a home and a marriage for 65 years with his soul mate Millie. He was a faithful member of this congregation and a volunteer servant and leader in several of its important programs, he was a role model to many, and at age, 85 – he received the "2005 Senior Lifetime Achievement Award" for his service to others.

About 12 years ago, I started working at Parsons Child and Family Center, only to find that Frank and Millie were there long before me. But they were not sitting at a desk – like me - but doing the real work of Christians - sharing a portion of their lives with some of the kids who lived at Parsons – kids who had so little of their own to share.

In the last moments that I spent with Frank, I opened the bible on his bed stand and read to him Psalm 112. It is the prayer of "a good man." It says, "they shine through the darkness, a light for the upright; they are gracious, merciful, and just." I thought to myself, "that sounds like Frank, 'gracious, merciful, and just'."

I wish that I could draw a lasting sketch of Frank's life that would provide us all with a permanent memorial to this man that I am honored to have called my friend – fortunately Frank has already drawn this sketch – drawn it upon the canvas of our lives. We can make the sketch that he has drawn so visibly for us, visible for others by honoring him who we called Dad, or Gramps or Frank - when we remember not only what he accomplished - but also what he was - a gracious, merciful, and just man. While he is no longer here to show us by his example - we do remember - and we follow his example when we choose to be gracious, merciful, and just.

When Frank was born, he cried, and those around him rejoiced. Frank lived his life in such a way that when he died, those around him cried. Being a man of faith, Frank rejoiced.

We all still live in the valley where the shadow of death casts its fears upon the living - not able to see the light that creates the shadow. Frank has passed through that valley - beyond the shadow and now lives in the light of the God he has faithfully followed. So even in our sorrow, we can rejoice for Frank. And we hope that one day we will rejoice with Frank. However, until that day

May you rest in peace Frank Doherty – Gracious, Merciful, and Just man.

2006.3   SUMMER GATHERINGS

In July 2006, Reg and I took the 1 hour and 15 minutes Ferry ride across the Long Island Sound from Bridgeport, CT to Port Jefferson, NY. We had made plans to meet three of our college classmates Grace, Jo, and Jeanie, in Riverhead, LI. We drove first to Mattituck to pick up Grace, who lived alone in a wonderful antique home. We met the others in a new restaurant on the Peconic Bay and because it was newly opened, we had no trouble finding a corner table facing the water or staying for hours reminiscing and updating each other about our lives.

From Riverhead, we drove westward to meet with the Straub clan in Nassau County. Seeing Donna reminding me of one of our many previous visits when Donna greeted me with a big hug and told me that I was her favorite. Her friend reminded her that she had just told Uncle Joe that he was her favorite. Without hesitation Donna replied, "I can have more than one favorite." Why didn't I think of that?

Our next stop was in Eaton's Neck, LI to spend some time with our Goddaughter Katie, her husband Andy, and their three daughters Corinne, Kristen, and Elizabeth. Katie is Graces' daughter, and we have met with her and her family many times at her house and at ours. We played pattern ball with the three girls, walked across the slanted shadows of the shaded paths, and enjoyed quiet meals with this lovely and loving family.

2006.4   RYAN'S 20TH BIRTHDAY

To Ryan Gerhard   11 Aug 2006

I look at a bird: I think our family is like a nest:
Safe, but not confining.
I look at a fruit bowl: I think our family is like an orange:
Each section distinct but united.
I look at vacation photos: I think our family is like a canoe:
Unsteady, but progressing because we all paddle.
I look at the sports page: I think our family is like a baseball game:
Slow, but not over until the last out.
Wherever I look: I think of you: a man, but still my grandson.

Happy Birthday, Grandpa Ron

2006.5   LEANN'S GRADUATION

LeAnn had completed her Bachelor's degree many years before and had completed the class work and needed only a final field project for a Master's Degree in Science. However, she thought teaching would be a good career to pursue because the schedule was perfect while Emily was in school and because her life experience convinced her that she had the skills and motivation that she would need as a teacher. Like her husband Brian, she attended Graduate School on a part time basis while working full time. When she graduated with a degree in Elementary Education in the spring of 2006, Reg, Greg and I attended the ceremony and later held a party at their home in Suwanee. Emily was beyond cute helping with the preparations and dancing with her Nia. LeAnn went on to become a model kindergarten teacher frequently winning the praise of her peers and often being asked to take on additional responsibility. We are all very proud of her. I hope that each of your children will have at least one teacher like LeAnn, the children love her, her peers admire her, and her supervisors respect her.

A good teacher is like a candle — it consumes itself to light the way for others.
Mustafa Kemal Atatürk

2007.1 & 1950   FAMILY REUNIONS

When we returned in April 2007 from a wonderful month at Brian and LeAnn's new cabin in Clayton, Ga. with Gregory, Brian, LeAnn and Emily we began spring-cleaning. The south wall of our contemporary style Delmar home had floor to ceiling windows. Our friend Frank Walsh installed the plate glass panes when we moved from Georgia to Delmar in 1978. He obtained the glass from a grocery store front that he was helping to modernize. It reminded me of the grocery store where Tony had worked in Central Islip.

(1950) I lived close enough to the Central Islip High School to walk home rather than ride the school bus like many kids in what was then a small rural community. After school if there was no ball game or practice session, I would often walk to Sam Holiday's Grocery Store on Carlton Ave. where Tony worked on Saturdays and five afternoons a week (after his regular job as cook at the State Hospital.) It was a very friendly place and tiny by today's standards, about 25 by 60 feet. This included the grocery section, a butcher shop, and the fruit stand where I worked one summer. Sam was gregarious and had a great Irish wit. The two butchers, whose counter was no more than twenty feet from the grocery counter, were always friendly, greeted each customer by name, and recommended a cut of meat that they knew the family enjoyed, or could afford. Tony was in his glory here, he never seemed happier than when he was behind the counter. So, it was obvious that something was seriously wrong when I walked past the window washer and into the store that spring afternoon. The mood was sullen and secretive as the men behind the counters passed knowing glances back and forth and Tony was nowhere to be seen. I looked at Sam cautiously, fearing the worst.

Sam nodded discreetly toward the young Italian man washing the outside of the large plate glass windows. Finally, he said, "See that man, that's Tony's son. Tony doesn't want to be seen by him and is hiding in the basement until he leaves." I was stunned and wanted to see Tony, but Sam insisted that he wanted to be alone. I hadn't known that Tony had a son from a prior marriage. Now I not only had a blood brother, Artie, and a half-brother, Richie, but also a stepbrother Tony Junior as well. I later learned that his son lived in Patchogue, L.I., N.Y., which was Tony's family home. He was born in 1928 and named after his father. I never saw him again and Tony never spoke of him or of that day when his two worlds collided at an unexpected and apparently unwanted family reunion. I can only imagine what Tony might have been feeling as he huddled in the dark basement with his first-born son just a few feet above his head. What could have caused such a schism in which father and son are so estranged that no words could pass between them?

(2007) With the windows now sparkling clean, I started on the landscaping in preparation for our family's reunions. Brian, LeAnn, and Emily were coming to Delmar for one week in July and Gregory with his girlfriend Lauren, for a week in August. We would share much of our time together with David and Michele in Voorheesville.

In order to enjoy a family reunion, you must first enjoy your family.
RJG

2007.2 & 1863   THE PINK KNEE

On July 17, 2007, I was in bed on the orthopedic ward of St. Peters Hospital when the phone rang. It was my favorite granddaughter, Emily: pure joy. I could picture her there with that smile like a sunrise, so big that it could swallow her face and so radiant that it could brighten the darkest day. I had my left knee replaced the day before and she wanted to know the color of my new knee. Only a young child could ask such a question. Knowing her penchant for pink, I told her that the doctor was out of pink and I had to take a regular white one. I heard the disappointment in her voice as relayed the sad news to her parents sitting next to her by the phone. "They were out of pink."

A few days later while recovering at home, I hobbled down the stairs on my crutches and found Reg making breakfast, just as she had done on so many previous mornings for the past 47 years. As I sometimes did, I gave our private tuneful greeting, "♪ Gooood Morning. ♪" As Reg is always very tuned in to my moods and feelings, when I gave the familiar cheery welcome, she knew that I was feeling better and that the pain had subsided. Reg not only has the power to improve her own mood, but she can make me feel better as well. Her smile lets me know that she's okay and my mood improves. Sometimes when I'm feeling low I give her our special cheery greeting, and she heals my soul with her smile, as surely as Dr. Abraham healed my knee with his blade when he replaced my knee.

The ends of the three bones that comprise the knee joint are replaced with a titanium "work-alike" joint in this major procedure. In spite of the fact that all of the many muscles, ligaments and tendons in the area were badly damaged and required months of rehabilitation, after a few days I was home, walking with crutches, and enjoying the fact that I would soon be more mobile and have less pain than I had before the surgery.

(3 July 1863) It was the third day of one of the bloodiest battles in American history. The fields were already covered with blood on July 3, 1863 as the battle of Gettysburg came to its climax. Fighting resumed on Culp's Hill, and cavalry battles raged to the east and south, but the main event was a dramatic infantry assault by 12,500 Confederates against the center of the Union line on Cemetery Ridge. Pickett's Charge was repulsed by Union rifle and artillery fire at great loss to both armies. 7,863 Americans were killed during the three-day battle and 27,224 were wounded. Among the wounded was Henrich Gerhards, my Great-Grandfather. A single rifle ball, embedded in his right groin, there was no major bone, nerve, or blood vessel damage and yet he spent the rest of life in pain and was so disabled that he and his wife Lena Eichwald Gerhards lived out their lives on his military pension.

I have copies of his medical records and believe that his problems resulted from the scarring and fusing of the several types and layers of tissue in his groin. His permanent disability resulted from injuries that could be easily repaired by today's medical professionals, while the surgery that I received could not even have been imagined much less performed by his physicians 144 years earlier.

(2007) When Emily's get-well card arrived a few days later, I saw Snoopy with his knees painted pink; and the wound covered with a real Band-Aid. Over the years, I'm sure that I have received thousands of cards of every description, but it is the memory of the pink knee that will always warm my heart and make me so thankful for the wonderful people who fill my life and for the brilliant healers who make it possible. Thank you, to both.

> If the only prayer you ever say in your entire life
> is thank you, it will be enough.
> *Meister Eckhart*

2007.3 & 1940   INNOCENCE

> *"There are some things children cannot know,*
> *because once they learn them they are no longer children."*
> *A. Brilliant*

At the age of five, both Emily and I were innocent. During my childhood innocence simply meant that I was naively unaware. Emily however remained innocent because she was unharmed; naiveté is no longer enough and perhaps impossible in this effusive age of information and communication. My insular screen protected me with the veneer of ignorance; Emily's LED screen exposes her to what lies beneath the veneer.

Society had changed the definition of innocence.

> *"Come mothers and fathers*
> *Throughout the land*
> *And don't criticize*
> *What you can't understand*
> *Your sons and your daughters*
> *Are beyond your command*
> *Your old road is*
> *Rapidly agin'*
> *Please get out of the new one*
> *If you can't lend your hand*
>
> *For the times, they are a-changin'."*
> *Bob Dylan*

2007.4   DAVE'S CHRISTMAS GIFT

Dear Dave,

December 23, 2007

Many of my most recent woodcarvings have been of animals and birds. As I was thinking about what to make for you on your 42nd birthday, I thought of the wonderful landscape you are creating at your home with blue stone steps, paths and patios and your desire to get back to working with your plants when all of the stone work is finally completed. So, I decided to make you a carving that includes both plant and stone.

The plant is a facsimile of a leaf from the corn plant that has been in our living room for many years and the stone is a chip from the blue stone walkway you built around our backyard pond. The glass bead symbolizes a drop of water that is there to nourish the plant and to cascade over the rock.

The leaf is a symbol of life, the water is a symbol of sustenance, and the stone is a symbol of strength.

Like nature, you possess these characteristics and like nature, you share them freely with us all.

Happy Birthday Dave, Love Dad

2007.5 & 1947   RODENTS AND OTHER HEATHENS

Yesterday two feet of snow fell and the backyard animals and birds huddled in their nests, tucked safely in the bows of the pine trees that we planted over the past 29 years. The yard was my church and I often wondered why so many consider a manmade structure, of brick and painted glass to be holier than this yard, tended to, but not created by man. If there is a sacred place, surely it is to be found in nature.

But, today the sky is clear and the air is still. The birds have returned to our feeder eating their corn and millet and suet. The mouse that lives with his family under the rock by the pond pokes his head out from time to time and scurries to the feeder to pick up the seeds discarded or dropped by the birds.

The squirrel, from the big maple tree also returned. I shooed him away, "Scat, there's nothing here for you, you little heathen."

(1947) It was a warm summer day, school was over, and we had recently moved into our new house on Pine View Blvd., the place that I would later refer to as my childhood home even though I had spent more than half of my youth living elsewhere. I had met all the neighborhood kids and was settling into my new life. There was still the nagging question of why I had a Tony instead of a Dad, but like so many other questions in my life at that time, it too was easily deferred.

There was quite a commotion at the end of the block; Father McGinn was home. (I learned later that he was a local hero, the small-town boy who became a Catholic Priest at a time when few from the village went beyond high school.) As I approached the yard, the largest and best kept in the area, I saw Father McGinn with most of the neighborhood kids talking and laughing in the back yard. As was his custom, he invited the Catholic kids in the neighborhood to an ice cream and cookie party during his annual homecoming visit with his parents. When he saw me looking in through the cyclone fence he said, "Scat, there's nothing here for you, you little heathen." Ice cream isn't the only way to cool down on a summers' day.

I guess we all need outsiders to hate; it makes the insiders seem so special. For some the outsiders are rodents who eat too much, for others its young boys who are offered too little.

2008.1   JURY DUTY

The county called me for jury duty several times in the past but this was the first time that I ended up on a jury. I was an alternate so I would not get to help decide the fate of the accused unless another juror was unable to continue. The charge was attempted murder. A drug dealer was robbed of his money including that which he owned to his supplier in the Bronx. The dealer's friends told him that he had only one option, "Leave Albany, and never come back, because the supplier will feel obligated to kill you even if he believes your story about being robbed." The dealer thought he could convince the supplier that he would make up the money if allowed to continue operations. As his friends suspected the supplier hired a "hitman" and together they drove to Albany and shot the bankrupt dealer. Although seriously wounded and permanently disabled, the dealer lived and called 911. The prosecuting attorney built what I thought was an airtight case against the "hitman" with three eyewitnesses, ballistic evidence, the weapon, an overheard jailhouse confession, and dozens of pieces of circumstantial evidence. After my dismissal, the 12 regular jury members began their deliberations. Each day I watched the newspaper for the results. A week went by before the judge declared a mistrial because one of the juries refused to find the man guilty because, unlike the cop shows on TV, there was no DNA evidence at the scene. I was stunned that someone could be so stupid; it reminded me somewhat of the O.J. Simpson case, except in that case the entire jury had a very different perception of what had happened than I did watching the trial on TV. A few weeks later, a second jury found the man guilty and the judge gave him a long prison sentence.

I was very impressed by the quality of the trial, the judge, the lawyers, the jury members, with one possible exception seemed to me to be very fair minded and competent, and I was honored to be a part of the process.

2008.2 & 1952   DRIVING MISS KEPPIE

In 1996 about a year after our long-time family pet Teddy died, Reg surprised me with a Christmas gift, Keppie, a gentle, loving, and nervous female Lab mix. She was named for the German mathematician and astronomer Johannes Kepler, (1571-1630.) Kepler demonstrated rigorously what Copernicus had only guessed to be the case that the sun and not the earth was the center of the solar system. Keppie was obviously very bright and I didn't think that Johannes would have minded being remembered in this way.

She loved to ride in the car. During her first few months with us, she would run all over the neighborhood whenever she managed to get outside without a leash. Our first attempts to catch her took hours but when I eventually realized how much she loved the car, I stopped chasing her and drove around block until she spotted me. When I saw her coming, I'd open the door and she'd jump in.

She loved to ride with her head out of the window, even in the winter. When it was very cold, she would whine for me to open the window. However, when she realized it was too cold she would go to the window on the other side of the car and whine again, I suppose that she was hoping that side of the car would be warmer.

In the summer Reg and I would occasionally drive to a nearby frozen custard stand. We would buy Keppie her own cup of frozen yogurt. She loved it and the kids in the nearby cars would howl with laughter seeing a dog eating her own frozen yogurt. On her birthdays, I would take her to McDonalds and buy her a hamburger. The celebration would last about 3 seconds.

(1952) Often in those moments of abundance and sometimes in moments of scarcity, I would remember when McDonalds first opened on Long Island, and recall with something approaching shame, that I couldn't afford to buy a $0.19 hamburger. I may have been finished with the past, but apparently, the past was not yet finished with me.

(2008) Keppie would climb the stairs with us each night and sleep in her own bed in our bedroom. Gradually as she aged, she was unable to climb the stairs but she would cry if we went upstairs without her. So, I would carry up the stairs in the evening and down again in the morning. Eventually she began to lose control of her bodily functions and we knew it was time to have her put down. I took her for a long car ride with many doggie treats and luncheon at McDonalds' drive thru for her last 3-second hamburger. At the vets, I sat with her on the floor as I had done with Teddy years before and held her head in my hands as she breathed her last breath. It was very sad to lose my favorite friend. Fortunately, my niece Donna had taught me that I could have more than one favorite. It was too cold to dig another grave beside Teddy's so we had her cremated and I sprinkled her ashes around pond, the path to the woods, and the grave marker of her predecessor.

There is no cure for birth and death, save to enjoy the interval. George Santayana

2009.1   SNOW BIRDS

We decided to extend our southern winter trip through most of February and March by dividing our time between Florida and Georgia. Our friends Jerry and Carol in Punta Gorda, FL were preparing to move from their home to a condominium and they let us stay at the vacant condominium, which abutted a golf course. We toured the costal islands with them and ate at several seaside restaurants. Jerry always knew the best places to eat.

When we returned to Brian and LeAnn's cabin in Clayton, GA., we hiked to the many waterfalls and along the Rayburn paved nature trail. Later we took Emily to play land where she slid, jumped, hopped, and ran for hours. After we returned her home to Suwanee, we visited the Foxfire Heritage Center in Mountain City, GA. In addition to the onsite museum, they produce a magazine, a book series, and an innovative approach to teaching. It also produces art festivals, workshops, and educational resources.

We had three family celebrations including a mock wedding for Lauren and Greg, St. Patrick's Day and an early 74th birthday party for me in a Clayton restaurant that is known for its key lime pie.

2009.2   LAUREN

The following was written to accompany the hand carved music box I made for Lauren Keating's wedding shower on August 19, 2009.

THE COUPLE

At first glance, the objects in this carving may appear to be two people, However, on closer observation it is seen that it is really just one. That is, just one couple. A couple is not merely a pair of individuals.

To become a couple, the pair must yield enough of their individuality to create a new entity. They become an entity, which contains all of the gifts of the individuals, plus the other-centeredness that makes the couple more than just the sum of its partners.

To become a couple, the partners combine their experiences from their pasts, share in the events of the day, and create a vision for the future.

The three heart shaped spaces within the sculpture represent the three levels of love which the couple shares.

> ➤ Agape love –   is unconditional and selfless where a person gives to another even if this act does not benefit her/him in any way.
> ➤ Philos love -   is based on friendship between two people that is the foundation of successful long-term relationships.
> ➤ Eros love -   is based on the strong physical feelings that lie at the heart of strictly romantic relationships.

Couples, unlike pairs, freely share all three levels of love.

2009.3   UMBRELLA

Umbrella is a non-profit agency that has been helping senior citizens and people with disabilities live comfortably, safely and independently in their own homes since 1995. Serving Albany, Saratoga, Schenectady, and Rensselaer Counties in upstate New York, Umbrella's award-winning program has been recognized by New York State and local governments alike for its excellence. In 2009, I began volunteering with Umbrella. I was a handyman prepared to provide whatever service my clients might need. Some assignments were as simple as changing a light bulb for a woman who no longer felt safe on a stepstool. Some as complex as designing and installing a small apple orchid, comprised of seven-year-old espaliered trees, for a 90-year-old man who knew that he would never eat the fruit from the trees that we planted together.

He who plants a tree plants hope.
Lucy Larcom

Espalier is the training of dwarf species to grow against a fence or wall. The technique was developed in the 16th century, out of the practical need for growing fruit in northern France and southern England. They discovered that horizontal apple-tree branches would direct energy away from vigorous vertical growth and produce lateral branches that eventually flower and produce fruit. In addition, by growing the tree flat against a wall or fence, they could create a favorable microclimate in which the wall radiated heat and provided shelter. As they do today, growers kept the trees dwarfed for ease of management.

I also painted walls, raked leaves, trimmed bushes, designed landscapes, cleared drains, and removed beehives. I volunteered my time and never charged the standard Umbrella handy man rate of $12 an hour. When we moved to LaGrange Rd., I left Umbrella, as there was much to do at our new home. Now I think that it may not be too long before I'm hiring a handyman rather than working as one.

> *"The best time to plant a tree was 20 years ago,*
> *the second-best time is now."*
> *Chinese Proverb*

CHAPTER 9   *TWENTY TEN*

Advances and changes of the era included economic globalization, the revolution in information technology, the nation's chronic deficits, and our pattern of excessive energy consumption. The disruption of many Islamic states in the Middle East has begun a process that will likely take decades to resolve, as dictatorial regimes crumble and competing forces battle to fill the vacuum. The worst earthquake in over 200 years killed 10s of thousands of people and destroyed much of Haiti's, already faltering infrastructure. An explosion of a drilling rig in the Gulf of Mexico created one of the world's worst environmental disasters. In 2011 a tsunami caused by a Pacific Ocean earthquake destroyed several Japanese cities and flooded a nuclear power plant causing the worst peacetime radiation disaster in history. In 2012, hurricane Sandy reaped havoc on the East coast of the United States causing damages that took years to repair and alerted the country about rising sea levels.

Best-selling books included "The Girl Who Kicked the Hornet's Nest," "Women Food and God: An Unexpected Path to Almost Everything", "Mockingjay", "Dead in the Family", "The Big Short: Inside the Doomsday Machine", "The Short Second Life of Bree Tanner", "Freedom: A Novel", "Sh#t My Dad Says", and "The Immortal Life of Henrietta Lacks."

An average new house cost $238,880

The average salary per year was $40,523

In 2010, a gallon of gas sold for $2.05, a loaf of bread cost $2.79 and the average cost of new car was 27,958.

The life expectancy of Males was 76.2, and for Females, it was 81.1 years.

The US Population in 2010 was 308,745,538

2010.1   THE FUTURE

At the turn of the century on January 1, in the year 2000, I thought of 2010 as representing the distant future where I would eventually reside. But today on January 1, 2010, I still don't reside there, as the future remains elusive forever beginning on the next page of my calendar. One thing doesn't change is that the future always turns out differently from what we expected, hoped for, or imagined. But its saving virtue is that it is real. Some see the future as a promise, where others, see only a threat. Perhaps it is both or perhaps . . . it is a self-fulling prophecy.

Life is what happens while you are busy making other plans.

John Lennon

2010.2 REUNIONS

In May of 2010, Reg and I took a trip to Long Island for a family reunion. We were Straubs, Gillers, Hettenbachs, Goodwins, and Gerhards. Carolyn and Richie Giller are gracious hosts and have a wonderful back yard which is almost all paved with bricks and a large in ground pool. There were 25 guests including eight kids who loved playing in the water. The weather was perfect and we spent the day eating, planning, and reminiscing.

In August, we drove from Delmar to Rhinebeck to meet at Mike and Sally's home and with Jo who took a train from Manhattan to join us. Mike was the best man at our wedding and Jo was Reg's bride's maid and roommate throughout nurses training. Mike's daughter, who is professional cook, prepared luncheon and we enjoyed touring their expansive home and estate and spending time with our old friends.

2010.3 ANNA MARIE ISLAND

Brian and LeAnn used their house swap credits to reduce the costs of renting four adjoining cabins on Anna Marie Island just west of St Petersburg, FL. The Island is a quaint Barrier Island nestled in the Gulf of Mexico, with beautiful turquoise waters  and white sandy beaches. It is a place where "old" Florida charm can still be found, flip flops are a way of life and the speed limit never exceeds 35mph. High rise condos and fast food restaurants are pleasantly absent from the pristine "get away from it all" island. The four families each had a separate modern cabin and Ryan and his girlfriend shared space with Dave and Michele. We spent a part of each day at the beach. Each family had some time to themselves and much time to share with the entire group of 10 Gerhards and guest. We toured Sarasota, which is a favorite haunt of Brian and LeAnn, and we ate in several fine restaurants. One evening we celebrated our being together with a silly hat parade. On one of our last days there, we took a cruise around the archipelago, leaving at dust and returning in the evening. We saw the sunset and nighttime skyline of the nearby towns and residential compounds from the bow of the boat.

2010.4 OLD FORGE

While we had spent many vacations and day trips in the Adirondacks and had seen many of its beautiful lakes and villages, we had never been to Old Forge, which lies in Herkimer County, west of our usually vacation spots. We stayed at a quiet old Inn, which was nearly vacant as the touring season had ended and the skiing season had not yet begun. The Enchanted Forest/Water Safari was closed for the season, which was fine with me, but we did witness the daily train robbery by the Loomis Gang aboard the Adirondack Scenic Railroad. We ended our extended weekend away at the Adirondack Museum in Blue Mountain Lake. The museum offers workshops on logging, boats, outdoor recreation, mining, craftsmanship, and fine arts. Historic structures range from a log hotel to a one-room schoolhouse. We walked through the landscaped grounds; toured the beautiful garden, with the spectacular view of the surrounding area in the background.

2010.5   HOME AWAY FROM HOME

After living on Greenwood Lane for 31 years, Reg and I decided that it wouldn't be too long before the large terraced and heavily landscaped yard, the multiple staircases, the detached garage and the size of house would be too much for us to maintain. We didn't want to be forced to live in whatever house happened to be on the market when we needed to downsize so we decided to begin looking at our leisure until we found a house that we would enjoy living in and still be able to manage with our aging bodies. When asked why we were moving I replied," I heard that most accidents occurred within a mile of home . . . so we moved."

After many months we found 14 La Grange Road in Delmar. We had looked at many ranch style houses but they each had major problems. This house with it large windows, screened porch, fireplace, attached garage, and huge basement seemed perfect for us. Dave and Michele helped us paint most of the rooms before we moved in and we were fortunate to find a buyer quickly for Greenwood.

I thought that leaving the old homestead would be difficult because there were so many memories there. But our new home was so perfect that we took our memories with us.

I made many upgrades to the new house and its mechanical systems and set up a woodworking shop in the basement. Reg took over the larger guest room for sewing and office work.

2011.1   THE AMERICAN DREAM

It seems catching up with the American dream is as improbable as catching up with the future. In the past 80 years, the cost of a new home has increased at more than twice the rate than the typical annual salary increased.

Year	Median Cost of New Home	Median Annual Salary	Number of years' salary needed to purchase a Home
1930	$3,845	$1,970	1.95
1940	$3,920	$1,725	2.27
1950	$8,450	$3,210	2.63
1960	$12,700	$5,315	2.39
1970	$23,400	$9,400	2.49
1980	$64,600	$19,500	3.31
1990	$122,900	$28,960	4.24
2000	$169,000	$40,703	4.15
2010	$221,800	$47,793	4.64

As the distribution of the wealth of our nation has gradually drifted upward, working class Americans are gradually receiving a smaller and smaller percentage of our bounty. Although the nation's wealth has increased over the past fifty years, it has not grown equally for all groups. Poorer families went from having no wealth on average to being about $2,000 in debt, those in the middle roughly doubled their wealth, about enough to keep up with inflation; while families near the top saw their wealth quadruple; and the wealthiest families grew six-fold. The changes in the distribution of

wealth are closely related to the changes in income. This chart from the Institute for Policy Studies shows how income has decreased for the poorest people, increased only slightly for the middle class, and increased greatly for the wealthiest 10% of Americans over the past 40 years.

2011.2   BRADY MILLS

Brady Mills Gerhard, our first natural born grandson, was born on 31 Oct 2011, it was Halloween, and he was definitely a treat. His red hair and blue eyes made him even more beautiful. Brady's middle, Mills, was taken from my mother's maiden name. It represents the Scottish side of the family which Greg seems quite interested in highlighting.

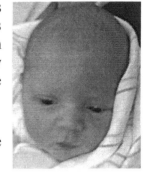

Brady's arrival made it perfectly clear why these little wonders are called "<u>Grand</u>" children.

2011.3   A MAN REAPS WHAT HE SOWS

The following text was given for my friend Paul along with a walking stick I carved for his 70th birthday.

(For Paul Troidle)
A Man Reaps What He Sows.
[Galatians 6.7}

You have sown support, love, comfort, aid, direction, beauty, joy, and security for others. I believe that you will reap that which you have sown

The walking stick I have made for you is a totem that symbolizes your life, how you have chosen to live it and the bounty that you reap.

➢ The strength of the Pole symbolizes the support that you supply for others

➢ The closeness of the Vine symbolizes the love that you share with others

➢ The Grip symbolizes the comfort that you extend to others

➢ The Strap symbolizes the aid that you minister to others

➢ The Compass symbolizes the direction that you provide for others

➢ The Gem symbolizes the inner beauty that you show to others

➢ The Whistle symbolizes the joy that you contribute to others

➢ The Tip symbolizes the security that you offer to others

2011.4   NEW YANKEE STADIUM ~ OLD YANKEE FAN

Reg has been a Yankee fan ever since her father brought her to the old Yankee Stadium when she was a little girl and she wanted to see the new stadium which opened in 2009. Her father had supplemented his income by working evenings as an usher at the old stadium. Ushers worked for tips and would escort fans to their seats and wipe off the dust from the city traffic. Later in the game when it was apparent which seats would remain empty, ushers would guide the more generous patrons to better seats. When Reg and I were dating, we would pick her father up at the subway station with his pockets bulging with coins. Today, ushers merely enforce seating restrictions, and on any given day, many box seats go wanting for fans.

By July 8, 2011, Derek Jeter had 2,999 hits. We were in the stands that day hoping to see him become the 28th player in history to have 3,000 hits. It was a bad day, Jeter didn't get a hit, the Yankees lost the game, and the bus took four hours to return to Albany due to road closures. However, the next day Jeter became  just the second player in Major League history to log his 3,000th hit with a homer joining Wade Boggs, who did it in 1999. We enjoyed our day at the park, ate junk food, and bought souvenirs for our grandchildren in Georgia

2011.5   ITS NOT JUST WALL STREET

The Albany Times Union rejected the following letter to the editor because it was too long. I hope it isn't too long for you to read.

In 2011, during of the worst economic crisis in a lifetime, between 20 and 30 million people were unemployed or under employed. Many had exhausted their savings, become a burden on others, or suffered problems with their health and relationships. When the costs of lost homes and job benefits are considered, the economic costs are stunning and the social costs are immeasurable.

During the last 30 years, workers, businesses, and government played by the rules that our economic system rewards, and by doing so, brought it to this disastrous result. Some took loans they couldn't afford, the government poured good money after bad, managers froze wages to increase profits, executives took astronomical salaries and bonuses, politicians scapegoated other parties, brokers made gains from others losses, and corporations used profits to influence the laws that shape our society. Everyone was doing what the system rewarded them to do. If a system produces outcomes that are unjust, unwanted, and unproductive, when we follow its rules, then the rules must be flawed. That's the definition of a systemic problem.

Our economic system has created great prosperity, but it is prone to periods of massive fluctuation. Periodically millions of people lose their jobs while the materials and equipment needed for work are idle. A stable economic system should be able to put the people wanting work together with the idle industrial capacity to produce the wealth needed to maintain society.

Because of a chronic labor shortage, the U.S. paid higher wages each year for 150 years. However, in 1970, computers and automation replaced huge numbers of workers, and industry began moving jobs to cheaper workers abroad. As jobs were decreasing, many women and immigrants entered the job market. Businesses didn't have to raise wages; there was no longer a labor shortage. As a result, the purchasing power for workers in 2010 was the same as in 1978. Workers responded by putting in more hours. Americans do more hours of paid labor per year than in any other industrial country. And they took on an unprecedented level of debt. In 2007, when many could no longer pay their debts, the crisis erupted. Businesses stopped investing and hiring workers because too few could afford their products. Corporations used their profits to collaborate with the political system to reward wealth with power and power with more wealth. As the wealth and power of the nation accumulated to an ever-smaller group, there was less wealth available for consumers. In 1945, for every tax dollar received from individuals, $1.50 came from corporations. Today corporations match that dollar with just 25 cents. In the 1970s, the top tax bracket was 70%. In 2011, it is 35%. We produced enormous wealth and we have given it to a small group of individuals and corporations. Tax reductions, together with over spending, have also created an enormous national debt. Of course, the solution to debt is wealth however; the wealth has been transferred to the richest individuals and corporations. So instead of taxing them, the government has to borrow from them because they have the money. Instead of paying taxes, they lend money to the government, which it has to pay back with interest. In 1980, the U.S. had one of the least unequal distributions of income and wealth among the industrial nations. Today we are the most unequal. We have killed the goose that laid the golden egg. Consumers do not have enough money to keep the economy going and the government does not have enough money to keep running. The distribution of wealth is not an egalitarian ideal; it is an economic necessity. The wealth must be shared in order for the system to work. Wealth doesn't have to be shared equally as communists proposed or concentrated in big government, as socialists prefer. It can be shared rationally as it was in the past to keep the economy running.

During the 1930's, the federal government created and paid for 11 million jobs which allowed people to keep their homes. The reluctance to tax the wealthy to pay for jobs assumes that taxes will take money out of circulation, reduce investment, and therefore reduce job creation. However, after over four years of recession there were still huge quantities of wealth sitting idle in corporate and private savings, awaiting customers to increase demand. Industry has failed to produce the needed jobs. Using a portion of that idle money to fund jobs will create the customers that the corporations await, the jobs that workers require, and the stimulus that the economy needs. The money is only sitting in those accounts because of the enormous transfer of wealth that the political industrial complex was able to promote in the name of simplifying the tax code. But it's not a free ride for us in the 99%. If the national debt is to be reduced to a manageable level, middle class Americans will also have to contribute more, once when the economy has improved.

We created the current system with its inherent limitations and we can improve it in the same way we improved other systemic national problems. America's response to many of the major challenges we faced in the past was "Increased Democracy." We have expanded the scope of our democracy since the country was founded. We've added voting rights for minorities (1870 and 1964), the direct election of Senators (1913); voting rights for woman (1920); voting rights for citizens of the District of Columbia (1961), and voting rights for persons 18 and older (1971). Our democracy recognizes that we all share responsibility for the policies that organize and control our lives.

Now we have a problem with the corporate policies that organize and control our work lives. The Supreme Court ruled that corporations are persons, entitled by the U.S. Constitution to influence elections directly. So, in addition to making enormous contributions in individual legislators through their lobbyist, corporations can also influence the outcomes of elections to ensure that they continue to receive their corporate subsidies and ensure that workers' rights to organize are further restricted and that their benefits are paid for by others. Boards of Directors control corporations, but the people with the largest stake in corporate policies, the workers, do not participate either as board members or in their selection. The Boards decide what, how and where to produce, and how to use the profits. The autocratic power of the Boards of Directors to control the fate of our country is comparable to the powers of the nobility of the past and is totally at odds with the democratic principles on which this country was founded. The same democratic principles that continue to improve our political and social systems can also be applied to improve our capitalistic economic system.

If workers, like managers had stock options, their elected representatives would give them a voice in the decision-making. The workers in corporations, would help decide the what, how and where to produce, and the distribution of profits. Democracy is people participating in the decisions that affect their lives. Work is one of the most important aspects of life; however, it is controlled by people who can manipulate outcomes to their own advantage, regardless of the implications for the people who produced the wealth. Corporate rights should not include the right to use the nation's resources as a platform to increase profits while ignoring the implications for the nation as a whole.

Would the workers stop raising wages to give a greater share of the fruits of their labor to wealthier shareholders? Minimum wage workers receive government benefits that are paid for by taxes. In this way, the federal and state governments are subsidizing big business whose profits increase because taxpayers provide their workers with health care, child support, food stamps, and a host of other benefits. Workers are disadvantaged again when they retire because the value of the benefits do not add to the workers' gross income so their Social Security benefits are much less, than they would be if business provided wages sufficient for workers to purchase the benefits for themselves. Would workers then vote to move their jobs to Asia or Mexico? Would they pay executives astronomical salaries? Would they lobby Washington for the right to pollute their own neighborhoods?

Monopoly law changes produced organizations that are too large to fail and so powerful that a few individuals can dramatically affect the social and economic fabric of the country. Fewer and fewer people have more and more control over the destiny of our country. Returning to a greater number of smaller companies would provide additional opportunities for local participation while increased competition would preclude failing to respond to broader national issues.

Democracy and diversity have improved our nation in ways that autocracy and exclusion could never achieve. There were outcries at all attempts to increase equality and justice. Cries of socialism, heresy, and doom will no doubt be heard again. But, as we recall our gains in political rights, civil rights, women rights, and other rights we can be encouraged as we strive now for workers' rights.

2012.1   LEWAYNE MAXWELL

This note was written to my daughter-in-law LeAnn on the death of her father Lewayne Maxwell.

> *LeAnn,*
>
> *I am so sorry that you have lost you father. I hope that your many joyful memories of him will give you some comfort. Memories remind us who we were, in the company of those we loved. Now we discover who are without them. But their lives echo within us and weave themselves into the persons who we are becoming.*
>
> *Love, Dad*

2012.2   APRIL IN PARIS

Paris, the city of light, has the well-deserved reputation of being the most beautiful and romantic of all cities, brimming with historic associations and influential in the realms of culture, art, fashion, food, and design. A large part of the city, including the River Seine, is a UNESCO World Heritage Site, which ensures that the city's charm will not be replaced by efficient condominiums. The city has many Michelin rated restaurants and contains numerous iconic landmarks, making it the most popular tourist destination in the world with 45 million tourists annually, which in 2012 included us.

We visited the Eiffel Tower, the Arc de Triumph, the Notre-Dame Cathedral, the Louvre Museum, Musée d'Orsay, Montmatre Sacré-Cœur basilica, The Avenue des Champs-Élysées the beautiful shopping boulevard, The Petit Palais (an art museum with an outdoor restaurant in the atrium) and the Palais Garnier Opera House, a 19th-century architectural masterpiece with ceiling paintings by Chagall. The late-night dinner cruise on the Seine River which ended with a light show on the Eiffel Tower. The couple at an adjoining table was on their honeymoon, and when they heard that we had been married for 52 years, they decided to return to Paris on their 50th anniversary. We hope to see them there.

The tree lined streets, the outdoor restaurants, the quaint building styles, the history, the art, and the marvelous food all combine to make Paris a wonderful place to visit. We chose a tour company that arraigned small sightseeing trips rather than daily large bus trips. This allowed us to explore Marie-Antoinette's Château de Versailles with its famous Hall of Mirrors, King's Apartments, Museum of the History of France, and manicured gardens as well as Monet's home and lily pond without the usual crowds. Most days we chose to travel alone by foot, by cab, or by subway. The sidewalk cafes seem to be the center of social life for natives and tourists alike. Our Hotel overlooked the avenue and provided the most varied and delicious breakfast feasts each morning. This is the city we would most like to revisit.

2012.3   RICHARD DESANT

My brother Richie had been seriously ill for several years. He suffered from diabetes and high blood pressure and had several strokes, which left him in need of braces and a wheel chair. His daughter Donna, didn't want a big gathering and Richie asked that his ashes be scattered in the bay where he used to fish.

The following was written to Donna Marie Clark and her family after the death of my brother Richie. Donna was Richie's stepdaughter. (22 Oct 2012)

Dear Donna, Anthony, and Danny,

For many years, one of our most important family traditions has been to plant a tree or shrub as a living memorial to a loved one who has died. We have enclosed a gift card so that our family may share with you a planting in your yard as a memorial for Richie.

I made the enclosed bowl from a branch of a tree that stood in our back yard for many years. Our hope is that this portion of our tree will remind you that Richie's northern family loved him and greatly appreciate all that you did to enrich his life and to ease his passing.

Ron and Reg Gerhard

2012.4   SWIFT PRESERVE

Reg and I went for a walk in this 21.6-acre wetland preserve in Delmar that was created to protect the wetlands after homes were constructed on neighboring parcels. The High School had once used it as an outdoor classroom. It has several trails and a kiosk at the entrance. The Mohawk Hudson Land Conservancy, which owns and maintains the preserve, was looking for a volunteer steward to help maintain the trails. Stewards conduct periodic visits, record the conditions of the land, including hazards and changes, keep the trails clear, and pick-up trash and litter, and report large scale dumping. Since I had resigned as a volunteer in the Umbrella program when we moved to our new home, I decided to volunteer. I did a lot of weed whacking and help build several small bridges. After a year, my knees were getting so sore that I was unable to walk the entire length of the various trails so I had to resign. I still help the organization by building a large workbench for the shed behind their office building on Kenwood Ave. and by donating hand turned wooden bowls for the annual silent auctions.

2012.5   CIRCLE OF FRIENDS

The Haines, who Reg and I met over 40 years ago, when Gail ran a nursery school in her home, had joined us for lunch in our screened porch. After a leisurely meal, they asked us to join a new couples group that they were in the process of forming. The group now meets monthly at alternating homes. The group uses a talking stick or other object that one must be holding in order to speak. This discourages people from interrupting or dominating the conversation. It clearly gives the floor to one person at a time, and encourages shared responsibility for participation. The object selected by the host couple is passed around the group. We talk about whatever is on our minds. There is no time limit and no obligation to speak, and no judgements or advice, unless requested. Some of the couples live many miles from Delmar and I often wonder if I should continue going. However, they are a very talented and diverse group and on the way home, I'm generally glad that I went.

2013.1   MOTHERS DAY

For Mother's Day, I bought Reg two tickets to see, and hear, Andre Bocelli at the Times Union Center in Albany. She invited me to join her; I had hoped she would. Andre sang 24 songs including selections from operas, Italian pop ballads, and Neapolitan folk tunes in a voice that is ideal for the sort of music he performs: he's the reigning global superstar of arena pop-opera. The music was technically perfect and artistically beautiful; but watching Reg's response throughout the evening was spellbinding. Like most things Reg does, she fully participates in life. I've come to be more comfortable with the fact that at many times I'm limited to being more of a spectator then a participant. I do love watching Reg; her Joy often spills over and I too get to participate, if only vicariously.

2013.2   THE SUMMER OF '45

I wrote the following account in August of 2013. My granddaughter Emily was writing an essay about what she did on her summer vacation. Her father Brian thought it would be fun for each family member to write an essay about his or her own summer vacation between the fourth and fifth grades.

THE SUMMER OF '45 by Ronald Gerhard (a.k.a. Papa)

In June of 1945, I began my forth summer vacation, but it was only the second vacation at our new home in Central Islip, NY where we had moved in 1944. I was glad that the winter was over because our new home had very little heat from the coal-burning furnace in the basement. Because of the war, we were not able to add radiators on the second floor where my brother Artie and I slept. All of the steel was being used to build the things needed to win the war even though Nazi Germany surrendered on May 8, the war with Japan, the war that my Uncle R.E was fighting, continued. But, it was good to be in the same house with the same people for more than one year.

In April, I had turned 10 years old and in May, there was a big celebration at the park to mark the end of World War II in Europe. Bicycles were decorated with ribbons and flags. There were bands in the park and many flags. The flag had only 48 stars, as Hawaii and Alaska were not yet states. It was a grand party.

The names of soldiers who were killed had been chiseled into the stone Memorial next to the Memorial from World War I. I didn't know any of the soldiers, but I knew where some of their families lived. In the windows of the homes of the fallen soldiers were small pennants with gold stars. The pennants for the soldiers who were still alive had blue stars. There were many blue star pennants around town. These would be removed when the soldiers came home, but the gold stars were forever. I felt lucky that no one from our family had gold stars.

We did have a blue star in the family that I was unaware of at the time. My father was a sergeant in the Army serving in Germany.

On Sunday afternoons, when Mom was at work and Artie was away with his friends, my stepfather Tony and I would work in the garden or in garage making things for the house. We would listen to Yankee games on the radio. There weren't as many teams as there are now and there were no teams west of St. Louis because traveling was so slow that many days would be wasted if the teams had to travel to distant cities. The Yankees didn't do very well that year and lost the American League Pennant race to the Detroit Tigers who beat the Chicago Clubs in the World Series. But I enjoyed being with Tony.

Sunday Jun 17th was Father's Day and Monday Jun 18 was Tony's 45th birthday so we celebrated them both on Monday, which was Mom's only day off. Mom baked a white cake with chocolate icing. Since the life expectancy for men was only 61 years for men and 65 for women, I always thought that they were both very old. Fortunately, they both beat the odds and lived well beyond their expected age.

On Jun 21, The Battle of Okinawa ended. A few months later, my uncle Robert E. Mills came home from the war dressed in his Marine uniform. R.E. participated in the invasions of Vella Lavella, Bougainville, Guadalcanal, and Iwo Jima. For a long time, Uncle R.E (as we called him) was my hero and he told me many stories about the war and about the injuries he had received and I thought that someday I would be a Marine. Fortunately, I never had to go to war even though I was in the Army for six years.

The rest of the summer was filled with news about the war, soldiers coming home from Europe, the atomic bomb, the surrender of Japan on August 15, and the beginning of the United Nations, which was supposed to prevent all future wars but so far, it's not working. This was a very big change from what I had heard for the previous six years. Most of the news that I had known until then was about the war and all of the terrible things that happened.

On Saturday mornings, I would listen to the radio for several hours of kid shows like: Let's Pretend, Buster Brown Gang, and Grand Central Station. They each had adventure shows about people who lived exciting lives. I still remember how exciting it was to hear the announcers' voices and the music when the shows began.

During the week, my friends and I would collect soda and beer bottles for the 5-cent deposit for large bottles and 2 cents for small bottles. If we were lucky enough to find enough bottles, we used the money to go to movies on Saturday afternoon in the next town 5 miles away. It cost 20-cents and candy was 5-cents. We usually hitchhiked because the bus was 20-cents each way and we rarely had enough money. The movies that I might have seen that year were cartoons like The Three Caballeros or short films with Daffy Duck and Porky Pig, war stories like Back to Bataan, adventures like Tarzan and the Amazons, and the musical State Fair. Every movie began with newsreels with pictures and stories about the war and other important events. When television became popular, the newsreels were discontinued because people could see the news at home.

The movie didn't cost much but people didn't have much money. Most of the people that I knew only had enough money to pay for their house, clothes and food. I never saw my mother or Tony go the movies, to a restaurant or take a vacation away from home. But we were happy at home and Mom was a great cook.

What Things Cost in 1945: A new Car: $1,220, Gasoline: 21 cents/gal, House: $8,600, Bread: 9 cents/loaf, Milk: 62, cents/gal, Postage Stamp: 3 cents, Stock Market: 152, Average Annual Salary: $2,600 and the minimum wage was $0.30 per hour.

No one had television in 1945 so we spent a lot of time listening to the radio. On rainy Saturday afternoons, when I couldn't afford to go to the movies (which was most of the time), I would listen to the disk jockeys play the top songs from the hit parade. Some of the many songs that were on the radio in the summer of 1945 were: Till the End of Time, On the Atchison, Topeka, & the Santa Fe, If I Loved You, You Belong to My Heart, Dream, Bell Bottom Trousers, Laura, The More I See You, Begin the Beguine, and You'll Never Walk Alone. The top singers were Perry Como, Frank Sinatra, Dick Haymes, and Bing Crosby.

I spent many days alone in the yard or in the woods behind my house, but I don't remember being lonely because I was always busy with some new project. I built a fort in the woods that looked like one I had seen in one of the many war movies that were shown in the past few years. It was complete with wooden machine guns built from scraps found at the town dump. I also built a bike from parts I found at the dump. I learned how to take apart the broken bikes and save all the working pieces. When I had all the parts I needed, I built my own bike from parts that others had thrown away.

My mother and stepfather both worked and my brother was rarely home so I had a lot of time alone or with my neighborhood friends. Some days we walked along the train tracks or to the vacant barns and garages next to the tracks. Occasionally we would find treasures like old railroad spikes or rings of rusted keys. Occasionally we would ride our bikes to the sand pit, where sand was mined. The pits were very deep and filled with green water. The sides were very steep and made of soft sand. It was very dangerous but we all pretended not to be scared and went home. I got a Monopoly game that Christmas and sometimes my friends would come to my house to play, because the house was generally empty. I liked to win.

Once a week I weeded, hoed, and watered the ¼-acre vegetable garden we had in the back yard. We grew many vegetables and my mother would take her vacation in the fall to can them and make many jars of spaghetti sauce. Tony was Italian and we had Italian food at least once a week. Our basement had many shelves that would be filled with food that my mother had canned each autumn. The food would last until the next spring.

Each month we would get a book of ration stamps from the government. You needed these stamps to buy food. The amount of food you could buy was limited by the number of people in your family. Many families had gardens in their back yards to supplement the food that they could buy at the store. Gasoline and many other items were also rationed. Since Tony worked in a Grocery store, I think we may have gotten some extra food. Some people would sell or trade their ration stamps in the black market. I didn't know what that meant but I heard it a lot on the radio.

Starting in 1942, American families were issued coupon books with stamps, both red and blue, that correlated to specific types of items. The system was complicated, with expiration dates, point systems—and food

shortages. Having a coupon didn't mean a commodity was necessarily available and coupons weren't the same as legal tender. Even with the right stamps, you still needed cash to bring home the groceries.

Red stamp commodities included meats, oils, butter, and certain hard cheeses. Blue stamps got you frozen and canned fruits and vegetables, juices, dry beans, and processed foods. Other commodities, including coffee, sugar, clothing, gas, tires, and shoes, had their own stamps. That left you predominately with eggs, milk, soft cheeses, chicken, grains, fish, and dried and fresh fruits and vegetables.

Victory Gardens produced as much as 40 percent of the produce consumed in the U.S. by war's end. And how's this for an unexpected bonus—today nutritionists believe that rationing during World War II resulted in temporarily improved nutrition, with a reduction in obesity and type 2 diabetes.

About once a week, I took the toy wagon to the icehouse four blocks away to get ice for the icebox. A 25-cent block of ice was about one cubic foot and would keep our food cold for several days. We didn't get a refrigerator until well after the war ended. The factories were making things for the war, and we couldn't by appliances, cars and many other items. We kept the icebox on the back porch because it was colder there most of the year and the ice would last longer.

All of the houses on my street had indoor plumbing. Only 55% of US homes had indoor plumbing in 1945, so we were very fortunate. A few years earlier, I had lived with my grandmother Hattie Mills, in South Carolina and her bathroom was an outhouse in the back yard. I was happy to have a real toilet. We also had a shower in the bathtub. This made it much easier and faster to bathe. I don't think people bathed as much before showers were invented as they do now.

In the evenings after supper, the kids from the neighborhood often played games in the street. We played Kick the Can, Red Rover, Hide and Seek or Ring-a-levio, (a game that originated in the teeming streets of New York City before World War I. It was taught to the kids by their immigrant parents who grew up in the tenement slums of lower Manhattan.) Once when my friend Joey G. was "IT," I nailed the can to the road so he couldn't kick it.

When the neighborhood girls joined us, we played "true, dare, consequence, promise, or repeat." A game that the boys never played by themselves. The girls liked to make us do or say stupid things, but we all laughed and never told the girls that we liked to play. Once I selected DARE and I was dared to go in the house and kiss my mother. I found Mom in the kitchen cooking and gave her a big hug and a kiss. It was the first time I ever remember kissing my mother.

My brother Artie brought a Red Rider BB gun from a friend and hid it in his closet. (Mom and Tony would never let us have a BB gun because we might shoot our eyes out.) Artie, who was three years older than me would never let me play with it but one day when he was out, I took it to the woods behind our house and shot at tin cans.

On some warm summer evenings, my friend Buddy P. and his father would take me with them to catch crabs off the Bayshore docks in the Great South Bay. We would tie a fish head to a long string and drop it over the edge of the dock. Soon I could feel a crab pulling at the fish head and I would slowly raise the string until it was just a few feet below the water. Using my other hand, I would slowly lower a net into the water and then quickly move the net to catch the crap. On a good night, we would catch a large pail full of crabs. On Holidays, we would watch fire works from the same dock.

For Christmas, Artie and I had received an 8-mm. movie projector. It came with several movies that we watched with our friends many times. The only movie that I remember is "Little Black Sambo." Sambo is a South Indian boy who encounters four hungry tigers, and surrenders his colorful new clothes, shoes, and umbrella so they will not eat him. The tigers are vain and each thinks he is better dressed than the others are. They chase each other around a tree until they are reduced to a pool of melted butter. Sambo then recovers his clothes and his mother makes pancakes out of the butter. The story was a children's favorite for half a century until the word Sambo was deemed a racial slur hurtful to black children. The names and pictures were changed and the story now continues without the hurtful stereotypes.

By Labor Day, I was ready to go back to school. The fifth-grade teacher was Mrs. O'Brien. She was a good teacher and I was glad to be in her class. I had enjoyed the summer, lying under the tree in my back yard, eating grapes in the arbor that Tony had built, sleeping late with my cat BoBo and playing with my friends. My days were filled with adventures, the adventures that I had created for myself. But now it was time to turn over the reins to Mrs. O'Brien and to see what adventures she could create for my classmates and me.

2013.3   UNCLE R.E

R.E. lived in Darlington, SC for most of his adult life. When we walked around town with him on some of our visits he waved at almost everyone who passed by, he was very social and well respected by his neighbors.

The following was sent to my cousin Robin Mills Sterling after the death of her father Robert on August 23, 2013.

In memory of Robert Edward Mills

Dear Robin,

I am so sorry that you have lost you father. I hope that your many joyful memories of him will give you some comfort. Memories, remind us of who we were, in the company of those we loved. Now we discover who are without them as their lives echo within us and weave themselves into the persons we are becoming.

For many years, one of our most important family traditions has been to plant a tree or shrub as a living memorial to a loved one who has died. Since it's not practical for me to send you a tree in memory of your Dad, I am sending you instead a wooden bowl.

I made the enclosed bowl from a portion of a cherry tree that was grown here in upstate New York. Our hope is that this portion of our tree will remind you that Robert's northern family loved and admired him and greatly appreciated all that you did to enrich his life and to ease his passing.

Ron Gerhard

2013.4 COLONOSCOPY

On a Thursday in September, I had a long overdue colonoscopy. The physician told me that I have a mass in my colon that had to be removed. He never mentioned cancer. Several days later during a consultation, my Primary Care Physician read to me the note that the Gastroenterologist had sent him that described the mass as probably being an adenocarcinoma (a form of cancer with a five-year survival rate of 10%.) For several days, I made what I thought would be my final financial plans. The threat was like a dark cloud that followed my every move and shaded my every thought. Several days later, the nurse called to tell the results of biopsy. There were no cancer cells seen, but a large precancerous mass about 2 inches in diameter that needed to be removed promptly.

The right half of my large intestine (which is about 2 feet long) was removed along with three dozen lymph nodes and other tissue. After eight of the worst days of my life in the hospital I finally came home, not knowing if my bowels would ever work normally again. However, week-by-week and month-by-month things gradually improved, and now I am close to being normal. I still have to be careful when I go out in the morning and be sure that there's a bathroom nearby. I feel very fortunate that my tumor did not require radiation or chemotherapy. I have two friends who did have cancerous growths and they suffered greatly by the extended treatments that they required. I hope that you who read this account will not postpone your colonoscopy or other tests. If I had had the mass removed 5 years earlier, it could have been snipped off during the colonoscopy, no surgery or lost bowel required. Please heed my mother's words, she once said, "If I knew I was going to live this long I would have taken better care of myself."

2013.5   COLIN EDWARD

When Colin was born on Nov 4, 2013, it felt like our family was finally complete. Greg and Lauren gave us the long-desired baby grandsons. Ryan was 12 years old when David and Michele were married, so his childhood belonged to his maternal grandparents. I loved holding Colin on our family get togethers. It is nice to know that the Gerhard name will likely continue. And at last, the Gerhard prophesy was fulfilled. My mother worked for many years in a psychiatric hospital where one of her patients claimed to be a prophet and predicted that Mom would have two more children; two boys each with red hair and blue eyes. Although my mother was too old to have any more children, the idea of two red-  haired, blued-eyed boys was so appealing that she held onto the dream for many years. I wish she could see these two, Colin, and his brother Brady; they are just what she always wanted, just two generations too late for her to enjoy.

Colin's middle name "Edward" is in honor his mother Lauren's father, Edward F. Keating.

2014.1   LAKE PLACID FAMILY REUNION

In July 2014, Dave, Brian, and Greg arranged for a family reunion. We shared a rental property with Michele's (David's wife) family. We stayed for the first 3 days and the Doherty's stayed for the second 3 days. Aside from some plumbing issues at the house and a rainy afternoon at an outdoor restaurant, the reunion was a great success. We had some time alone with Emily and lots of time with Brady and Colin including a ride on the local scenic railroad and its merry-go-round. The photo was tahen on the pier after a boat ride on the lake.

The second half of the week was spent in Voorheesville at Dave's pool and fire pit and at our house in Delmar. This was a great time with the entire family together. I wish we could do something like this every year. I really like these people! (Photo left to right, top: Brady, Greg, Lauren, Colin, Michele, David, me, bottom: LeAnn, Emily, and Reg.)

In September, Reg and I booked a room at the Leo House in NYC. It's a guesthouse, operated a Catholic charity, which serves travelers for stays of up to 14 days. It provides a congenial and inexpensive place to stay and a hardy breakfast. It's on 23rd St. in the Chelsea district one block from a subway, and two blocks from the High Line urban park. We walked along the High Line that is so well designed and landscaped that it's hard to believe that it once was an abandoned railroad track. The entire area from the High Line west to the Hudson River is being renovated and gentrified. I don't know who is being displaced by the construction or where they will go, but the area that they are leaving behind is beautiful.

We spent a few hours at the Air and Space Museum on the Aircraft Carrier USS Intrepid. Then we headed north to spend time at Strawberry Fields in Central Park. I used Reg's phone to call my cell phone, which plays "Imagine" as its ring tone and listened to a local musician perform a much better version. Later in the day, we had a private tour at the Metropolitan Museum of Art by our old friend Jo who is volunteer docent there.

The next day we visited The Museum of the City of New York, and I remembered bringing the children from a Harlem day care center there in 1958 as part of a Developmental Psychology course. In the afternoon, it was down Fifth Avenue to the Guggenheim Museum, where we saw many stunning works of art. One object in particular caught our interest, a painting by a French artist presenting a charming young girl beckoning to us from her rural countryside. We imagined what it would be like to step inside the painting and walk with her along the path that led to her home. We would share stories with her about our life on this side of the canvas, but mostly we would listen to her as she told us about her life and of her hopes and dreams for the future that would never arrive in her land of warm colors and frozen time. We are all forever bound to the canvas on which we live and by the time and space, that frames it.

Then it was on to St Patrick's Cathedral and a quick supper at a restaurant adjacent to the Rockefeller Center Ice Rink.

In the evening, we saw The Book of Mormon, which may be the most vulgar, and irreverent play ever written; but it is also the funniest thing I had ever seen, my sides hurt from laughing so hard even though I missed many of the punch lines because of the laughter from the audience.

On our last day, we revisited the World Trade Center, which a few years ago, was merely a huge hole in the ground, but is now beautifully transformed into a park, a memorial, and an education center. The reflecting pools are a spectacle that needs no explanation. The park that encircles the site contains a grove of newly planted and carefully manicured trees surrounding a fenced area protecting the single tree that survived the conflagration 13 years earlier.

A stroll around Battery Park provided us with the opportunity to reflect about the World Trade Center and all that has transpired since and to plan our return home.

2014.3   HOMEBODY

While rereading what I have written thus far, I realize that a reader, who didn't know me well, might get the impression that my life was a continuous series of major events because that's what I have written about. Actually, the trash goes out more than I do. I am a home body who would much perfer having a few friends in for diner then going out to eat in a restaurant. I don't feel lonely when I'm alone and my best friend is my wife Regina, who I spend time with most every day.

2015.1   LACROSSE AND CRISSCROSS

We spent much of the month of March in Georgia enjoying the first signs of spring that would not arrive in New York for another month and crisscrossing the suburbs of northwestern Atlanta from Suwanee to Decatur to spent time with Brian's and Greg's families. We took Colin and Brady to a petting zoo and a playground but spent most of our time with them playing in their backyard and reading to them.

We watched our favorite Granddaughter, Emily, play Lacrosse several times, and have come to understand why her teammates and friends call her "the hammer." Off the field, she is quiet, gentle, and personable, and on the field, while assertive, she plays with much grace and eloquence and still gets things done for her team; perhaps she should be called "the velvet hammer."

2015.2   OCTOGENARIAN

April 14, 2015. Today I turned 80, and it's the oldest I've ever been and the youngest I'll ever be and since you're only old once, I've decided to enjoy it. Actually, I feel the same as I did yesterday.

> *'Age is an issue of mind over matter. If you don't mind, it doesn't matter.'*
> *Mark Twain*

> *'Life is full of misery, loneliness, and suffering - and it's all over much too soon.'*
> *Woody Allen*

> *'Life is not measured by the number of breaths we take, but by the moments that take our breath away.'*
> *Vicki Corona*

> *When I was born in 1935, my life expectancy was age 61*
> *today at age 80 my life expectancy is age 88.*
> *So, it appears that the longer we live, the longer we are expected to live, so if we live long enough we'll never die.*
> *My goal is to live forever, so far so good!*
> *Ron Gerhard*

2015.3   ITALY

We flew from Albany to Philadelphia and then on to Venice where we took a ferry from the Italian mainland to the main Island of Venice, which lies amid a group of 117 small islands that are separated by canals and linked by bridges. Our hotel was on the Grand Canal a few blocks from St Mark's Square (Piazza San Marco), which is the center of the historic district. The following day we had guided tours of Saint Mark's Basilica, the Doge's Palace (Palazzo Ducale), and the Correr Museum (Museo Civico Correr). We strolled along the waterfront, ate in small cafes, and rode in a water taxi to the Rialto Bridge. We also had a side visit to Murano Island and the Murano Glass factory, which ended with a souvenir ring for Reg. Murano glass has specialized in fancy glassware for centuries. It led Europe for centuries, developing technologies which the artisans of today still employ.

The quintessential Venetian experience was the gondola ride through the canals, which glided past ancient palazzi and magnificent cathedrals on a handcrafted gondola, while musicians serenaded us with Italian ballads. Our tour companions from California took a video and emailed it to us. The last evening in Venice was spent at a wonderful restaurant where wine flowed like water.

A ferry ride to the train/bus station began our trip to Florence. We rode across northern Italy's rolling hills and rivers stopping for lunch at a vineyard that grew its own olives and served wine made on the premises. After a little too much wine, it was off to the tipsy tower of Pisa which was not quite worth the lengthy trip.

We arrived in Florence at dusk and stopped at an overlook with a gorgeous view of the entire city. Even from this height and in the fading light it was clear that Florence is an extraordinary city. Our hotel was across from a waterfront park on the River Arno. The next morning, we visited Galleria dell'Accademia, which houses Michelangelo's *David, a* highlight of our trip. To the people of Florence, the statue symbolizes the defense of civil liberties but to me it symbolizes our son David who is named for this masterpiece of Carrara marble.

Next was a visit to the Magnificent *Uffizi Gallery*. One of the world's top art museums, it houses some of the most important works of the Renaissance, including works by Leonardo da Vinci, Giotto, Raffaello, Cimabue, Botticelli and Michelangelo and a large collection of early Greek and Roman sculptures. Our guide helped us get an overview of the collection and a rich sampling of the various collections. The museum is so huge and so rich with history that it would be overwhelming if attempted alone without a guide.

We walked the narrow streets and listened to our guide describe its history and snacked at local cafes. On our free afternoon, we walked through the Arno riverside park and watched the children play as the kayakers glided by. If I were ever to live in Italy, I would choose Florence by the river Arno.

After two days, it was off to Assisi where Reg's brother Gerry had studied while writing his book about St Francis. We tried to find one of his books at the cathedral book store to take a picture of Reg reading it in Assisi, but we wound up at the wrong bookstore and we had to move. Because a nearby convention of chocolatiers had concluded earlier that morning and the small city was too crowded to really enjoy. But we both were glad to see the place were Gerry had studied and the cathedral which Reg had used as a model for a wall hanging that she had made for him years before.

After lunch, it was on to Rome. There is evidence of human occupation of Rome from 14,000 years ago, and today the streets are like living museums where every turn provides a history lesson, a spectacular work of art, or occasionally, both.

The Vatican, the smallest independent state in the world houses the Vatican palace and garden, the Vatican Museums and the Sistine Chapel, St. Peter's Basilica, and St. Peter's Square. Michelangelo's Pieta and the altar in St. Peter's Basilica were highlights for me, but the scale of the church and its' riches are overwhelming and somewhat embarrassing as the wealth is beyond imagination.

The Colosseum was inaugurated in 80 AD. It was large enough for theatrical performances, festivals, circuses, and games, which high officials watched from the lowest level, aristocrats on the second, the populace on the third and fourth. A fifth story was reserved for woman who were not tax payers and therefore were nor entitled to free admission to the main seating areas.

The Pantheon is the best-preserved monument of Roman antiquity it's remarkably intact for its 2,000 years.

Walking through the forum, now in the middle of a throbbing modern city, is like stepping back two millennia into the heart of ancient Rome. Although what survives of this center of Roman life and government shows only a small fraction of its original splendor, the standing and fallen columns, its triumphal arches, and remains of its walls still impress, especially when you consider that for centuries, the history of the Forum was the history of the Roman Empire and of the western world. Roman political and religious life was centered here, along with the courts, markets, and meeting places. After the seventh century, the buildings fell into ruin, and churches and fortresses were built amid the ancient remains. Its stones were quarried for other buildings and it was not until the 18th and 19th centuries that systematic excavations brought the ancient buildings to light from under a 10-meter layer of earth and rubble.

Throwing a coin into Rome's largest fountain the Trevi Fountain is a tradition that is supposed to assure your return to Rome. I guess we won't be going back; the fountain was closed for repairs when we were there. We had lunch at one of Rome's most characteristic squares Piazza Navona that houses a beautiful Baroque fountain.

On Monday evening, we took a taxi across the city to a small family style restaurant. The site was selected by our friends Paul and Jan Troidle from Ballston Lake, NY. They just happen to be in Rome that day with Janet's sister and we arranged to meet for dinner. We had a great time with them and laughed at the fact that we both happen to be in Rome at the same time. Just another day in the life of the Jet Setters.

2016.1   GEORGIA AND FLORIDA

In March, we drove to Georgia to be with the southern contingent of our family. We also made plans to visit with our friends the Bush's from South Carolina but illness prevented them from making the trip to a point midway between SC and GA. But we did get to visit with our friends the Zolezzi's from Florida who we met at a motel in southern Ga that lies midway between our homes. Our visit with Greg and Brian was cut short when Reg became ill. During our visit to Georgia, the year before I was sick and spent three days in bed at our motel. Old age seems to be catching up with us; perhaps we need to run faster.

Later in the year Greg, Lauren, Brady, and Colin spent four days with us in Delmar. Then they went on to Hampton Bays to spend time with Lauren's family at their summer cottage.

2016.2   THROMBOCYTHEMIA

In August, I received the news that I was suffering from Essential Hemorrhagic Thrombocythemia, a form of chronic leukemia. Although it's called, suffering, I feel fine and it can only be diagnosed by examining my blood under a microscope. There are too many platelet-producing cells in my bone marrow, which results in an overabundance of platelet cells or thrombocytes in my blood. It's caused by a genetic mutation in the Janus Kinase 2 gene.

(Genes are the basic unit of heredity and are made up of DNA, which act as instructions to make proteins. We have between 20 and 25 thousand genes, which vary in size from a few hundred DNA bases to more than 2 million bases.) The Janus Kinase 2 gene regulates blood cell functions. It sends messages telling the bone marrow to make more cells, or to stop when the body does not need more cells. The mutation causes too many blood cells to be produced, which can clog the blood and make it sticky. The gene mutation occurred in early blood-forming cells after conception, so it is not an inherited disease.

In September, I began treatment, which includes Chemotherapy and a weekly analysis of my blood to determine exactly how the drug is effecting my blood. So far, I do not have any side effects from the drug, which I have been taking for 2 weeks. The goal is to adjust the amount of medication to keep the Platelets at an acceptable level without causing major decreases or damage to other types of blood cells that are produced in the bone marrow and are also effected by the medication.

Actually, the doctor told me that it would take about 20 years for this disease to kill me. Since I'm 81 now, I figure I'm good until age 101. This is great news because previously I was likely to die by age 89, so by getting this disease I've increased my life expectancy by 12 years. That's what I like about statistics, with a little imagination there's a number to suit every occasion.

CHAPTER 10

The table beginning the next page compares my progress through eight decades to the progress predicted by Erikson's stages of psychosocial development:

	STAGES	AGES	CHALLENGES AND OUTCOMES
1	Infancy	0–2 years	Trust vs. Mistrust
2	Early childhood	2–4 years	Autonomy vs. Shame/Doubt
3	Preschool	4–5 years	Initiative vs. Guilt
4	School age	6–12 years	Industry vs. Inferiority
5	Adolescence	13–19 years	Identity vs. Role Confusion
6	Early adulthood	20-39 years	Intimacy vs. Isolation
7	Adulthood	40–64 years	Contributing vs. Stagnation
8	Maturity	65 – Death	Integrity vs. Despair

In spite of all of the unique circumstances of my life, it clearly follows the general patterns and themes that we all share.

Human Family[1]

... In minor ways we differ,
in major we're the same.

I note the obvious differences
between each sort and type,
but we are more alike, my friends,
than we are unalike.

We are more alike, my friends,
than we are unalike.

We are more alike, my friends,
than we are unalike

Maya Angelou

[1] *Last 10 lines of 40-line poem.*

ERIKSON'S 8 STAGES	MY LIFE EXPERIENCE
Infants whose needs have been met develop trust, see the world as safe and predictable, and see hope for the future. When their needs are not met, they see the world as unpredictable, unsafe, and have little hope for life to improve in the future.	**1930-39 (Ages 0-4)** I remember little about life as an infant. I suppose that's good as infants spend much of their time in dire need of something. I assume my needs were met and that I ended infancy dry, rested, satiated, and trusting in my caretakers. Whatever trauma I experienced as our core family dissolved at age three seemed to have healed without leaving any notable scars to retard my future development. There was always someone to love, even though it wasn't always the same person, the attachment seems to be more important than the face behind it. I do wonder if I might have achieved more if, I had a greater capacity to persist in times of stress. I always felt comfortable working independently and undertaking new projects and learning new skills. I suppose this indicates that I passed preschool development.
Toddlers learn to control their actions to get desired results and establish their independence. If denied this opportunity, they may develop low self-esteem, feelings of shame, doubt and the loss of the will to persist.	
Preschoolers learn to master basic skills and principles, develop courage and independence, and want to begin and complete their own activities. They may feel guilt or frustration when their efforts do not have the desired results and develop negative or aggressive behaviors. If encouraged and supported in making realistic and appropriate choices, they develop independence.	**1940-49 (Ages 5-14.)** Because I moved so often, I was left with the feeling that I didn't really belong anywhere. In spite of difference circumstances, I think my feelings were very similar to my classmates. Although, I remember feeling inadequate during much of my elementary school years, I believed that at that age many felt the same way so I didn't feel generally inferior.
School age children compare themselves with their peers. They develop pride in the accomplishment of schoolwork, sports, social activities, and family life. Success instills a sense of personal competence that is carried into the future. If children do not learn to get along with others or have negative experiences at home or with peers, an inferiority complex might develop into adolescence and adulthood, which will prevent them from feeling competent in the future.	**1950-59 (Ages 15-24)**, I often felt insecure and somewhat different from the other kids. But, as I look back, I believe that we were all going through the same changes. Some, thought they

Adolescents are developing a sense of self and struggle with questions such as "Who am I?" and "What do I want to do with my life?" Most adolescents explore various roles and ideas, goals, and attempt to discover their adult selves. Success at this stage gives a strong sense of identity and fidelity to core values and beliefs. When adolescents fail to make a conscious search for identity, or if they are pressured to conform, they may develop a weak sense of self and will be unsure of their identity and confused about the future.

Early adulthood is about journeys from naïve to wise, idealist to realist, and immature to mature. Having developed a sense of self in adolescence, young adults are ready to share life with others. If other stages have not been successfully resolved, young adults may have trouble developing and maintaining successful relationships that are based on love that respects the needs of others.

The **mid-adult years** are involved with finding life's work and contributing to the next generation, through childbirth, caring for others or engaging in meaningful and productive work. Those who do not master this task may experience stagnation and feel as though they are not leaving a meaningful mark on the world and they may care little for connections with others and have little

were simply unique. Others, who were provided with positive experiences to counteract the difficulties of growing up, believed that they were unique, just like everyone else. A comedian said, "If I had an inferiority complex, it wasn't a very good one." I had several supporting players who helped me find an identity that would not self-destruct and I was able to set the stage for a future that was unclear but not unwelcome.

1960-69 (Ages 25-34), I finally felt that my life was chosen by me rather than by circumstances. Our family was almost complete; we waited only for Gregory, I was proud of my career and in addition to being the perfect wife for me, Reg was a marvelous mother. She is the fire in the middle of our family who provided us all with warmth.

I think I failed coming of age for at 25, I was still naïve, idealist, and immature. My youth still dwelled just below the surface, waiting for an opportunity for yet another embarrassing encore. Sometimes instead of acting my age, I acted my shoe size.

1970-79 (Ages 35-44) Our family was established and Reg and I were content. I taught at several colleges, gave over sixty presentations in seventeen different states. I also wrote eleven monographs and had eight articles published in professional journals and collaborated in the writing of chapters in two books. But I was unable to meet my own aspirations, for my quest was not bounded by reality, but by the desire interest in productivity and self-improvement

People in **Late adulthood** reflect on their lives and feel a sense of satisfaction or of failure. Those who are proud of their accomplishments feel a sense of integrity, and they can look back on their lives with few regrets. Their knowledge and experience gives them a sense of Wisdom. Those who are not successful may feel as if their life has been wasted. They focus on what "could have" been. They face the end of their lives with feelings of bitterness, depression, and despair.

The privilege of a lifetime is to become who you truly are.

C.G. Jung

to move forward, success was always one-step away.

I was offered several leadership positions in other states, but I declined them all as I did not want to make the boys move again.

1980-89 (Ages 45-54) After 20 years of building a safe nest for our three children . . . they left. Reg and I learned to live with only each other to care for. At first, I roamed the empty rooms depressed with loneliness. Eventually I gave up the hunt for the past. I continued to write monographs and computer simulations and make presentations to fill the gap created as my career shifted from leading change agent to technocrat.

1990-99 (Ages 55-64) As my life evolved I wondered if it had a central theme or was my core self just a mirror responding to happenings around me. Is there something that is mine and not defined by circumstances? After I retired from Mental Health, I started new careers that I might have always enjoyed but didn't pursue because of the low wages.

2000-09 (Ages 65-74) While I feel proud of what I accomplished at home and at work, I still have the gnawing feeling that I might have done better at both. My family seems to love me, my work has helped a few, and perhaps its' remnant will provide a stepping-stone for future improvements and yet . . .

CHAPTER 11   *THE FINALE*

I have often joked that, "My goal is to live forever, so far so good!"

One day however, the trap door will spring again and I will be gone, not to another new and exciting time, but into the timeless unknown.

When Reg and I die, our children may be bereaved. Even mature adults can feel the pain of midlife orphanhood when their parents are suddenly gone. Because this rite of passage highlights our own mortality, and may expose unresolved issues of guilt, sorrow, and anger, and create changes of identity, or roles, it may prove to be more grief filled than you thought it would be.

Grief is what we feel and mourning is how we act in response to the grief. Try to find a way to mourn that will help soothe rather than exacerbate the pain of grieving. Somethings that may help are recounting memories, completing tasks or goals that we left unfinished, or honoring our birthdays with surviving family members, and my favorite, resolving sibling conflicts and carrying on together.

Let the journey be what it is and let your new grieving self be whatever it may be. Stay close with each other for we are stronger together than we are apart.

CHAPTER 12 *FROM A DISTANCE*

Like the Winter Wheat, my life story took several seasons to germinate. There was much editing and revision to produce what I hoped would be a better rendering of my story. I wish I had begun editing my life's story earlier, as I was living it; I could have produced a much more productive and interesting version of my life. But, you don't have to wait; it's never too early or too late to begin revisions to a life that could be improved.

The past, like any other viewpoint, will be better understood when seen in proper perspective. When I look back on the lives of my grandparents, I see farmers, factory workers, storekeepers with what we view today as very simple lives, their days were filled with chores and challenges, and their nights with loves and losses just as ours are today. I can no more imagine what the lives of my grandchildren will be like, than my grandparents could have imagined me sitting at this computer writing a message in electrons for persons who may not yet exist. I do know that the context in which you live will be markedly different from that in which I find myself. However, I suspect that the content of your experience will as closely resemble mine, as mine resembles that of my grandparents and their grandparents before them. This is why classic tales such as the Iliad are still relevant today, almost 3,000 years, after they were written. We experience life in our mind and in our hearts, and our minds and hearts are more alike than different. I hope that my story helps to open your mind to new possibilities, for the most costly thing that anyone can own is a closed mind.

Humankind is like a flowing river with many currents and eddies; each person is but a single drop, whose ripples spread, and soon diminish, and vanish, and few will be remembered. However, we find comfort in knowing that what we have done well may trickle down to future generations before fading away, just as the lives of our ancestors have influenced us in ways that we may never precisely know. My life has been greatly enriched by the foundation given to my generation by our ancestors; I hope that one day you may find something of value in the legacy of my generation. You need not long for the romantic idea that the "olden days" were somehow better, for there is no future in the past. Let history inform your destiny but, do not let your history define your destiny. You cannot control where you came from nor can you change the past, but you can control where you go from there. The future is not a gift, but an achievement to be invented, not predicted. You are both the hero and the author of your story, so write yourself an interesting plot and let the life that you lead be in service to the character you would like to become.

You are complete and do not need my advice, but I hope you will heed the words of Elie Wiesel the Nobel Laureate, Holocaust survivor, and author of fifty-seven books who once said, "Think Higher, Live Deeper."

Live simply. Love generously, Care deeply, Act justly. RJG

DESCRIPTION ABOUT WINTER WHEAT

Literally: Winter wheat is a form of the grain planted in the autumn to germinate and develop into young plants that remain in a dormant phase during the winter and resume growth in early spring. Classification into spring or winter wheat is common and traditionally refers to the season during which the crop grows or lies dormant in the Northern Hemisphere.

Symbolically: Winter wheat represents hope in the tenacious nature of human kind to survive enumerable hardships, to endure in the face of scarcity, to prevail in the presence of adversity, and to thrive in times of abundance. This hope is based on the thoughts and beliefs that are informed by the evidence amassed through many lifetimes of our collective experiences.

Metaphysically: Winter wheat represents the self-evident belief that we are created with the innate capacity to flourish and to share in the material, spiritual and psychological bounty which life has to offer. This belief is based on a faith that requires no evidence but its own existence. My friend the late Father Henry Tansey, a Mill Hill Missionary priest from Ireland, called this "Expectant Faith."

ABOUT THE AUTHOR RONALD J GERHARD

Winter Wheat chronicles one man's journey through a time when all things seemed possible; but only for those few whose provenance provided the resources and opportunities needed to succeed.

He had no advocate or grand plan to guide him, but a discontent born of frustration kept him moving toward a goal that he hoped he would recognize when it came into view.

Not strong enough to succeed alone, he needed to find a loving and supporting wife who would affirm, inspire and encourage him, with whom he could create a family that would not abandon him. And, he needed to find a fulfilling career where he would no longer feel like a bit player in someone else's story.

Most of all, he needed to find himself.

R

Made in the USA
Middletown, DE
13 May 2017